SCIENCE/TECHNOLOGY DIVISION
CHICAGO PUBLIC LIBRARY
400 SOU

D1074425

DISCARD

Shipping Company Strategies

Related books

Sea Change Sea Liner Shipping
M.R. Brooks

Globalization and Strategic Alliances: The case of the Airline Industry
T.H. Oum, J.-H. Park and A. Zhang

Related Book Series

Handbooks in Transport
Editors: D.A. Hensher and K.J. Button

Research in Transportation Economics
Editor: M. Dresner

International Business and Management Series
Editor: P. Ghauri

Related Journals

International Journal of Transport Management
Editor: A. Bristow

Journal of International Management
Editor: M. Kotabe

Transport Policy
Editors: M. Ben-Akiva, Y. Hayashi and J. Preston

Transportation Research A : Policy and Practice
Editor: F.A. Haight

Transportation Research E: Logistics and Transportation Review
Editor: W. Talley

For full details of all transportation titles published under the Elsevier imprint please go to:
www.ElsevierSocialSciences.com/transport

SHIPPING COMPANY STRATEGIES
Global Management under Turbulent Conditions

Dr. Dr. h.c. Peter Lorange
President IMD
The Nestlé Professor

2005

ELSEVIER

Amsterdam – Boston – Heidelberg – London – New York – Oxford
Paris – San Diego – San Francisco – Singapore – Sydney – Tokyo

ELSEVIER B.V.	ELSEVIER Inc.	ELSEVIER Ltd	ELSEVIER Ltd
Radarweg 29	525 B Street	The Boulevard	84 Theobalds Road
P.O. Box 211, 1000 AE	Suite 1900, San Diego	Langford Lane, Kidlington,	London WC1X 8RR
Amsterdam, The Netherlands	CA 92101-4495, USA	Oxford OX5 1GB, UK	UK

© 2005 Elsevier Ltd. All rights reserved.

This work is protected under copyright by Elsevier Ltd, and the following terms and conditions apply to its use:

Photocopying
Single photocopies of single chapters may be made for personal use as allowed by national copyright laws. Permission of the Publisher and payment of a fee is required for all other photocopying, including multiple or systematic copying, copying for advertising or promotional purposes, resale, and all forms of document delivery. Special rates are available for educational institutions that wish to make photocopies for non-profit educational classroom use.

Permissions may be sought directly from Elsevier's Rights Department in Oxford, UK: phone (+44) 1865 843830, fax (+44) 1865 853333, e-mail: permissions@elsevier.com. Requests may also be completed on-line via the Elsevier homepage (http://www.elsevier.com/locate/permissions).

In the USA, users may clear permissions and make payments through the Copyright Clearance Center, Inc., 222 Rosewood Drive, Danvers, MA 01923, USA; phone: (+1) (978) 7508400, fax: (+1) (978) 7504744, and in the UK through the Copyright Licensing Agency Rapid Clearance Service (CLARCS), 90 Tottenham Court Road, London W1P 0LP, UK; phone: (+44) 20 7631 5555; fax: (+44) 20 7631 5500. Other countries may have a local reprographic rights agency for payments.

Derivative Works
Tables of contents may be reproduced for internal circulation, but permission of the Publisher is required for external resale or distribution of such material. Permission of the Publisher is required for all other derivative works, including compilations and translations.

Electronic Storage or Usage
Permission of the Publisher is required to store or use electronically any material contained in this work, including any chapter or part of a chapter.

Except as outlined above, no part of this work may be reproduced, stored in a retrieval system or transmitted in any form or by any means, electronic, mechanical, photocopying, recording or otherwise, without prior written permission of the Publisher. Address permissions requests to: Elsevier's Rights Department, at the fax and e-mail addresses noted above.

Notice
No responsibility is assumed by the Publisher for any injury and/or damage to persons or property as a matter of products liability, negligence or otherwise, or from any use or operation of any methods, products, instructions or ideas contained in the material herein. Because of rapid advances in the medical sciences, in particular, independent verification of diagnoses and drug dosages should be made.

First edition 2005
Reprinted 2005

British Library Cataloguing in Publication Data
A catalogue record is available from the British Library.

Library of Congress Cataloging in Publication Data
A catalog record is available from the Library of Congress.

ISBN: 0-08-044611-6

Working together to grow
libraries in developing countries
www.elsevier.com | www.bookaid.org | www.sabre.org

ELSEVIER   BOOK AID International   Sabre Foundation

∞ The paper used in this publication meets the requirements of ANSI/NISO Z39.48-1992 (Permanence of Paper).
Printed in The Netherlands

CHICAGO PUBLIC LIBRARY

R0407324344

CONTENTS

CHAPTER 3
The Drive toward Non-Commodity Segments

FOREWORD

The shipping industry is both special and fascinating. It is special, above all, because of its truly global nature, the huge discrete investments needed, the highly cyclical markets at play, and the unique competitive structure, with many determined players. It is fascinating, above all, because fortunes are made—and lost—at a fast pace, with some of the most risk-willing owners also serving as decision makers.

This book is the result of at least seven forces that have shaped my interest in shipping corporations and their strategies. The first is purely personal. Early on, my grandfather, Rudolf Ugelstad, co-founder of the Norwegian shipping company Olsen & Ugelstad, awakened my interest. In the 1950s and 1960s Olsen & Ugelstad was one of Norway's largest shipping companies, with a fleet of more than 50 wholly owned ships. I also had many interesting conversations on shipping strategies with my uncles, Trygve and Rolf, and with my cousins, Rudolf and Paal. My mother's cousin, Sam Ugelstad, who ran his own shipping company, S. Ugelstad, also provided me with many important ideas early on.

During my graduate studies in the United States, I met Victor Norman, and we both had a common interest in shipping management issues. We were particularly interested in the question of attitude toward risk taking among ship owners. We co-organized a conference on shipping management and shipping strategies in 1972, which led to an early book on the topic, *Shipping Management* (Lorange and Norman, 1973). Previously we undertook initial research on shipowners' propensity toward risk (Lorange and Norman, 1971a and 1971b).

A third important influence on my interest was my cooperation with Paul L. Eckbo and Arlie Sterling on the forecasting of shipping market cycles in an attempt to better understand the development of such cycles, particularly "turning points." This collaboration led to the formation of the forecasting company Marsoft in 1982. I have thus worked with Paul Eckbo for approximately 30 years on issues relating to how the ship markets work, and I know the evolving development of Marsoft and its methodology. Occasionally, I have also contributed to Marsoft. I therefore feel confident regarding Marsoft and its usefulness, which has been a major reason for the relatively extensive use of Marsoft as the basis for examples and illustrations in this book. Marsoft's approaches must, of course, be *complemented* with other approaches, above all judgmental inputs. The owner and his/her feel for the market is critical. Marsoft can only provide simulations that give the owner better confidence in the end that he/she is well adjusted to the market. Today, Marsoft is, arguably, the world's leading ship market forecasting company. Over the years I have had stimulating conversations with many of Marsoft's staff, including Paul L. Eckbo, Arlie Sterling, Paal Monsen, Tasos Aslidis, Costas Bardjis, Kevin Hazel and Evangelos Efstathiou.

A fourth important influence on my interest in shipping was a number of assignments as director on several shipping company boards:

Olsen & Ugelstad, Oslo, Norway: I served as a director from 1974 until the discontinuation of business in 2003. It should be noted that this company ceased operations in 1980, as a result of the worldwide shipping crisis at the time. Here, I would like to point out that Olsen & Ugelstad never went bankrupt, but merely ceased to operate. Kristoffer Olsen, Ole Lund, as well as the many Ugelstads already mentioned, all influenced my understanding.

Jebsens, Bergen, Norway: I served on the board of this company, which specializes in smaller bulk carrier ships, from 1990 to 1993. Jebsens' dynamic CEO, Atle Jebsen, has been a great source of inspiration to me.

Knud I. Larsen (KiL), Copenhagen, Denmark: I served as board member in this publicly traded company from 1994 to 1998. KiL focused on contained feeder ships, gas carriers and smaller special-purpose tankers. I learned important messages at this Danish firm, particularly from KiL's chairman, Jan Erlund, from board members Steen Krabbe and Jens Christian Lorentzen, and from CEO Finn S. Larsen.

Royal Caribbean Cruise Lines (RCCL), Miami, Florida: I served as a director of this company from 1995 to 2000. RCCL is the world's second largest cruise company, now with 14 large cruise ships operating worldwide. Being on the board was tremendously stimulating and provided a lot of learning, particularly from the major shareholders and board members, Arne Wilhelmsen, the late Jay Pritzker, and Samuel Ofer; the chairman/CEO, Richard Fain; and fellow board members Kaspar Kielland and Thor Arneberg.

Fifth, I have benefited from deep discussions with leading practitioners in the shipping industry. Here I would like to mention in particular Tom Erik Klaveness, Morits Skaugen, Jr., and Jens Ulltveit-Moe.

The final, and perhaps the most important, industry-specific source of influence for my interest in shipping strategies comes through my involvement on the ownership side with the ship owning company S. Ugelstad, founded in Oslo, Norway in 1929. I inherited 50% of the company in 1987, and subsequently purchased the remaining shares. The company now owns and operates a fleet of four platform supply ships (PSVs) for the offshore industry as well as one reefer ship in worldwide trade. I have been influenced by several sources here:

- The board of directors, in particular the stimulating cooperation with Hans G. Haga, Thure Svensson and the late Kaare Wikborg.

- S. Ugelstad's leaders—with its managing director Odd Settevik, my son, Per F. Lorange, and Per Lindseth—have been critically important in developing my own understanding of the shipping business.

- The relationship with ship brokers, particularly R. S. Platou. Here, Per Engeset has played a major role. My understanding of the offshore supply shipping business is largely a function of all my discussions with him.

- The banks, in particular Nedship Bank. Here, I have gained important insights through discussions with Jan Hjellestad and Oyvind Holte.

This brings me to the last and most general reason why I think I might have something to add to the subject of strategic management of shipping companies—namely, more than thirty years of academic work in the area of strategic management. My three decades of teaching and researching strategy have given me an exposure to many of the current theories in strategy, organizational behavior and finance. They have also given me a chance to discuss various industry-specific strategic challenges in broader contexts with colleagues at leading academic institutions with which I have been affiliated, such as the Sloan School of Management (MIT), the Wharton School and IMD. Over the years I have studied and discussed many industries, many companies and their key leaders. In this book I have drawn on my years of thought, reading, research and discussion around the theme of growth in organizations—either you grow or you stagnate, even die. Particularly important here has been my work with Professor Bala Chakravarthy.

The rationale for the book, in a narrower sense, is understanding the success of global shipping corporations, i.e., how to become a winner in this industry. As such, it is relevant to those active in shipping—practitioners and academicians alike. In a broader sense, the book is also about how to manage in the face of global turbulence. Understanding how to deal with the growing forces of instability will be key, not only for executives from the shipping industry but also for many executives from a wider set of industries and corporations.

In Chapter 1 we shall briefly set out some key strategic challenges of a shipping corporation. A conceptual model for developing strategies in shipping companies will be developed, illustrated by a historical exposé of the successful, but turbulent, evolution of two leading shipping companies, A. P. Moller-Maersk and Leif Hoegh & Co.

The next three chapters deal with the specifics of strategy formulation and implementation in shipping firms In Chapter 2 we shall discuss commodity-based shipping strategies, underscoring how the shipping firm must adapt to volatile market conditions to proactively take advantage of movements in the market. Speed and flexibility will be critical here. In Chapter 3, we shall discuss the move toward niche strategies, where the shipping firm attempts to position itself *away* from the commodity markets and instead to develop services vis-à-vis specific customers, which in turn may allow the firm to charge higher prices and secure stable returns. In Chapter 4, we shall discuss the overall portfolio strategies of the shipping firm, where the key challenge will be to put a set of chosen business strategies together in a deliberate way to create a better balance. These may be commodity-based business approaches and/or niche business approaches. The key is to develop an overall balance that provides an acceptable overall risk profile and overall better long-term stability for the firm.

In Chapter 5 we shall discuss several organizational issues, largely to do with the implementation of the shipping firm's flexible strategies. After all, it is people, working together in organizational teams that make strategies happen, particularly in today's turbulent world. We shall thus discuss how the shipping firm might choose different strategic forms, depending on the types of strategies it wishes to pursue. The role of key players and personalities, including the owners, the chief executive, the internal entrepreneurs and the board of directors will also be discussed.

Chapter 6 deals with the ownership side, with particular emphasis on whether the shipping firm can benefit from being public, or whether it might have a better opportunity as a privately held corporation. We note that privately held firms are still rather prominent the shipping industry. The pros and cons will be discussed. Perhaps heavy risk-taking and coping with extreme turbulence can be better handled in privately held firms? Finally, we discuss the future of the industry and outline the contours of the shipping company of tomorrow. Focus on speed, agility and flexibility will be key hallmarks.

Many people in addition to those previously mentioned have provided specific inputs to the book, including: Terje Andersen, Eric André, Per-Ola Baalerud, Gerhard Binder, Michael Bonner, Lars-Erik Brenøe, Didier Cossin, Sean Day, Jan-Erik Dyvi, Sverre Farstad, Richard Fain, Arvid, Grundekjøn, Thor Jorgen Guttormsen, Robert A. Ho, Leif Hoegh, Westye Hoegh, Kevin Irvine, Maersk Mc-Kinney Møller, Bjorn Möller, Carsten Mortensen, Nobuyoshi Norimoto, Henning Oldendorff, Oscar Rosendahl, Tor Ståle Moen, John Syvertsen, Tonny Thorsen, Sigurd Thorvildsen, Felix Tschudi, Alex Wilhelmsen, and others. Lindsay McTeague edited the manuscript, supported by Gordon Adler. Eva Ferrari and Annette Polzer typed the many versions of the manuscript. I would like to thank all of the abovementioned people. And there are many others I cannot mention here for lack of space, but who have, nevertheless, made significant, if anonymous, contributions. I hope that this book will not only offer insights that are practically relevant but also lead to the stimulation of new strategies and further breakthrough research in shipping.

Peter Lorange

Lausanne, Switzerland

August 2004

*This book is dedicated to
Maersk Mc-Kinney Møller, outstanding leader and entrepreneur,
in recognition of his outstanding contribution
to the development of the field of shipping strategy.*

CHAPTER 1

A TRULY CHALLENGING INDUSTRY: SHIPPING COMPANY STRATEGIES

Strategy is to be prepared; strategy means choice. —*Lorange, 1980*

HISTORICAL BACKGROUND

When the shipping industry began, first during the era of the great sailing ships and then with the advent of steamships, the captain was, in essence, an independent entrepreneur. He undertook the chartering of the ship and ran the commercial operation around it. Often, the captain also owned a significant share in the ship. So it follows that, in those early days of the industry, most shipping companies were relatively small—typically one ship, or a few at most. And, significantly, entrepreneurialism was a key to success. We shall argue that it still is! (Walton, 1987)

With the advent of new technologies for hulls and engines, such as, initially, steel ships, and then steam engines, internal combustion engines and turbines, the capital intensity of the shipping industry increased drastically. This evolution in technologies led to a major consolidation, and with it, the "death" of many traditional players. At the same time, opportunities for new shipping players emerged, and several important "modern" shipowners ("entrepreneurs") came to the fore (Christensen, 1997).

It is probably fair to say that the competitiveness in the shipping industry is extreme, and that it has always been very competitive—a true approximation of a worldwide "perfect" *competitive* market situation. It is also *global* (Bhagwati, 2004; Wolf, 2004) and there is a strong competitive *transparency* and high *connectivity*, in the sense that ships can be used in most trades and by most shippers in a fully interchangeable way. Further, the industry is highly *capital intensive* and highly *cyclical* (*Der Spiegel*, June 7, 2004).

As we can see from Exhibit 1.1 the degree of concentration, measuring the four largest owners in each major segment within the shipping industry, is generally very small. This underscores the fact that the industry is highly competitive. We shall discuss this in Chapter 2.

Exhibit 1.1: Market Share of the Four Biggest Owners Relative to the Group of the Ten Largest Owners in Particular Ship Segments

Market Share	Ship Segment
28%	Container > 3,000 TEU
28%	VLCC
27%	Chemical Tankers
27%	Suezmax Tankers
26%	LNG Tankers
22%	Cape-size
21%	Aframax Tankers
12%	Container < 3,000 TEU
11%	Panamax Tankers
11%	Panamax Bulkers
10%	Handimax Bulkers
9%	Handy-size Bulkers
9%	Product Tankers

Source: Marsoft, 2004

There are two exceptions:

- Niche segments: When one can "own" the consumer, such as in the cruise business, with heavy branding; in the container business, with link-up with overall logistics for the customer, including door-to-door logistics services, etc., i.e., when it comes to particular *niche* businesses, as we shall see in Chapter 3, there may be relatively less competition, at least for a while. It should be noted, however, that niche businesses can almost always be copied and that, therefore, they soon tend to be competitive too.

- Commercial consolidation, primarily through pools. We have seen more development of pools as of late. This means operational consolidation. It should be noted that this does not seem (yet) to be ruled out by anti-trust/anti-competition ruling bodies in the US and Europe. The pools give the owners a chance to enjoy operational scale without the risk of owning the entire fleet, since the ownership side will be split among the pool participants. The pool thus provides larger units, for negotiation purposes, on the supply side.

Examples of important pools on the tanker side would primarily be Tanker International for VLCCs (very large crude carriers), the Connecticut pool for Aframax tankers, with particular focus on the Caribbean trade, and the Dorado pool for product tankers. In the dry bulk market, examples of major pools would be the Klaveness pool, as well as Starbulk (Westfal-Larsen and Grieg).

Consider now the challenging issues facing the modern shipping industry today, which lead to the realization that we must cope with increasing turbulence, more volatile competitive forces, such as unexpected movements in the stock market, abrupt macroeconomic swings, severe political issues and so on. Let us briefly discuss these macro trends, and then ask how our shipping business might be exposed when it comes to all of this.

Macro Issues

A number of macroeconomic factors drive the development of shipping markets. In addition, several specific trade issues have an impact on various niches/trades. Taken together, they tend to have an important influence on the overall markets. Part of this is the financial markets, which should be specifically mentioned and which are, of course, intertwined with the shipping markets. And lastly, developments in certain technological factors typically have significant impacts on shipping markets as well.

The level of economic growth in the world, the development of trade worldwide, in short, the economic health of the world economic system has an impact on shipping markets. As we know, economic development goes in cycles—often described as worldwide booms and depressions. There are, of course, also differences from one geographic area to another. And political factors influence the shipping market, too. Major global political crises, as well as more localized political crises, can have a critical impact. Typically, shipping markets tend to strengthen during a political crisis, yet they tend to react adversely to a weak economic climate.

Extremely high growth, beyond normal expectations, tends to go hand-in-hand with very high profitability in shipping, through high market conditions. Normally, however, when growth is *not* high, the industry tends to be *extremely* unprofitable. Growth is, therefore, fundamental for determining the positive swings in shipping markets and a given for the shipping sector's ability to "produce" strong financial returns. Today, for example, much of the global shipping boom stems from growth in China, particularly from raw material imports to support Chinese manufacturing and infrastructure growth. Shipping growth is also being fueled by growth in container line shipping that supports the export of products manufactured in China (Hale and Hale, 2003).

It should be noted that China today is the only country with (a) a *flat* demographic position, in contrast to all other developing countries, which face heavy demographic growth; (b) *strong* macroeconomic growth, with a 7% to 8% GNP growth per year; and (c) with a relatively efficient political structure, i.e. *one* political party which can get things done, and fast (*World Competitiveness Yearbook*, 2003).

Not only the economic but also the political stability of each country is, of course, important. Here the major countries, such as the US, Japan, the European Union (EU) and China play increasingly critical roles. Above all, a slowdown in the US tends to have negative effects on developments in the shipping market. Emerging countries, such as India, Brazil, etc., also play increasingly important roles. Local political uncertainties, such as the ones experienced recently in the Middle East, can also have a significant effect on the development of shipping markets.

More specifically, China's economic development is important for the world's shipping markets. China is a relatively easy country with which to do shipping business, and much foreign-registered tonnage has been employed there. Still, the Chinese are becoming more and more self-sufficient. In terms of relationship marketing, it may thus become harder to break into China. They now have their own networks and do not really need non-Chinese participation. They have also built up an impressive national shipping industry. For the owners and managers of shipping companies, a long-term view of China is, therefore, probably a vital element of successful strategy. Seaspan, for instance, is taking a long view with its container ship fleet on long-term charter to China Ship Owners' Corporations. Skaugen is taking a long-term view with its barge business on the Yangtze River. To handle relationship marketing with major clients, Oldendorff has a small office in Shanghai and Klaveness has one in Beijing.

Iron ore and steel imports to China will continue to be critical for developing the dry bulk market. Only five years ago, the Organization for Economic Cooperation and Development (OECD) countries dominated the steel trade; China was a minor player. In 2002 and 2003, China began emerging as a key force, and the OECD's role started shrinking. Over the next few years, Chinese trade growth is likely to dominate in steel, which will be essential for strong growth in dry-bulk market demand. Exhibit 1.2 provides an interesting picture of how steel consumption (per capita) rises as countries become richer. China clearly has a long development ahead. Exhibit 1.3 provides a picture of how steel output drives freight rates, again underscoring the importance of steel and China.

Exhibit 1.2: Steel Intensity Rises as Countries Get Richer

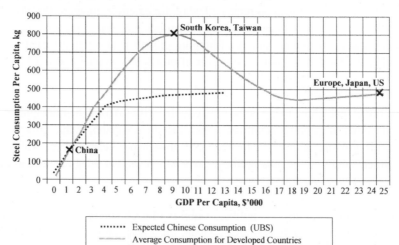

Source: Marsoft, 2004

Exhibit 1.3: Steel Output Drives Dry Cargo Rates

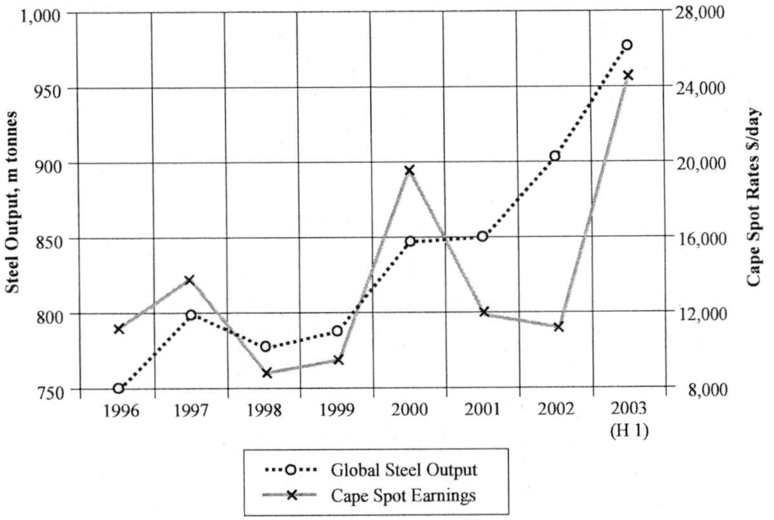

Source: Marsoft, 2004

As far as the demand side goes, in reality, it is rare for only one factor—China's imports—to be decisive in determining the entire world's market levels for dry bulk. This applies directly to Panamax ships, but "trickles down" to smaller ship categories, too. How can we find out more about the development of this truly critical demand-side factor? Perhaps we could send people to the various steel plants, to better understand their plans, their ordering activities, their inventories, in short, their outlooks. It is important here to remember that this sort of macro-analysis in the specifics is probably more valuable than looking at aggregated official economic statistics numbers.

Additional issues here would deal with getting a clearer understanding of Chinese infrastructure project developments, particularly how long they can be expected to go on (it is likely to be many years), and harbor capacity developments, expansion plans, congestion problems, etc. Further, it is important to understand Chinese shipping itself, as well as the country's shipbuilding. According to *The Economist*, in the 15th century China was a big maritime power. It roamed the Pacific with ships six times larger than those of Christopher Columbus (*The Economist*, February 19, 2004). China's five-year plan calls for it to become the world's leading shipbuilder by 2015, displacing South Korea and Japan. It is already a leading builder of simple dry cargo ships. And it is starting to build more complex vessels, such as tankers and container ships.

Waigaoqiao, a shipbuilder in Shanghai, has orders for more than 25 heavy bulk carriers, each of 175,000 deadweight tonnes (dwt), the most yet for a Chinese-built ship. It will next begin work on an oil tanker. By the end of 2004, Shanghai shipyards expect to have increased production by two-thirds over the year before. China State Shipbuilding Corporation is constructing a shipyard that will be able to produce 8 million dwt of ship per year by 2015, making it the largest such yard in the world. In 2003, Chinese shipyards accounted for one-tenth of world output. In 2003, Shanghai and Shenzhen (near Hong Kong) became the world's third and fourth busiest ports, trailing only Singapore and Hong Kong (*The Economist*, op.cit.).

Turbulent Conditions

Violent Political Forces

There is no doubt that the geopolitical scene is changing. Things are becoming more turbulent—not less—after the collapse of the former Soviet Union and the emergence of the United States as the sole superpower. A major reason for this has to do with increased regional geopolitical instability. Consider, for instance, the tensions in the Indian subcontinent; China and its relationship with Taiwan; Korea—North and South; the Israeli-Palestinian conflict; Iran–Iraq; the many gruesome local and civil wars in Africa, conflicts in Central America; the Balkan situation—with several years of terrible wars just behind us and tensions still continuing... We could go on and on.

Terrorism is another dimension, heightened after the September 11, 2001 attacks in the US. Despite the efforts of many of the established world powers, it seems to be difficult to limit this threat of terrorism, whether it be in Russia, the Arab world, Spain, the US—anywhere. An immediate sense of violence and political instability is the result.

China and India are becoming increasingly important players in today's global economic scene. The question that many ask is: Are these countries politically entirely stable? China is run by what many see as an authoritarian regime, although it is certainly more and more pragmatically liberal in its views on economic matters, but still not a democracy. Will the present balance last? Are we talking about a rather feeble stability here? Similarly, India—being the world's largest democracy—is still fraught with tensions. Can relative stability remain in this enormous country? Will the path toward more economic liberalism continue?

We could go on speculating about the political forces that are currently at play, or are latent. Clearly, this has an impact on the business order. Political stability is a condition for economic stability and prosperity, as well as for investment attractiveness and meaningful economic value creation by each particular firm (Courtney, 2001).

Truly Global Competition

Markets seem to be becoming larger and larger—and trade barriers seem to be becoming less distinct. This is, to some extent, a function of multinational, multilateral agreements, creating larger homogenous trading blocs, such as the European Union, covering large parts of Europe; NAFTA, covering North America; ASEAN, covering Southeast Asia, etc. Also, competition is becoming significantly more global due to the migration of economic activities to low cost areas, such as manufacturing to the former Eastern Europe, India and China, development of software to India, service activities such as call centers and accounting to India, etc. All in all, markets are becoming more global. It is certainly increasingly hard to find a sustainable local niche in this global world.

Again, the paradox seems to be that volatility is becoming more extreme. We have strong economic ups and downs within each trading bloc, for instance. In Europe, for example, the "locomotive" Germany has experienced problems maintaining its economic dynamism. The same can be said of the second largest economy in Europe, France.

In North America, the entire economy has gone through large swings, with extended periods of depression and so on. Again, the true globalization of competition seems to call for global adaptation by corporations, but it also seems to imply exposure to local ups and downs in various parts of the world, at various points in time. When things are good in one place, they are not so good elsewhere, the global portfolio strategy of corporate activities being rather volatile (Fischer, 2004).

Increasingly Capital Intensive

Many industries are becoming more capital intensive. Partly this is driven by the need to maintain physical plants that are becoming larger and larger, and more and more sophisticated, to secure the necessary economies of scale to be cost competitive. Many such plants now cover vast regions of the world. Global sourcing and reconfiguration of the manufacturing-based part of the value chain seem to be high on the agenda. The days when plants were focused on each national economy seem to be largely gone. One consequence is, of course, that the investment requirements per installation are becoming higher.

Similar arguments can be made when it comes to research and development (R&D) investments. They typically call for more substantial commitments of resources in order to be able to come up with new products and/or processes that increasingly can have a global reach. R&D today seems to be a matter of going for larger gains and a global scope, but also with larger financial commitments—and risks!

Similarly, developing global brands costs a lot of money. Corporations will increasingly have to allocate funds to such global brand development. Multi-local is simply not good enough any more for leading companies in many industries.

This pattern of resource intensity is further accentuated by the fact that most industries are experiencing even more rapid obsolescence. Technologies are changing faster, which calls for ongoing modification of plants, even total obsolescence. R&D is leading to new developments all the time, calling for shortened life cycles to recuperate the R&D investments. Brands are evolving, requiring more resources to be allocated to the maintenance and development of a dynamic brand presence, etc. More abundant financial resources are necessary to cope with the increasingly rapid changes—and indeed more turbulence!

Global Capital Markets

Corporations are increasingly able to tap global capital markets. Capital is available at more or less similar rates everywhere—and the cost of capital has come down. It is increasingly difficult for individual nations to implement their own fiscal policies, for example, by imposing schemes for rationing capital, or increasing interest rates and the cost of capital to limit inflationary spending, etc. Further, capital seems to be rather abundantly available. If a project is good, then the capital can generally be found.

The consequence is that it is relatively easy for new entrants to an industry to come on the scene. From a financing viewpoint, a new corporate entity can easily be established to push a particular new strategic project, as long as the basic business rationale and the managerial capabilities are there. This again means that there might be less and less "protection" built around an already installed capital base. Smaller competitors can come in all the time and can be rather effective in competing with the larger corporations, now that they enjoy more or less the same cost of capital as the larger ones. This results in more effective competition—but again also in more turbulence!

Government Actions

We have already pointed out that individually driven governmental fiscal policies seem to be less and less possible to carry out. The EU, for instance, is regulated so that fiscal policies cannot be used to transfer "economic burdens" from one country to another. Interest rates, inflation, and the like are more or less determined for the entire union. Budgetary fiscal soundness is called for, to ensure balance in each country's national budget. Still, there are some government opportunities for impacting the conditions that industries and corporations face. The primary one perhaps relates to taxation. Corporate tax rates differ widely from country to country. And some industries are also granted particular tax preferences within given countries. Further, personal tax rates, wealth taxation, inheritance taxes, etc. can differ, making some industries more attractive than others because the executives needed to run them face lower taxes in some geographic locations.

Subsidies are also still quite prevalent in many industries. They can take the form of investment subsidies for large new projects, or of so-called investment stimulants such as more favorable financing, guaranteed lower interest rates, introductory tax breaks, etc.

Finally, customs barriers are still prevalent. Countries are still using trade tariffs to attempt to boost their own economic regions, of course at the expense of other countries.

Even though there seems to be general agreement among nations on a world order base to minimize local idiosyncrasies, there is no doubt that these still play a very important role, which is perhaps even increasing in importance. This can impact business in significant ways and can be critically important for some types of corporations and can even affect their potential success or failure. Again, turbulence seems to be a factor to cope with here too.

Timing Is All—Its Value as a Competitive Dimension

Time to market is increasingly a key dimension for competitive success. When a corporation, or an industry for that matter, has developed a unique new value proposition, it now typically takes less and less time before alternatives are available in the marketplace. There is typically a shorter and shorter period of "grace."

Similarly, timing investment decisions, say, when it comes to capacity expansion, seems to be becoming increasingly critical, so as not to "invest" out of sync with the economic cycles. Timing relative to the economic cycles is more and more becoming a key factor for success. To enter certain markets ahead of others, but also to be able to cash in, or even exit, while on top seems critical.

With the emerging changes in world patterns of manufacturing—with much of it now being relocated to so-called low cost countries, of which China is perhaps the premier example—the issue of trading also becoming even more important. To develop trading capabilities to be able to make long or short positions when it comes to procurement and supply is becoming increasingly vital.

Risk management is also linked to all of this. "Value-at-risk" is becoming a standard way of looking at investment portfolios for asset management companies. The so-called Basel II convention for management of risk in financial lending corporations is gradually being phased in. Risk management is a central part of the management function today.

All in all, this again means volatility—and of course also new ways for agile management to secure success through better timing! (Grove, 1997; Strebel, 1992).

Global Human Resource Management

Companies and industries are certainly becoming less and less nationally based. To succeed globally today, it is no longer sufficient to have a national corporation and, say, a number of local subsidiaries internationally. The company itself needs to become truly global, seeing itself more as a network of activities, drawing on human resource talents from all over the globe, without being confined to having a dominant group of people from a particular headquarters location and country of ownership. We may thus be talking less about host country dominance in human resource management today. Rather, we may consider welcoming all types of human resource talents, irrespective of where they come from, as long as they can do the best possible job.

In this sense, we can talk about the emergence of the "stateless corporation." The consequence is, of course, that human resource policies are also becoming more adjusted to this global reality. Performance, not cultural or geographical preferences, seems to dominate more and more. One might say more turbulence! (Evans et al., 2002).

Strong Leadership Is Key

To lead these emerging flat, networked corporations—which typically tend to be less hierarchical, more project oriented—requires charisma and drive from the top. The leader today will have to have global appeal. He or she will need to have impeccable stakeholder acceptance and a profile that creates broad bonding with various talent groups worldwide. Leaders from the old national orders seem to be less effective. It is key that today's leaders are truly inspirational, not tied to a particular narrow national tradition.

Headquarters organizations similarly seem to be rather small and highly professional. The firm seems to be being restructured in a different way, along important project initiatives and ad hoc temporary organizational units. The modern corporation is perhaps more and more built around being "large" *and* "small." Rather autonomous smaller entities are being created to safeguard entrepreneurialism and drive. They are, however, often supported by "shared services" in order to take advantage of the size and scale advantages of larger firms.

The net effect of this is again more flexibility and ability to deal with change. There will be less stability in formal organizational structures. Net effect: More turbulence!

Extreme Volatility in Value Creation

Interestingly, huge fortunes are being created today with remarkable speed. Similarly, established fortunes are being wiped out—also rather regularly and at amazing speed! The so-called rich are often "newly minted," while the established, traditionally wealthy individuals and families are tending to become relatively less important. Again, we see quite a lot of turbulence here, with new players coming on the scene, typically self-made, representing a brand of professionalism applied to the new opportunities that have arisen worldwide relatively recently. The bottom line again is a pattern of increased turbulence—on the ownership side!

Now consider this. Shipping is one of the few industries that would be faced with all of these mega trends. My claim is that more and more other industries—and thereby also more and more corporations—will become exposed to an increasing number of the above factors. Turbulence and global shipping go together. Hence, it may be valuable not only for shipping executives to try to comprehend the factors behind this. Executives more generally might benefit from analyzing the global shipping industry carefully to learn from successful strategies here. Understanding the shipping industry is thus not only a matter of those executives who are particularly drawn to this rather unique industry being prepared for success in this arena; it is also a much broader challenge for executives active in other business arenas. Understanding key lessons from the shipping industry will be vital in order to be prepared to manage turbulence and dynamic change more generally. The shipping industry can lead the way toward a better understanding of how to handle turbulence for a broad range of executives.

Let us now consider the examples of two shipping firms that have survived through turbulent times by focusing on both the *markets* and *niches*. Entrepreneurship has been part of their success throughout. The two firms are Leif Hoegh (Oslo, Norway) and A. P. Moller-Maersk (Copenhagen, Denmark). Since their beginnings, both companies have grown into multinational corporations, and tracing their ascent is a good way to understand the major trends and developments of the global shipping industry from the early days of the 20th century to the present. And this understanding can serve as a platform for considering the strategic, organizational and ownership issues that today's shipping companies face.

Leif Hoegh & Co.

Leif Hoegh & Co. was founded in 1927 (Hoegh, 1970; Bakka, 1997). At first, the major emphasis was on chartering out crude oil tankers to oil companies on long-term charters. Timing—judging the peaks of the freight market—was, of course, important, but so was financial management. Leif Hoegh's focus on long-term charters was not unusual, since a significant segment of the industry at that time aspired to long-term charters and financing ships with as much financial leverage as possible. With this double focus, several shipping companies built up their asset bases in spectacular fashion. Among them were industry giants: Aristotle Onassis, Stavros Niarchos, Andreas Sohmen-Pao, and several Norwegian companies, including Bergesen and the so-called Bjorge Group (Olsen & Ugelstad, Meyer, Berg and others).

In the late 1920s and early 1930s, long-term charters also offered a significant plus for the oil companies: By using long-term charters, an oil company could enter into off-balance sheet financing for significant parts of its crude oil transport, offering the shipowners in return a "guaranteed" return on investment (ROI), typically around 8%. It is interesting to note that, since then, oil companies have realized that they can squeeze the shipowners even further by demanding shorter charters, or even no long-term charters at all, thus relying on the shipping industry's typical extremely elastic supply (there will always be new owners, available capital and thus new ships to step in).

By the mid-1930s, diversification had become the name of the game for shipping companies. Some went into tramp shipping, others into liner services. From 1936 onward, Leif Hoegh, for instance, seeing liner shipping as counter-cyclical to tankers, and thus complementary, started its liner activities. After a decade of diversification, following World War II the shipping industry entered into what turned out to be several decades of boom conditions. These years of strong growth in shipping ran in parallel with decades of worldwide economic growth, which should not surprise us since, according to research, shipping markets tend to show strong returns—"beyond expectations"—during periods of strong *overall* economic growth.

During the boom decades, there were several constraints on building new ship capacity worldwide. Shipyards were generally old-fashioned and often run down. For Leif Hoegh, this constraint meant taking a more opportunistic approach to shipping, an approach that consisted of finding market-oriented niches, such as in overseas liner services (geographic expansion), and "playing" the commodity markets more systematically. This constraint was further accentuated by Leif Hoegh's dedicated investments in large tankers. Although this marked the company's return to its founding strategy, it nevertheless continued to recognize the importance of the markets, the timing and the commodity orientation of most shipping segments.

Starting in the 1960s, many shipping companies began managing themselves more professionally. They hired analytical executives who focused more sharply on the financial dimension. They also brought in professional ship engineers, who added much-needed technical expertise. The pattern here was clear: Shipping companies were trying to add new competences to their existing bases, perhaps in order to be able to bring into practice their own, unique strategies. By adding new competences and looking to realize unique strategies, many shipping companies thus ended up focusing more on niches, where they could apply their competences from a "platform" of thorough analysis, stricter performance hurdles and more stringent efficiency targets. It would not be outlandish to claim that the era of unilateral opportunistic capitalism was now on its way out, and that professionalism, often around several diversified, more tightly focused niches, was on the way in.

Many shipping companies, both old and new, tried to take advantage of the boom years, but by the late 1970s and early 1980s, most were saddled with massive over-investments. As we know, in the early 1980s, the industry slid into a slump that lasted ten years. Many of the "new" shipping companies went out of business. A good number of these had, as indicated, been running on a model best described as "professionalism within traditional niches," and it turned out that, with their commodity base, they lacked the robustness to withstand the recession. So, for many shipping firms, the 1980s meant finding a survival strategy. So it was with Leif Hoegh, which finally reached an agreement with its creditors in 1987.

Strategically, Leif Hoegh has thus gone from being a diversified shipping company to becoming a highly focused one over the last decade. Several key strategic choices have been made. In the past, commercial activities were present in a broad range of segments, such as tank, OBO (ore-bulk-oil), RoRo (roll on, roll off), RoroHual (Hoegh Ugland Auto Liners), open hatch bulk carriers, Hoegh Lines (including West Africa Lines), LPG (liquid petroleum gas), LNG (liquefied natural gas), traditional bulk carriers, reefers, and a large stake in the Norwegian America Line Cruise business. As noted, this old strategy was based on being engaged in several different shipping segments in order to spread the risk. The focus over time became to develop activities in a specific area, and then split this off, typically as a separate firm and with its own board. There were several examples, with Leif Hoegh owning various percentages:

- Bona Shipholding—42% ownership; operated tankers and OBOs.

- HUAL—50% ownership; RoRo segment.

- Cool Carriers—75% ownership; reefer.

- Hoegh Lines—100% ownership; open hatch.

- Gorthon Lines—majority ownership; paper transport.

This structure made it easier for Leif Hoegh to subsequently spin off these holdings, as well as giving the company more flexibility regarding timing.

The new strategy started with the purchase of 50% of HUAL from Ugland, for US$390 million. This was the biggest investment in Leif Hoegh's history. This in turn led to a further optimization of the firm's resources:

- Financial resources were more focused, for growth

- Scarce leadership resources had fewer business activities to concentrate on

- More profitable segments within the shipping industry were targeted

- Let the investors balance their own risk profiles. This finally led to the privatization of the company in June 2003, with only two family owners holding shares, and other family members pursuing their own investments.

Ultimately, this led to a focused strategy, based on only two segments, RoRo and LNG, which we shall discuss further in Chapter 4. The focused strategy involved several important steps:

- 1999 saw the sale of Bona Shipholding to Teekay, initially in Teekay's shares, which were subsequently sold. In retrospect, one might speculate whether perhaps Leif Hoegh might have been able to utilize the stock market more aggressively in connection with its merger of Bona, which it controlled with Teekay. It might perhaps even have established a stronger ownership share in Teekay, based on its well-established ownership position, when Bona was merged into Teekay rather than exiting.

- Cool Carriers was sold—the software to J. Lauritzen and the 13 ships asset by asset.

- Hoegh Lines was sold to Oldendorff in 2001—the part that served Indonesia/India to the US West coast.

- Gorthon Lines was sold in 2001.

- All the remaining open hatch ships were transferred to Saga Forest Carriers, a free-standing company dominated by Leif Hoegh, but with its own structure, so that Leif Hoegh could have more flexibility in disposing of it or making other strategic moves involving this entity later.

Today, HUAL represents 70% of the firm's turnover. It gives critical mass within this segment and allows the company to develop a global service network. Leif Hoegh is pursuing three sub-segments in this business:

- New cars

- Used cars (POW)

- Tall and heavy vehicles.

Several recent strategic moves have been made at HUAL, including the acquisition in 2001 of Kiwi Car Carriers for the transportation of used cars from Japan to New Zealand. It also ordered five huge PCTCs (pure car and truck carriers) in Korea in 2002 and 2003, entered a joint venture with Louis Dreyfus for a RoRo carrier to Airbus, and took on five more new PCTCs on ten-year time charters from other owners in 2003.

Leif Hoegh has thus shown a strong willingness to follow its fundamental beliefs regarding the development of the various shipping markets, and then to take the consequences of this by getting out of several types of shipping activities and focusing primarily on the automotive transportation segment—a market its board and management truly believe in!

Today the global automotive industry is opening up more, and there is strong expansion. There is also much more trade, with car models being shipped worldwide. There is thus a strong expansion in the trade of cars globally.

The implication for Leif Hoegh is that it can invest more or less whatever capital it has available in this one segment, given its strong growth. This was not the case, say, some eight years ago, when the automotive industry segment was not growing much at all—above all due to restrictions within the industry. Then the industry was less global in its trade patterns; it was also more focused on specific automotive manufacturers using only one shipping company, i.e., tighter links between shippers and producers. Now, by contrast, the global brands are "crisscrossing" more between the various shipowners, with less tight links between the automotive firms and the shipowners. It has become a more attractive segment over time for the owners, as the global automotive industry has prospered.

In the LNG segment, Leif Hoegh won a 20-year contract for two LNG ships from Statoil/TotalFinaElf (TFE) for carrying gas from the Snovit field in the Barents Sea off Norway. This contract was run together with Mitsui Lines.

There are important historical lessons here. One is that, in a predominantly commodity-based industry, *timing* is essential. Another is that shipping companies *always* need to understand the "worst case" scenario, for only with this understanding will they have enough resources to withstand an extended economic downturn, whenever it happens. Further, shipping companies need to have good personal relationships with the financial markets—something the relatively few companies that survived the painful decline of the 1980s appear to have had, i.e., a cooperation between the financial sector and the shipping sector. And, finally, focus means everything. A simple, robust strategy seems to be important. "Strategy means choice" (Lorange, 1980). This can be summed up in Exhibit 1.4, which compares the financial results of Leif Hoegh before and after the significant refocusing strategy. One can see that by concentrating on a few business segments, the company indeed achieved much stronger results.

Exhibit 1.4: Leif Hoegh & Co. Results

	1999 (old strategy)	2002 (new strategy)
Turnover	490 m$	670 m$
EBITDA	64 m$	160 m$
Operating Profits	23 m$	88 m$
Owned Ships	37	52

Source: Guttormsen, 2003

The Country of Location: Example–The Norwegian Maritime Charter

It is interesting to see how the general economic development in certain shipping companies has led to—perhaps unintended—shifts toward more speculative shipping. Let us take the case of Norway. Norway has always been a large shipping nation, with a considerable part of the global shipping fleet controlled by Norwegian shipowners, and with many sizable globally successful shipping companies headquartered in the country. During the years after World War II, the wages of Norwegian seamen were relatively reasonable, even on a worldwide comparative basis. Over the years, wage levels grew rather rapidly, however. This applied not only to direct wages but also to the accompanying social costs as shown in Exhibit 1.5 (Seland, 1994, p. 163).

As wages increased, the economic returns for the Norway-based shipowners thus gradually diminished. In order to "compensate" for these added costs, many Norwegian shipowners gradually entered into more short-term, market-based speculation for its ships. The overall composition of the Norwegian fleet was increasingly determined by "asset play" rather than long-term relationships with shippers, which had in large part been a basis for the initial success of the Norwegian shipping-based industrial sector. With more asset play and more focus on short-term market conditions, the risks were, of course, also higher. The result was, indeed, the economic collapse of many traditional Norwegian shipping companies. Only relatively few maintained a strong focus on market relationships and a systematic, long-term market-based focus.

Exhibit 1.5: Norwegian Price and Salary Development 1954–1966

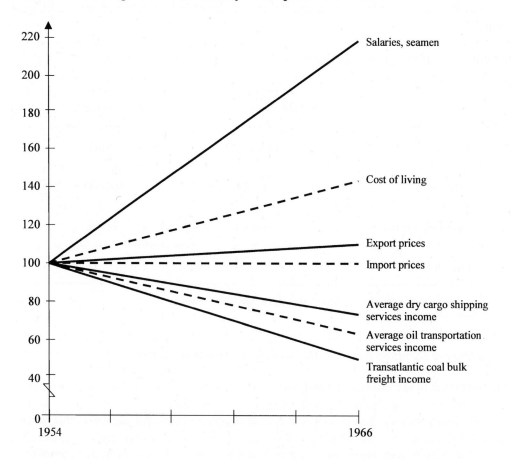

Source: Seland, 1974

At the same time, it is interesting to see that the wages of Norwegian white-collar workers seem to be relatively low on a comparative basis. It is thus still relatively inexpensive to run the headquarters functions of global shipping companies from Norway. One can attract capable executives to staff the international shipping firm, operated out of Norway. It would be relatively much more expensive to run such firms out of many other world economic centers, for example London, New York or Tokyo. One must underscore the importance of strong investments in the human resource development function in countries such as Germany, Denmark and Norway, not least in order to "compete" for the talents. It may thus be impossible to attract experienced ship officers and white-collar talents without stimulant public sector supported investments in such countries' human resource strategies (Wilhelmsen, 2004).

Exhibit 1.6: The Norwegian Maritime Cluster

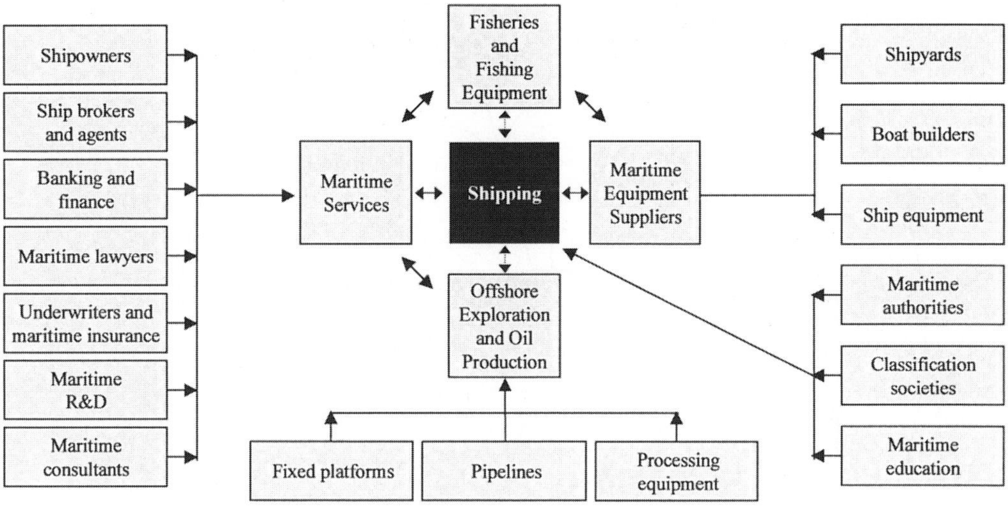

Source: Ullring, 2003

Exhibit 1.6 illustrates the key interrelationships in the Norwegian Maritime Cluster. Norway has 0.1% of the world's population and represents approximately 1% of the world's economy (GNP), yet it accounts for around 10% of the world's seaborne transportation. As one can see from the exhibit, one postulates that there is strong positive reinforcement between the various activities in the Norwegian Maritime Cluster. Such clusters can be a source for enhancing a country's competitiveness.

It should be pointed out that many of the ships controlled by Norwegian shipping do not actually fly a Norwegian flag, but may sail under various "flags of convenience," including that of the Norwegian International Ship Registry (NIS), which provides a number of advantages when it comes to taxes, crewing, etc. Thus, a major issue has to do with the maintenance of the Norway-based headquarters for various shipping companies. A key problem here has to do with the personal taxation of owners and senior executives. Without liberalization here, it may be doubtful whether the Norwegian Maritime Cluster will continue to exist in its present dominant form.

This has been demonstrated through research done by Michael Porter of Harvard Business School (Porter, 1998), and has also been applied to specific countries, for example Norway (Reve and Jakobsen, 2002; Jakobsen, 2003b). Another way to illustrate the Norwegian Maritime Cluster is through Exhibit 1.7, which lists the various players in a different manner.

Exhibit 1.7: The Norwegian Maritime Network

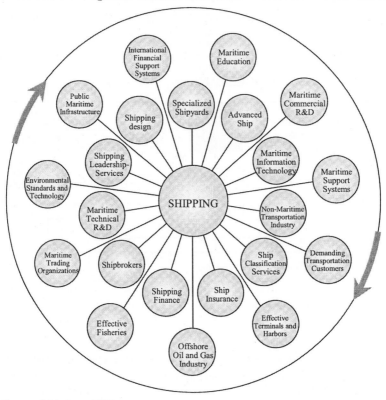

Source: Reve and Jakobsen, 2002

A. P. Moller-Maersk

The steamship company A. P. Moller-Maersk, as the name suggests, was founded by A.P. Moller and his father in Svenborg, Denmark, when they established the Steamship Company Svenborg in 1904. Moller established another steamship company eight years later (Steamship Company of 1912) because he did not feel entirely comfortable with the input from his board of directors of the first company. Both companies grew into enormous shipping giants that were merged during the spring of 2003 under the new name A. P. Moller-Maersk Corporation, to form one of the largest shipping companies in the world (Hornby, 1988).

A. P. Moller-Maersk started business in a modest way—mostly small steamships in the tramp shipping business. With personal flexibility and prudence, A. P. Moller himself was able to build up the organization and take advantage of the turbulent environment of World War I. After the war, the company was an early adopter of diesel-powered vessels and added many newbuildings to its fleet, particularly from A. P. Moller's own yard, Odense Steel Shipyard. Through this link with his own yard, Moller was able to have ships built when there was a need for them. This was vertical integration, with the company gaining control over a large part of its value chain, which thus allowed it access to new ship capacity when needed and also offered more stable employment in the wider "Danish ship industry cluster." In 1928, A. P. Moller-Maersk added a tanker business, built mainly around long-term charters, and a liner service. Thus, the more stable liner and tanker services complemented the traditional tramp business, with its heavy short-term exposure.

After World War II, A.P. Moller-Maersk expanded forcefully, ordering many large liner ships and several new tankers. These were largely built at the company's new yard, Lindoe, opened in 1959 as a new division of the old Odense Steel Shipyard. The vertical integration was not always a success, however. The series of large, double hull VLCC tankers built at Lindoe were technical wonders, but commercial disasters. In retrospect, it seems that these ships were built ten years ahead of their time. Ironically, with today's call for double-hull ships as protection against potential spills, Moller's first double-hulled tankers would be just the right tonnage; but ten years ago, this was not so. The company also expanded into other non-shipping activities, such as oil and gas exploration, and production, as well as various industrial activities.

A. P. Moller-Maersk has since diversified into a number of areas in the shipping value chain, including IT services, and consolidated its own position in others. Its Maersk Sealand is the largest container shipping operation in the world, with a capacity of more than 800,000 TEU and employing more than 30 POST PANMAX, so-called mega-ships, all built at the Lindoe yard; it is now the cornerstone of the group (*Der Spiegel*, June 7, 2004). This also includes ownership in terminals, trucking, IT support, etc., i.e., an integrated global transportation services concept. A long-term view clearly drives the build-up of all of this. Gas carriers, car carriers, VLCCs and product tankers, as well as offshore supply vessels, drilling rigs and a number of other types of vessels are all part of a fleet of more than 250 vessels, with a total deadweight of approximately 12 million tons. By 2003 the group had more than 60,000 employees in over 125 countries.

Looking back over A.P. Moller-Maersk's one-hundred year history, it is interesting to note that the pragmatic business focus of the group seems to have prevailed, leading to repeated commercial success through the decades. Still, even outstanding performers like A.P. Moller-Maersk make mistakes. For example, the fleet of geared Panamax ships did not seem to work out. The fleet of small gas tankers bought from Westfal-Larsen was ill timed. And the double hull VLCC tankers were also ill timed, as noted above.[1]

The shipping industry is, of course, full of examples of ill-timed decisions, and it is easy—but not constructive—to be overly "insightful" in retrospect. A valuable insight, however, seems to be that success in the shipping industry stems, to a large degree, from a willingness to take risks, to make specific moves, so that ship assets are in play when opportunities arise. But with the willingness to take risks, of course, comes the risk of making the wrong decision, too. At the same time, however, the willingness to take risks needs to be backed up by well-

---

[1] Today, A. P. Moller-Maersk seems to be taking a rather opportunistic approach to its VLCC tanker ownership. In 2004, for instance, it sold four of its 1990s double-hull ships to Greek owners. In December 2003 it was reported to have ordered three VLCCs from Chinese shipbuilders (*TradeWinds*, 2004).

thought-out, conservative financial policies. This prudent, focused approach is captured well in a letter from A. P. Moller to his son, Maersk McKinney-Moller, on December 2, 1946: "My old saying: no loss should hit us, which can be avoided with constant care, this must be a watch word throughout the entire organization." (Hornby, 1988).

The company has consistently pushed for the development of larger and more advanced ships. The way it competes in the offshore supply business—where it is one of the world's leaders—can serve as an example. A. P. Moller-Maersk is here primarily focused on the anchor handling tug segment, particularly the very large ones. It has traditionally been seen as one of the leading companies in developing bigger and more powerful ships. The company takes pride in going for size and state-of-the-art equipment, defending its market dominance through more advanced ships. This is clearly a large, aggressive organization with its own culture, and the competition can at times find it hard to understand A. P. Moller-Maersk's pricing decisions. For the company, however, securing a competitive position is important, even at the cost of having to settle for a relatively modest rate at times. During peak periods the company, with its size, will always benefit.

As we know, after the slump in the shipping industry in the 1970s and 1980s, the early 1990s saw the return of stronger shipping markets. The markets have of course fluctuated since then, as they are bound to do: There have been upturns, followed by extended downturns, although never of the same length and depth as those that hit the industry in the 1980s. By the 1990s, many shipping companies, including Leif Hoegh and A. P. Moller-Maersk, were again benefiting from the upside in the market, enjoying strong financial returns from their basically commodity-oriented strategies. It was a welcome period of consolidation, indeed.

As noted, today A. P. Moller-Maersk is No. 1 in the world in container ships over 3,000 TEU (11% of world capacity), No. 4 in container ships under 3,000 TEU, and No. 7 in VLCCs. The company thus not only is big in each of the various segments where it operates—so that it can enjoy scale and cost efficiency—but also has the ability to serve large oil company customers when it comes to their various demands, i.e., it has a customer focus. This is similar to Teekay, which has the size to be efficient and also the customer focus to meet its customers' needs.

Looking retrospectively at the ups and downs in the shipping industry since the early 20th century, as well as at the shipping companies' response, it seems safe to say, in summary that until the early 1990s most shipping companies had a predominantly commodity-oriented focus. This meant that when the market stayed down, they had relatively few corporate-driven options. In many ways, the market dictated their options. Further, much of the technology in the industry was 30 years old by the end of this period—since the 1960s there had been only marginal improvements. The industry was low margin; short-lived peaks in rates, associated with peaks in economic growth, did not change the picture.

For many shipping companies, including Leif Hoegh and A. P. Moller-Maersk, the last decade and a half have thus involved trying hard to find specialization niches. Searching out and taking advantage of such niches has meant that shipping companies have had to try to leverage their strengths in new geographic markets and add "bolt-on" technologies to their established base of strength. Much of this leveraging and bolting on has also led shipping firms to focus for the first time on building their businesses on truly independent business "legs." In other words, many are now following a portfolio strategy. In the past, the so-called commodity strategy collapsed because *all* of a shipping company's businesses sank when the shipping market fell. Shipping companies now appear to be basing their portfolio approach on the assumption that the robustness and cyclical independence of the separate business legs gives them a strength they lacked when they focused almost exclusively on the commodity side of the business. The niche focus means that the independence of the various business legs may well now be more of a reality than ever before.

For shipping companies, it would be good if this history of shipping being a fundamentally low margin business did not repeat itself. Nevertheless, there seems to be strong evidence that strong shipping markets depend on strong trade growth in general. Thus, without growth in worldwide trade, shipping markets tend to be down. It is only truly exceptional growth— beyond what the majority of players in the industry expect—that leads to exceptional, positive shipping market rates.

Traditionally, the bulk of the world's shipping activities was led from Europe and, to some extent, from the US. But have the changes in shipping company strategies and the patterns in world economic growth over the last decade resulted in any new region of the globe coming to dominate the shipping markets? There has, in fact, been a marked shift toward the Far East. Japan has played a critical role for several decades, and its growth has dramatically funneled the strengths of shipping markets in the early to mid-1990s. Similarly, Korea, Taiwan and Southeast Asia have played key stimulating roles. Today, China is particularly critical, being a major source for funneling economic growth worldwide, and with a positive impact on world shipping markets.

Let us also consider that, today, new shipbuilding capacity is high, so owners can rapidly order and receive new capacity, essentially in all niches of shipping. Commoditization of all niches has accelerated. Further, the access to cheap financing has never been easier. One significant financing option is so-called limited partnership capital (*Kommanditgesellschafts-kapital*), available to private investors in Germany and some other countries (Norway and Denmark—*komandittselskap*, or KS), which provides considerable tax advantages for individuals. See Chapter 3 for further explanation. Thus, a shipping project can actually yield a negative return, while the return to the investors can still be positive. This "dream" of hitting on a project with positive returns fuels the rapid evolution in the shipping industry toward commodity, from niche to niche. In general, the shipping industry is mature, with relatively poor returns, except for those rather rare, often short, market cycles when the market truly skyrockets and offers exorbitant returns. As noted earlier, these relatively atypical cycles tend to coincide with periods of economic growth, either globally or, more specifically, within a particular industry or geographic segment, such as in the past when the world economy was faced with crude oil shortages (which has happened several times), and in the near future when the rest of the world will have to contend with China's economic upswing.

Looking at the cyclical nature of the shipping industry and the importance of timing, it seems reasonable to ask why forecasts and scenarios, such as those supplied by Marsoft, are valid at all. Markets are, of course, always hard to predict. What companies like Marsoft, which provides strategy, risk management, investment advisory and market analysis services to the maritime industry, can do is to give a *spectrum* of forecasts. These are based on the best data available, regarding both the aggregate supply side—such as supplies of goods based on developments, say, in the availability of ships of various types—and the demand side—based on, say, demands for oil transportation or bulk cargo handling services, etc. The value of this approach is that it *complements* the judgment of the individual decision-maker, by providing analysis, as far as it can be taken, regarding market developments and turning points.

THE STRATEGIC CHALLENGE

What lessons about strategic challenges can we draw from the history of ocean shipping in general over the last century, as well as from the specific histories of Leif Hoegh and A. P. Moller-Maersk and the like? Although we will explore these challenges more profoundly in later chapters, here are four tentative conclusions that will also serve as the basis of the later discussion in the book:

Cyclicality and turbulence characterize much of the shipping industry, but successful shipowners see these two forces as an *opportunity*, not a threat. Taking advantage of the opportunity, however, requires understanding how to execute an effective commodity strategy. Successfully executing a commodity strategy rests on three principles:

- Right timing is everything—short term (spot) and long term. In and out!

- Cut the losses—run with the winners.

- Squeeze the margins out of the business.

There are opportunities for carving out niche strategies in shipping, i.e. for identifying market segments where the competition is unlikely to be very strong, and where adding the right unique competences will allow a shipping firm to serve a set of customers more or less alone. Thus, the drive for non-commodity niche strategies also seems to be an important part of the successful shipping company's overall strategic menu.

Strategic niches tend to create only short-lived bonanzas. Other shipowners tend to "copy" the initial niche pioneers, which causes a general move toward commoditization of niche strategies over time.

A shift toward professionalism has occurred—clear and strong—with financial analysis, better market insights and consistent risk-taking approaches now prevailing. Nevertheless, to succeed, today's shipping company must still have the old entrepreneurial *Leitbild*. There is still an abundance of strong-willed—often even flamboyant—individuals who set their imprimatur on this business, perhaps more than in any other industry. It seems clear that "power" at the top through decision-making ability is critical. This leadership style must, however, encompass a clear vision, clear creativity and a clear ability to be consistent over time.

Our brief historical analysis of shipping markets and the shipping companies' responses to them has thus led us to four key lessons about the strategic challenges in the shipping industry. With these key strategic challenges in mind, let us now push further to analyze the *context* for good shipping strategies. More specifically, let us look in more detail at a model of shipping company strategies. Once we have established a working model, we will explore key macro issues, a few trade-specific issues and key characteristics of the financial markets as they relate to shipping strategies. This brief overview will end with a short review of the major relevant technological developments, important contextual realities for how shipping strategies can be shaped.

Shipping Company Strategies: A Model

Exhibit 1.8 depicts a model for business development in shipping companies. Professor Bala Chakravarthy and I developed this conceptual scheme to shed light on the internally generated growth process in industrial corporations (Chakravarthy and Lorange, 2004). As we shall see, the model is easily adaptable to shipping companies' strategic challenges.

Exhibit 1.8: A Conceptual Model for Shipping Strategies

	To be developed	**Leverage** ("Commodity Niche")	**Transform** ("Speculation Niche")
Market Understanding			
	In place	**Protect & Extend** ("Commodity")	**Build** ("Niche")
		Appropriate	Need to develop

Know-How Resource of the Shipping Firm

Source: Chakravarthy and Lorange, 2004

As noted, we can characterize shipping markets as typically consisting of established markets, such as the classical tanker markets, containers, liners and/or bulker markets. Here, perfect atomistic competition prevails (we shall discuss this more in Chapter 2). Alternatively, we can think about new shipping markets within highly specialized shipping segments, such as special-purpose bulkers, heavy lift ships, certain types of supply ships, special-purpose tankers, etc. Here, we might expect more specialized markets, imperfect competition, less atomization—indeed, what we would call niche markets (we shall say more about this in Chapter 3). The horizontal axis of Exhibit 1.8 picks up on this aspect of specialization, when a company specializes by (potentially) adding proprietary competences, know-how and technologies.

But we can also think about distinctive competences applied to the core activities in shipping. Typically, a shipping company will cover the core activities relating to running ships in the atomistic marketplace. This means not only the technical side but also having the prerequisite competences in-house to have an understanding of the market mechanism at play. The bottom left square of Exhibit 1.8 reflects this.

Alternatively, a shipping company can add new activities, such as new market insights, more intimate contacts with specific shippers, new technologies for loading and unloading and for understanding how to operate highly specialized types of ships, etc. The vertical axis of Exhibit 1.8 reflects these options.

Think about developing a model for shipping as making choices between four potential categories:

- The **Protect and Extend** category (lower left quadrant of Exhibit 1.8, as already noted) is for doing the atomistic business "as usual," which is essentially a commodity strategy. It is key to attempt to identify successful examples of a Protect and Extend strategy where there is a good link between, on the one hand, market contacts and appropriate know-how and, on the other hand, the shipping firm's ability to deliver on this.

- The **Leverage Business** category (upper left quadrant) is for entering new ship market segments, based on repeating a success strategy already developed under Protect and Extend.

- The **Build Business** category (lower right quadrant) is for adding new technologies to an already successful strategy developed under Protect and Extend.

- The **Transform Business** category (upper right quadrant) is for adopting both new technologies and new market segments together. This can typically be rather speculative. According to Chakravarthy and Lorange (2004), this study is often associated with failure.

Leverage business, Build business and Transform business are niche strategies. Unfortunately, in classical shipping, the opportunities for entering these categories of business development are typically rather small. A main focus will thus *always* have to remain on Protect and Extend, where the atomistic market will be in full play. What does this mean? Simply that, under most circumstances, following a commodity strategy well is key. There will often be relatively few opportunities for unique new markets and/or unique new distinctive competences (we will look at this again in Chapter 3). The commodity nature of the Protect and Extend business, to be discussed extensively in Chapter 2, more or less delineates the classical strategic arena where much shipping business plays out.

Some time ago McKinsey undertook a study for the Norwegian Shipowners Association and the Norwegian Science and Technology Research Council (McKinsey, 1985, 1989). They proposed a model for different types of shipping companies, pursuing different types of strategies, which would be based on the significance of achieving economies of scale, as well as on an ability to achieve a degree of specialization/differentiation. Exhibit 1.9 gives an overview of their proposed strategic archetype map. As one can see, these would be special shipping, contract shipping and industry shipping.

Exhibit 1.9: McKinsey's "Shipping Map" for Shipping Firms

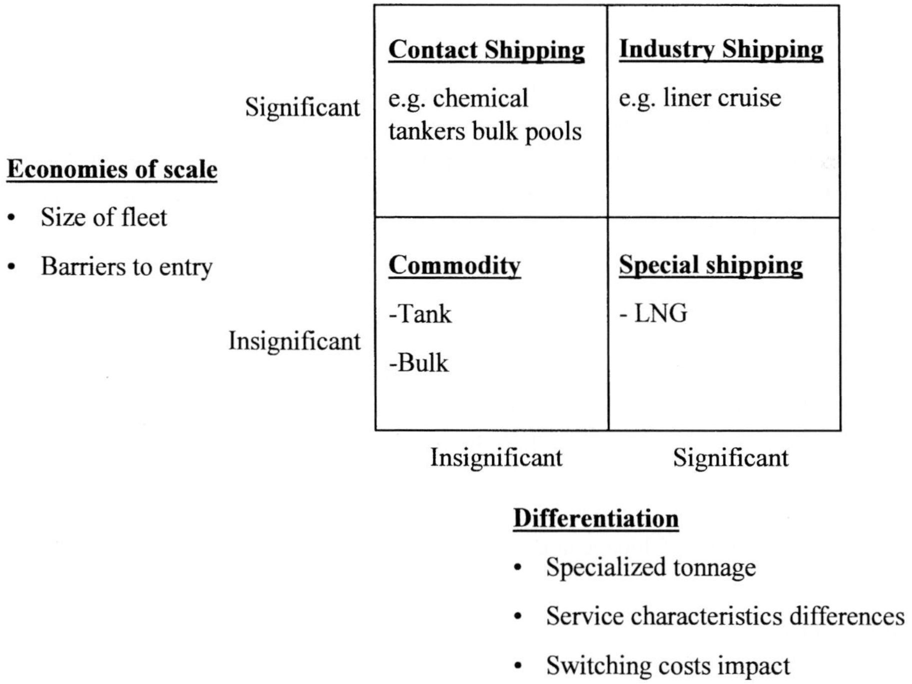

		Contact Shipping	**Industry Shipping**
Economies of scale	Significant	e.g. chemical tankers bulk pools	e.g. liner cruise
• Size of fleet			
• Barriers to entry	Insignificant	**Commodity** -Tank -Bulk	**Special shipping** - LNG
		Insignificant	Significant

Differentiation

• Specialized tonnage

• Service characteristics differences

• Switching costs impact

Source: McKinsey & Co., 1985, 1989

The McKinsey model has several similarities with what we have proposed in this book. Above all, it stresses the importance of commodity shipping versus other types of shipping. The key difference, however, is that the differentiation dimension proposed in their model has been developed further in this book, where we have introduced *both* a technology dimension *and* a customer dimension. The economies of scale dimension proposed by McKinsey is, by contrast, not seen by us as being typically all that significant. Clearly we recognize, however, that barriers to entry do now and then exist, as will be discussed in Chapter 3. For commodity shipping the most critical success factor is developing a clear strategy regarding second-hand asset play, according to McKinsey. Thus, while emphasizing the "in/out" strategic dimension, the "long/short" chartering dimension seems to be less heavily emphasized in their model.

For complex segments McKinsey emphasizes "industrial" shipping strategies, combined with asset play. There are many similarities here with what we propose.

As an overall factor for success, McKinsey recommends, organizationally, strong analytically based strategies, combined with a managerial bias for action, a recommendation we wholeheartedly agree with.

TRADE-SPECIFIC IMPACTS ON THE MAJOR SHIPPING MARKETS

At the extreme, it seems safe to conclude that each trade will set its own market. There are, of course, strong interdependencies between freight rate markets, but for all practical purposes, the major trades tend to be the market setters for what can be seen as their own broad shipping freight rate markets. And all of these major shipping markets can be classified as commodity markets. There are, nonetheless, observable differences.

Coal

Coal is an important commodity. It is, in particular, a major driver of the development of bulk freight rates. Factors such as stock building when it comes to steam coal can, for instance, be important. It might make sense, therefore, to monitor this development. Micro factors, such as for instance the temporary closing of Japanese nuclear power plants, can also play an important role in the potential revival of the coal trade. Other factors, like lower imports into—and any exports from—China, can be important, too.

Steel and Iron Ore

Here, as noted, an increase in, for instance, China's iron ore imports can play an important role in the development of shipping markets, since iron ore is a key raw material in China's steel production. In other words, there are close links between iron ore and steel.

Increased shipbuilding in countries such as China and South Korea can thus also play a role. Direct steel products imports into South Korea and China can, of course, further impact the bulk ship freight rate market.

Grain

Grain, another commodity, can have a significant effect on the bulk freight rate markets. Trends show that grain imports into Russia, for example, have strong effects on the shipping market. Natural factors such as drought in Australia can also play an important role. Changing trade patterns, such as relatively more imports from South America and Australia, versus relatively lower imports from the US, say, into Eastern Europe and Russia or, say, into China, means longer shipping legs, or routes, and can also have important effects on the shipping market. The relative length of the shipping legs can change, and the bulk shipping rates will change accordingly (the longer the shipping legs, the higher the bulk shipping rates).

Crude Oil

A key driver for this will be a number of factors that have an effect on the supply side for oil, such as the policies of the Organization of Petroleum-Exporting Countries (OPEC) and other producing countries, or factors relating to geopolitical events, like the impacts of restrictions caused by threats of war (or actual acts of war). In the long run, oil exploration will, of course, fundamentally also affect the supply side. Consider Exhibit 1.10.

Exhibit 1.10: Correlation between Middle East Output and VLCC Spot Rates (Monthly, Dec 1999–Oct 2003)

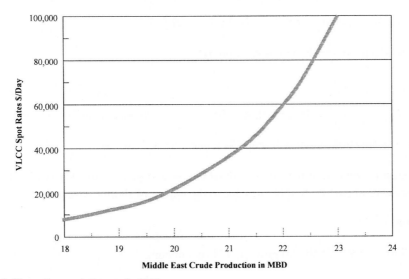

Source: R.S. Platou Economic Research, 2003

This exhibit indicates a correlation between Middle East output and VLCC tanker freight rates. One sees that when crude oil production is up, freight rates also tend to go up. It is, however, generally not only the supply side, but rather the demand side that above all determines oil tanker freight rates. Here, local consumption in the various industrialized parts of the world will be important. Equally important will be the effects of meteorological developments, such as low temperatures that result in higher consumption of heating oil. The general economic climate in various parts of the more industrialized world will also have an impact on oil consumption. In total, the pattern of factors that determines the freight levels for oil tanker services will thus be different from those that have an impact on the freight levels for the bulk carrier segments. Nevertheless, it will be true for both that the freight rates tend to be volatile and it will thus remain difficult to predict with any degree of certainty or exactitude how they will develop.

Shipping Rate Forecasting—Marsoft Example

Forecasting alternative scenarios for the development of various shipping markets is, of course, very difficult. Nevertheless, a number of organizations are in the forecasting business, and one of the leading ones is Marsoft. Marsoft provides regular alternative scenarios for each of the main bulk size categories, the main oil carrier categories and the main container ship categories. Here's an example: For a Cape-size 150,000 dwt ship, the spot rates between Brazil and Rotterdam for iron ore, Marsoft offers three alternative scenarios, a base case, a low case, and a high case.

Base Case

- Economic growth in the US will pick up over the next 12 months.

- Chinese steel output will increase by 10% per year.

- The steam coal trade will grow strongly.

Low Case

- European Union (EU) growth will diminish to 0.5% per annum in 2003 and 2004.

- EU steam steel output will drop 2% relative to the base case.

- Grain exports from the former Soviet Union will pick up quickly (which will have a negative impact on freight rates due to the impact of shorter voyages).

High Case

- Chinese steel output will grow by 13% per annum.

- Total Chinese dry bulk imports will rise by 15% per annum (please compare this with a rise in imports of 22% in 2002).

Based on these general forecasts for supply and demand, as well as on these three scenarios, Marsoft forecasts the rate developments for the Cape-size 150,000 dwt ship, spot rates Brazil/Rotterdam (see Exhibit 1.11).

Exhibit 1.11: Cape 150,000 dwt Spot Rates (Brazil/Rotterdam—Iron Ore)

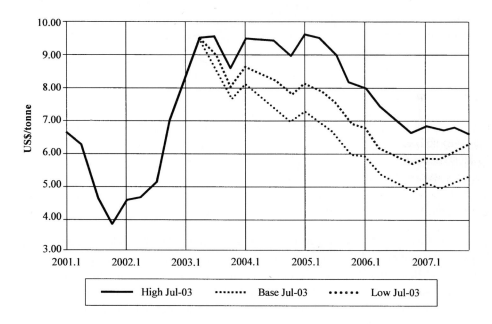

Source: Marsoft, 2003

One can question the accuracy of Marsoft's forecasts. For instance, one might compare the forecast given in early 2003 (Exhibit 1.11) for the freight rates of a 150,000 dwt Cape-size ship going from South America to Holland, and the same forecast given a year later (Exhibit 1.12). We see here that Marsoft's initial forecast was far too conservative. We see that the two forecasts provide dramatically different pictures regarding the scenarios. For example, the absolute height level that the freight market reached is much higher in the latter case. This is above all a reflection of the key assumption relating to the Chinese economy. We can also infer from this that the second-hand value for large bulk carriers turned out to be much larger that initially forecast by Marsoft. When it comes to the development of the market from the peak around January 2004, we see that Marsoft does expect a drop in the market—and this is under both scenarios. The key, as we see, is to be able to come up with reasonable key assumptions behind the forecasts.

Exhibit 1.12: Cape 150,000 dwt Spot Rates (Brazil/Rotterdam—Iron Ore)

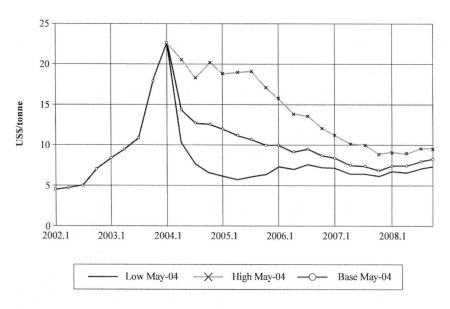

Source: Marsoft, 2004

It is useful in this respect to distinguish between the basic model, the underlying assumptions that go into the model, and the forecasts thereby being generated. The assumptions will drive the model and determine the specific outcomes for the forecasts. Thus, to set meaningful assumptions is critical. As we shall see, Marsoft did not set entirely realistic assumptions regarding the development of the Chinese market. This turned out to be a major reason for the less accurate forecast. However, subsequent testing of the basic model by Marsoft, putting in the correct assumptions regarding China on a post facto basis, confirmed the basic Marsoft model was indeed rather good.

Consider now the assumptions as they relate to the China-based market situation. In early 2003, the bulk carrier fleet was highly utilized worldwide, say, at a level of around 96%. The expert assumptions indicated that China's economy would, in all likelihood, slow down, and that one would not get the continuation of the growth in China that one had previously seen. Instead, the opposite happened. The effect of this was that the overall bulk carrier utilization rate went up by another estimated 3.5%. In addition, there was an effect of delays in Chinese ports, which would mean another estimated 3%. To counterbalance this, however, there was a shift from oil tanker to bulk carrier utilization for the worldwide OBO fleet, which meant 1% less overall utilization, due to this added capacity. On top of this, there was less scrapping, meaning another 1% less utilization.

The net result was that the overall utilization of the world's bulk carrier fleet went up 4.5%, i.e., to full utilization, an absolute maximum. This is in contrast to the original assumption which indicated that the utilization would be expected to go down. As we know, the result has been an exceptionally strong dry bulk market. Marsoft missed this!

The issue of developing key assumptions is, therefore, a critical one. Marsoft utilizes leading analysis houses worldwide, various economic experts and available resources from a broad set of sources. This is the basis for their assumptions setting.

FINANCIAL MARKETS

Financial markets can also have a direct effect on freight rate markets. For instance, currency rates can directly impact shipping rates. They can also have an indirect effect through an impact on major commodities, such as oil prices. Further, currency rates can have important effects on shipbuilding prices—they can potentially stimulate or dampen newbuilding activities, which, in turn, can have an impact on freight rate markets. Interest rates can have many of the same effects. In short, understanding the developments in financial markets, particularly currency and interest rate fluctuations, has become an increasingly integral part of understanding how freight rate markets develop. For instance, since many shipping transactions are consummated in US dollars—including newbuilding and second-hand prices for ships—a general appreciation of the dollar relative to other currencies tends to lead to a lowering of shipping rates. Further, when interest rates go up, shipowners incur higher overall costs, and this may lead to an increase in freight markets to compensate.

TECHNOLOGICAL DEVELOPMENTS IN SHIPBUILDING AND SHIP DESIGN

Technological developments can also have an important influence on shipping markets. Despite the fact that shipowners are often conservative here, a number of broader developments in technology have had an impact on the shipping industry. For instance, the price of building new ships has steadily gone down. The replacement cost of vessels has, in general, thus also come down, not just because shipbuilding has become more cost efficient but also because of various kinds of government subsidies. Thus, the asset values of ships have, at times, declined above and beyond the normal depreciation effects of aging. For instance, over the last ten years, there has been a 33% decline in replacement value for building new ships of most types (I. M. Skaugen Annual Report, 2002). This decline has been accentuated by the increase in new shipbuilding capacity, which has led to both lower shipping freight markets and higher depreciation costs for shipowners which, in turn, has dampened the newbuilding activities that many traditional owners can afford. Instead, new owners with "fresh" capital have entered the industry aggressively. The design of the ships themselves has led to higher speeds and lower fuel consumption as well. All these factors have been leading to downward pressure on the ship freight rate markets, with both a capacity effect and a productivity effect setting in.

CONCLUSION

In this chapter we have drawn an overall picture of the shipping industry, with its strong global focus and the fierce competitive forces. We illustrated the evolution of successful shipping company strategies with two case studies—Leif Hoegh & Co. and A. P. Moller-Maersk. We then introduced our conceptual model for developing strategies in shipping companies. As we shall see, this represents one of the cornerstones of this book. And finally we discussed the challenges of rate forecasting, using Marsoft as an example.

In the next chapter, we shall examine in more detail how shipping companies may develop strategies for competing in commodity markets. We shall see that a keen understanding of freight market developments, particularly having a feel for the turning points, can provide the basis for commodity-based shipping strategies. Key strategic decisions on how the ships might be employed will be in/out decisions, as well as long/short decisions. We shall also see how important a consistent profile of risk will be, including strong discipline. The need to keep costs at an absolute minimum will also be discussed. Commodity-based strategies represent the backbone of most shipping companies—hence, the discussion in Chapter 2 will be important and detailed.

CHAPTER 2

COMMODITY-BASED SHIPPING: PLAYING THE MARKET

The art of prophecy is very difficult, especially with respect to the future. —Mark Twain

The shipping market is so volatile and margins so uncertain that consistent success in chartering and investments demands is a very disciplined decision-making process.
                    —Dr. Arlie Sterling, Lloyd's List, May 6, 2003, p. 7

Shipping is a hot topic because the world is short of ships.
                    —Financial Times, *March 12, 2004, p. 12*

MARKET VIEW

For a long time it has been almost a truism in shipping that supply and demand for shipping activities should ideally be more or less in balance. Too much supply, i.e., too many ships available, causes the freight markets to fall. Too much demand relative to supply causes the ship market to go up. Demand rarely exceeds supply over a long period, however. Rather, there tend to be relatively short peaks in the freight market. Shipbuilding technology has exacerbated this phenomenon: Huge capacity is available for building new tonnage—and fast. The high capacity thus further tends to shorten the peak periods for ship freight rates. Finally, ample financing tends to be available. Banks appear to be eager to give loans—they can, indeed, often be seen as rather effective drivers of new shipbuilding activities, which in turn also tend to dampen the freight rates. In general, this is unfortunate for the shipping industry, since supply generally tends to outstrip demand. The result is long periods of rather depressed freight markets (Stopford, 1997).

Well-consolidated companies typically have the luxury of going anti-cyclical. Because of their financial strength, they can be less dependent on the banks. Often companies in this category become bigger and bigger until, perhaps, greed kicks in. It is in general hard to be small and to play the market successfully at the same time.

We should remind ourselves here that the visible volatility of the market, as reflected when the swings in the time charter rates are be plotted, would be a function of the time horizon. The volatilities are much more extreme when observed over short-term, spot market conditions; the average evens out over longer time periods (hence also the more "average" freight rates for long-term charters). The overall "mean" for the charter market's moves will, of course, remain the same. Note, however, that market plots of charter market rates are normally skewed toward the low end, reflecting the fact that charter markets tend to go through relatively long periods of low freight rate levels, combined with some extreme, positive peaks. This bias toward the low end is, of course, highest for the spot market.

The forecast for the freight rate developments for the spot rate, iron ore Brazil/Rotterdam for a 150,000 ton deadweight (dwt) Cape-size ship was given in Exhibits 1.11 and 1.12, and the corresponding historical rate distributions are given in Exhibit 2.1, illustrating the tendency to be "skewed to the left."

Exhibit 2.1: Historical Rate Distribution of Spot Rates 1990–2003. Cape 150,000 dwt (Brazil/Rotterdam—Iron Ore)

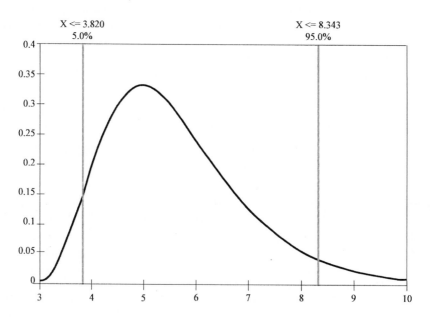

Source: Marsoft, 2003

A cumulative probability distribution can be developed out of this, which provides a measure for evaluating likely rate developments in the future, based on the historical rate performances (as indicated in Exhibit 2.1), as well as for future expectations, as indicated in one's forecasts, such as the ones given in Exhibits 1.11 and 1.12. This same picture of the cumulative probability distribution can be seen in Exhibit 2.2.

Exhibit 2.2: Future Expectations—Cumulative Distribution of Spot Rates

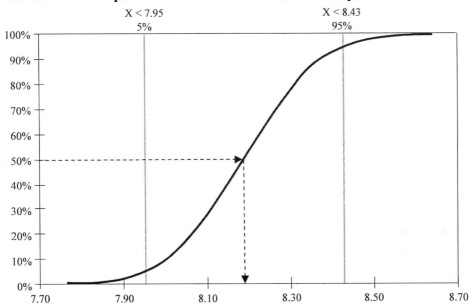

Source: Marsoft, 2003

As Exhibit 2.2 shows, there is a 50% chance that we shall achieve a spot rate of US$8.20. There is a 95% chance that the spot rate will be less than $8.43. And there is a 5% chance that the spot rate will be as low as $7.95 or less. This means that when we are calculating a certain spot rate expectation, we can easily go in and see how this equates with past history and future forecasts.

As noted, shipping markets tend to be atomistic markets; they exhibit more or less perfect competition. The price offered for the freight service determines (in large measure) who gets the deal—the lower the offer, the better the chance. There tend to be many suppliers, with very little concentration in the shipping industry structure. Further, there tend to be many sources of demand for shipping services—again with relatively little concentration on the demand side of the industry. All in all, these tendencies add to an atomistic—or highly fragmented—pattern, with both many suppliers and demanders. Finally, the various ship types—basic oil carriers as well as bulk carriers—are usually more or less similar, i.e., interchangeable, which adds to the pattern of commodity orientation that is typically used to describe shipping markets and services. There are, of course, various types of ships when it comes to size, speed, age, etc. Nevertheless, there tends to be a strong correlation between the freight rates for these various types. For instance, a falling market for very large ships also tends to push down the freight rate markets for categories of smaller ships, although typically with a lag. Also, rates for newer ships tend to fall, along with rates for older tonnage of similar type.

CLASSIC SHIPPING SEGMENTS

Let us now discuss more specifically the major shipping markets. There are typically different general markets for tankers, as opposed to bulk carriers, container ships or liner shipping, each of which will be analyzed in more detail below (Zannetos, 1966, 1999).

Tanker Markets

In tanker markets there appear to be cycles, not trends, and these cycles seem to be pronounced. Over the long term, however, there seem to be neither clear upward nor clear downward general trends. The long-haul trade mix relative to the short-haul trade mix is also important, as noted. Presently, there seems to be a relative decline in the long-haul trade side in tankers, not least due to the emergence of several large-capacity pipelines. What is truly important here is the owner's ability to secure back haul business.

Within the tanker category, there are at least four major sub-markets—all, as noted, somewhat correlated:

- VLCCs (very large cruise carriers)—ships with more than 200,000 dwt capacity

- Suezmax market—ships typically of around 100,000 to 125,000 dwt

- Aframax/Panamax market—ships of 60,000 to 80,000 dwt

- Product tankers/Handy-size market—ships typically around 30,000 to 45,000 dwt.

Tanker regulation is now an issue. In the European Union (EU), tankers will have to have double hulls by 2005—brought forward from the previous deadline of 2010—and they already have to have double hulls to enter US ports. The EU has already imposed a ban on single hull tankers carrying heavy oil shipments to EU ports. This came into effect in July 2003, after the sinking of the *Prestige*, a 26-year-old Greek-owned tanker, in Spanish waters in 2002. Furthermore, if a single hull tanker is more than 28 years old, it cannot operate in European or US waters. The EU is also interacting with the International Maritime Organization (IMO), which regulates world shipping, to adopt these EU guidelines for phasing out single hull tankers.

The cost of complying with the new regulations will be high for shipowners. A case in point is Teekay Shipping Corporation—the world's largest tanker owner. It recently stated that it would write down the value of its fleet by about $50 to $60 million because of the required phasing out of some of its single hull tankers. This non-cash write-down stems directly from the IMO's decision, on December 9, 2003, to bring forward the phasing out of single hull tankers. Nineteen of Teekay's tankers are affected by the new rules (*Gulf News*, December 15, 2003, p. 45). The salient questions are: Will other countries adopt these rules? And will the oil companies prefer the newer, better maintained ships, or will they go for the lowest rates, when it comes down to it? The latter largely seems to be the case so far.

The new IMO regulations are scheduled to come into effect in April 2005. They impose a more rigorous inspection regime for all tankers, and ban the carriage of heavy oils on single hull tankers. A majority of the non-double hull tanker fleet would be phased out by 2010 as a result. The immediate effect is that approximately 32 million dwt, or 10% of the existing world tanker fleet, is expected to be banned from worldwide trading when the regulations come into force. A further 87 million dwt, or 27% of the world tanker fleet, are expected to be excluded from the majority of oil tanker trades by 2010. This accelerated phasing out schedule could lead to increased commercial discrimination against older, non-double hull tonnage, thus helping to maintain the tight balance between supply and demand (Teekay Annual Report, 2003, p. 19).

The phasing out of single hull tankers can significantly affect the crude tanker freight market—and most likely lead to improvements.

Bulk Carrier Markets

The dry bulk carrier market can be broken down into three major segments:

- Cape-size bulk carriers—comprising ships of more than 80,000 to 100,000 dwt

- Panamax market—typically comprising ships of around 55,000 to 80,000 dwt

- Handy-size market—typically comprising ships of 25,000 to 35,000 dwt.

Ship safety is a concern here, too. Regulations for bulk carriers are thus also being tightened. The IMO has decided that from 2007 bulk carriers must be built with double hulls, but the phasing out of single hull vessels has not been addressed yet (Whittaker, 2003).

The three major iron ore producers (Companhia del Vale Rio Doce (CVRD), Brazil; BHP, Australia; and Rio Tinto, UK) are accelerating the introduction of more iron ore production capacity. Indeed, they have a higher concentration in this trade than OPEC ever had. Hence, they could be able, hypothetically at least, to push the prices up, which could have the effect of reducing global trade and lowering shipping markets. Today's superpowers do not seem to mind, however, that the receivers of the goods, in this case primarily China, seem to have to pay, and that this country's (and others') economic growth might be negatively affected by this. The ore producers' expansion projects have speeded up significantly in response to the heavy demand in growth in general and, as noted, in particular from China. The result: More iron ore in international trade and higher freight rates.

As noted in Chapter 1, the closure of 17 Japanese nuclear plants in the Tokyo area represents an example of how short-term discrete events may further drive the freight markets up, in this case due to higher coal imports. Five plants are now back in operation; the rest are not meant to come into operation again until later, but the closures resulted in a 15% to 20% increase in coal imports to Japan.

How much further up can bulk shipping markets go? What are the turning points? How can we manage the risk of exit and/or long-term charter fixing at this point? Historically, the market peaks have been short, and the downturns brutal. Ore imports to supply the Chinese steel industry seem to be the key to understanding the overall market cycle this time. As with electricity, the critical importance of shipping is easily forgotten until there is not enough of it. Industrial uses of ships, for example by oil companies, mining companies, steel mills and power utilities, fostered a belief that shipping would always be readily available at low cost, and many companies decided not to take longer-term cover for their shipping needs. "The industry became highly transactional, and short-term thinking prevailed." (*Financial Times*, March 12, 2004, p. 12).

While the tanker markets and bulk freight markets tend to be largely independent of each other, there are of course also interdependencies here, above all due to the effects of newbuilding activities in the shipyards. The yards tend to deliver the type of capacity in one of the two ship types that happens to be the most advantageous for the yards at a given time in terms of the price that they can ask for a newbuilding. This, again, is a function of the freight rate outlook as seen from an owner's eyes. This expectation regarding the likely development of freight rates for the ship type will thus impact the owner's appetite to place orders, and also his willingness to pay the yard a reasonable price for the ship. This, in turn, tends to lead to too much newbuilding ordering in this particularly popular category of ships. Further, over time, this tends to bring the freight rate down in this category, now making other ship categories relatively more attractive for the owners, thus evening out the long-term differences between tanker rates and dry bulk shipping rates—indeed, in general, between any types of ships.

Container Markets

Container shipping has revolutionized the shipping industry and transformed the shipping business over the last decade and a half. In the past we had break-bulk liner activities. Emerging containerization, which started some 25 years ago, has, however, dramatically changed the liner business, and has also strongly affected the reefer business (because of the adaptation of reefer plugs in the container ships, allowing them to carry refrigerated containers), as well as large segments of the classic bulk shipping business.

The impact of containerization on the shipping business cannot be overestimated. Traditionally, containerization led to spectacular growth in this shipping segment, coupled with strong development of the technology behind the container ships. The segment has also been highly profitable. At the same time, the size of ships has gone from around 1,000 TEU to more than 8,000 TEU for so-called mega ships. The speed has also increased. Initially, the container shipping business could be seen as a specialized niche business; today, it has many of the characteristics of a commodity business. A growing fraction of container ship capacity is today run in the open market, on either short-term contracts or time charter/bare boat charter contracts, as opposed to being part of a specific liner business' operations.

China, with strong exports of manufactured goods, is coming into play very strongly in the container market, too. Low Chinese labor costs are critical for locating manufacturing there, with a marked migration of manufacturing from Japan, the US and other sources. Shipowners' response to this general upturn in container ship freight rates has, however, followed traditional patterns: aggressive new building contracting. Today, a significant proportion of new container ships has been built on speculation, not based on the specific demands of liner companies, which was traditionally the case.

What would a downward, worst case scenario for the container shipping segment be? The risk of acts of terrorism in a major consumer country, such as the US, might lead to a downward adjustment of consumers' activities, and with it, a corresponding slowdown in imports to the US, particularly from China. In the end, it will be the overriding developments of the final consumption patterns in industrialized countries that could represent the biggest sources of vulnerability for the container business.

Container lines are also attempting to be cost efficient, above all by operating larger container fleets to achieve economies of scale and also to integrate forward into port operations, storage, even door to door trucking delivery. The trend in container lines is thus generally one of going for larger and larger ships, often with higher and higher speeds, complemented by smaller feeder ships, warehousing, door-to-door activities, etc., and building a strong *brand* to support this. Competition among the various players is fierce. A. P. Moller-Maersk has approximately 11% of the world's capacity for container ships—over 3,000 TEU—followed by MSC and Evergreen.

According to Marcus (2003), one can perhaps distinguish between three tiers of container liners, based on a number of factors:

- The *first tier* carriers, which would be the industry leaders, offer a differentiated product, based on price and/or service with large container ships, modern terminals, worldwide information systems, and a number of add-on value-creating possibilities through warehousing, trucking, etc. Maersk Sealand is No. 1, as noted, with an overall capacity of more than 800,000 TEU; MSC, from Switzerland, is No. 2 (500,000 TEU); and Evergreen, from Taiwan, is No. 3 (440,000 TEU) (*Der Spiegel*, June 7, 2004).

- The *third tier* of carriers, by contrast, are very much focused on narrow market niches, where they go for specific cargo types, often bringing in chartered vessels with specialized technology and having close relationships with the shippers. Shallow draft ports are often a reality, calling for tailored, special-purpose ships. Thus, typically these third tier carriers operate in isolated geographic locations. An example of this might be the Norwegian firm Lys-Line.

- The *second tier* carriers, in between, seem to represent a rather vulnerable group. They would be highly at the mercy of general market conditions, having to play to a mass market focus, but with limited resources—often with suboptimal ships and restricted inland services—and also with limited information services. Perhaps an example of this might be Hapag-Lloyd, which is ranked No. 15 in the world, with a capacity of 160,000 TEU (*Der Spiegel*, June 7, 2004).

Thus, strategy means choice and an ability to have the resources to back up one's choices within the container liner industry.

Interestingly, one of the shipping industry's largest groups of players, the Norwegian shipowners, are largely absent when it comes to this segment. Why have Norwegian shipping companies not entered the container shipping segment in a significant way? From a historical point of view, Norwegian owners largely seem to have stuck to pallets as a transportation solution. Also, several Norwegian players focused heavily on RoRo ships. Norwegian owners thus seem to have got "trapped" in these transportation concepts, and have thus largely missed out on the booming growth in the container market.

Liner Shipping

The liner shipping business has traditionally been a basically non-commodity market, where new ship designs, speed, tonnage increases, etc. were important. Have we, however, seen more commoditization here, too? Recall that in this segment we have high capital costs, long ship life and highly effective operators. Price wars are not uncommon. To gain/defend market shares, liners might give much of their margins away. As soon as they gain efficiency, they will thus have to turn much of this over to the customer because of the need to protect their own market share.

The liner industry thus seems to have more or less disappeared in its classic form. It was heavily based on the so-called liner conferences, which attempted to set an elaborate system of pricing for the different participants in the various liner trades, thus in effect restricting competition by stipulating rates. A number of "new" types of liner activities have now, however, emerged:

- Container lines are based on a scheduled service, from various ports to various others, with high speed and regularity. It thus allows shippers a high degree of convenience and predictability.

- Special chemical carriers are also often run as liner operations, with scheduled departures within a fixed pattern of trading—from a certain number of locations to another number of locations. Often each shipping company will have its own storage tanks ashore. Branding is key!

- Car carriers are also typically run according to fixed schedules and through a global pattern of operations, indeed a liner operation. Again, branding plays a role here too.

As we have already noted, liner shipping in the past was largely a non-commodity business. For many years, liners competed on the design of the ships, the size, the speed, different cargo, handling capabilities, cellular layouts, etc. Today, the ships are basically the same. Costs are absolutely key now. To gain cost advantages, bigger ships are coming on line all the time. They are often supported by container ship "feeders," which are generally chartered in. All in all, there are lower barriers to entry, which "invites" price wars.

Is the structure of the liner industry changing? The industry leaders seem to be growing bigger and bigger. The second tier liner firms are, however, seemingly becoming neither big enough nor small enough. The third tier companies might be in even greater need of becoming more focused, and so on. The degree of commodity orientation would be inversely related to this. The big winners are the global giants Maersk Sealand, Evergreen, etc.

In general, modern liner operations are based on developing strong brand names, with a focus on getting close to the customer—often in fact integrating one's own services with the logistics value chain of the customer. It is thus more a value chain concept that is driving the modern liner operation, rather than the classic "conference"-based liner concept, which limits competition.

As indicated, there are clear interdependencies between the various ship categories *within* each of the bulk carrier, tanker, container and liner ship markets. Hence, executives active in any of these markets must follow the specifics of all, in the sense that they can explore shorter-term differences. Companies such as Marsoft accordingly provide specific rate development forecasts for each of three general market categories—tankers, bulkers and containers—and with specific rate forecasts for various ship sizes within each major type.

It is key that we consider the dynamism of shipping strategies here. One can thus think about *acquiring* a position (say, a second-hand ship, an order for a new ship) *now*, in order to be in a position to make meaningful market-based moves later, say, in six months' to a year's time, when the shipping market has, one hopes, gone up. For instance, one can contract a newbuilding order now, and then enter into a time charter or a bare boat charter 6 to 12 months from now, when the shipping rates are higher. Similarly, one can buy a ship now, and then run it in the spot market for a relatively short time, and then sell it and/or charter it out on time charter/bareboat charter when the market is higher.

Effective shipping strategy thus depends on *anticipating* the "turning points" and having a reasonably good feel about when to build up the appropriate tonnage to be in a position to do business at higher freight rate levels later. It is of course nerve-racking for some people to have to make moves that may involve large commitments of investment funds without a corresponding fixed income stream, to have to pay financial charges without having a corresponding revenue stream associated with these commitments—in essence, merely to have an "open" position for later on. For effective shipping company strategies, this kind of positioning is, however, critical. It goes without saying, nevertheless, that a shipping company's ability to expand along these lines via proper timing and positioning tends to be limited by what the banks are willing to provide in financing, given the fact that, when acquiring a ship, there will be no secure cash flow associated with the position taken for a certain period of time, until the ship is later fixed or sold.

SHIPOWNERS' CLASSIC RESPONSES—PLAY THE MARKETS

Let us refer again to our conceptual scheme initially articulated by Chakravarthy and Lorange (2004) for developing strategies in shipping companies, as illustrated in Exhibit 1.8. The specific challenge in the shipping industry is to develop a realistic strategy for the commodity segment: Protect and Extend. This is conceptually illustrated in Exhibit 2.3.

Exhibit 2.3: A Model for Commodity Strategies

	Leverage	**Transform**
New		

Shipping Markets	**Protect and Extend: A Commodity Strategy**
	"Understand the market better"
	   - Timing decisions
	   - Turning points
	"Do good even better"
		Build

Established	Marginally improve market position
	   - Product extensions
	   - New product offering
	   - Marginally strengthen existing
	     competencies
	   - Squeeze the margins	

	In place	Must build

Distinctive Competences

Source: Chakravarthy and Lorange, 2004

The message here is that the aim is to improve marginally on one's position, squeezing the margins, via a better understanding of the markets—in/out and long/short—*and* to have superior distinctive competences in cost and efficiency performance. One might say that this is to attend to the core business for many shipping companies (Zook, 2001) and to maintain an open, innovative mind when it comes to this core business (Rigby and Zook, 2002). A number of examples illustrate this strategy well.

The first example is Fairmont Shipping, Hong Kong, which focuses on the Handy and Handimax bulk sectors. Fairmont follows a very focused strategy in the bulk carrier segment. It has relatively low debt per ship, seeing high liquidity as a clear objective with its shipping activities. Each ship is financed individually and is "ring fenced" as much as possible. Some ships are on long-term charters, but most are on spot or very short term charters. Fairmont Shipping is part of a family-owned conglomerate, with heavy emphasis also on real estate, which tends to be less liquid and require longer holding periods than most shipping activities. It also has a shipyard and crewing activities through other affiliates. Fairmont has activities in five countries and is thus not overly dependent on the Chinese regulatory or political situation. Its shipping activities are deliberately focused on the commodity-based markets; it achieves its portfolio strategy through other means.

The way that Fairmont Shipping—and many other shipowners for that matter—has traditionally responded to the classic atomistic shipping market conditions has been to try to detect and utilize imperfections in these markets in order to, for instance, make better timing decisions in chartering, new ship orders, second-hand sales and purchasing, etc. Above all, there could well be a "battery" of decision parameters for Fairmont and other shipowners to consider in order to effectively operate with classic shipping strategies:

- Chartering: In/out; long/short

- Purchase and sale of ships

- Withholding capacity

- Operations and/or asset play

Chartering

In chartering, timing decisions (cycle management) are vital to success. When it comes to market cycles, one has to consider when to get *in* and when to get *out*, and also whether to go *long* or *short* in the market cycle. In/out and long/short considerations are the key to timing decisions. Exhibit 2.4 gives an overview of how cycle management can be conceptualized.

Exhibit 2.4: Cycle Management—The Right Positioning Changes with the Cycle. Getting It Right Requires Anticipation, Flexibility and Action

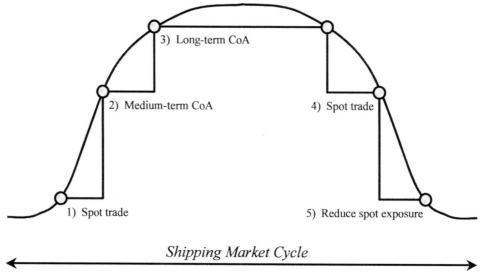

3) Long-term CoA

2) Medium-term CoA   4) Spot trade

1) Spot trade   5) Reduce spot exposure

Shipping Market Cycle

Source: Marsoft, 2003

Specifically, one initially needs to determine whether to go for the spot market, or whether to enter into longer-term charters, typically time charters, but also bare boat charters and/or contracts of affreightment (CoA). The key here is to go for the short-term spot market when the market is going up, and then to fix the ships on longer-term charters when the market is high, in order to achieve higher rates when the spot market subsequently falls. In falling markets, the smart strategist always tries to achieve longer-term charters, although the lower the market falls, the more necessary it is to anticipate a market swing back upward. Throughout the cycle, the timing of decisions can be easy to misjudge. For instance, Klaveness took over a "portfolio" of 11 ships with contracts of affreightment from A. P. Moller-Maersk during the summer of 2001. This turned out to be ill timed and was, indeed, a major factor in the actual net loss of the entire Klaveness group in 2002. Later, however—as we have seen—this decision proved to be excellent, since it allowed Klaveness to benefit from the strong upturn in the bulk market in 2003. It also gave Klaveness significant access to the Chinese bulk market, including the takeover of A. P. Moller-Maersk's former office in Beijing.

Purchase and Sale of Ships

Newbuilding contracts are critical, and the timing is key here as well. Newbuilding contract prices tend to fluctuate wildly, depending on the backlog in newbuilding orders and general freight rate levels. The appropriate timing means achieving favorable ship purchase prices and financing, as well as having the new ship—with its new capacity—enter the market when the general freight markets are high.

One challenge with newbuildings, as noted, stems from the deflation in newbuilding prices. When newbuilding prices fall, there could be a problem with the cost of capital for an individual ship investment, as well as for the portfolio/fleet. Even though the cost of capital of the newest ship will be lower, the *average* cost of capital for the fleet will be higher. A traditional LNG (liquefied natural gas) ship, for instance, used to cost $250 million to build. Now one can be had for $150 million. This potentially represents a huge "loss"/added cost of capital for the owners of existing ships.

As far as newbuildings go, many yards, particularly in Korea and perhaps also in China, seem to push hard for volume by always attempting to have full order books. They may not be as focused on price alone, which perhaps seems to contribute significantly to pressing the newbuilding market downward toward further commoditization. This aggressiveness may be tipping the balance between supply and demand, particularly in light of the huge new shipbuilding capacities that are being added in these countries.

The purchase of second-hand tonnage is also very important. When freight markets are high, second-hand ship prices are, of course, also high. The successful purchase of second-hand tonnage thus tends to occur when these ships are relatively cheap, i.e., when the market is down, but when a turnaround in market rates is expected to come relatively soon.

Timing the sale of ships is equally critical. The trick, of course, is to sell when the market is high. Unfortunately, many shipowners end up selling their ships when the market is down. Partly they can be influenced by a generally pessimistic outlook and "lose their nerve." Partly they can be pressured by financial lenders—given the general economic conditions—to ease up on their overall financial commitments and exposure, get their debt financing more under control, and sell old ships to make room for newbuilding programs, etc. Successful shipowners tend to be good at timing decisions for the sale of second-hand tonnage, however, and generally resist selling under such price distress.

Withholding Capacity

Shipowners can decide to lay up their ships, thereby withholding capacity. Given the atomistic nature of the shipping markets, one shipowner's decision to lay up a ship does not, of course, impact the freight rates per se. The decision parameter for the shipowner is thus simply whether the costs of running the ship are higher than keeping the ship idle. Fuel costs, insurance and crew costs are the most important variables here. It is expensive to lay up a ship, and it costs money to reactivate it later on. Laying up decisions are, therefore, often difficult to make (Mossin, 1968). A variation on the laying up decision is the decision to go slow speeding. Again, given the atomistic nature of the markets, the impacts on the freight rates are negligible here. The major saving will be in bunkers' fuel consumption costs.

Finally, scrapping can also be important. When a ship is old, scrapping may be the best alternative, depending on what scrap price can be obtained—typically based on tons of steel in the ship—relative to the running costs of the ship, and also whether it is worthwhile to wait for a future upturn in ship markets. Keep in mind that the economic life of a ship is finite, often no more than 25 years. Beyond this, several costs can become excessive: rapidly increasing ship classification fees, repairs, replacement of steel plates and parts, insurance, fuel inefficiencies due to technological semi-obsolescence, and the shippers' general insistence on newer tonnage. The decision to scrap a ship is, in the end, usually driven by the scrapping prices one can obtain. These prices are indeed cyclical, too, depending on the supply and demand for ships to be scrapped, as well as on general steel prices, which are, at least in part, a function of the freight markets. Here again we see the interconnectedness of the shipping markets.

Operations and/or Asset Play

The decision to focus primarily on operations or on asset play is perhaps the fourth dimension shipowners need to think about when they consider implementing classic shipping strategies. To make profits out of operations, the shipowner must run a particularly efficient operations department, with a clear focus on the costs of running each ship. The choice of which flag to run the ship under, above all to get the crewing costs down, the choice of nationalities of the crew, etc., matter here. Typically, ship operations have moved away from high cost areas, such as Scandinavia and Europe, to lower cost areas, such as the Far East, and/or to flags of convenience, such as Liberia, the Bahamas, etc. Many high cost countries have reacted by establishing their own international ship registers, which tend to give the owners more flexibility on crewing, while allowing them to fly perceived "high quality" flags.

Asset play, by contrast, simply means that the owner tries to make the bulk of the money on the purchase and sale of ships. Clearly, the right timing is indispensable here. The holding period, when the ships need to be operated, would of course still be managed as economically as possible. Still, in an asset play strategy, one could even conceive of incurring losses when it comes to the periods of operations. Typically, an asset play strategy means that the ships tend to be on shorter-term charters or operating in the spot market. Operations type strategies, on the other hand, often tend to imply longer-term charter strategies.

In general, the classic strategic choices under atomistic conditions in a classic shipping market will call for a close focus on understanding the markets better, above all, anticipating the turning points, and "doing good even better" in operations. But what does this mean in the context of a model for business development and growth strategy assessment in shipping companies? Simply that there are *two* major categories of activities that shipowners will have to focus on. First, as noted, they must *understand the market better*. This means having as clear a notion as possible of the relevant timing decisions and trying to establish a clear understanding of what the potential turning points in the developments of the various markets might be. This is in line with what has already been discussed, as illustrated in Exhibit 2.4. In the next section, we shall go into even more detail on this.

Second, they need to *do good even better*. This means, when it comes to running the firm, always trying to marginally improve one's operating position, with more efficient ships for a given commodity trade. This might mean taking a broader viewpoint than focusing on only each specific ship. Other elements might be included—for example, improving transportation offerings, say, through new unloading equipment that reduces the time needed for unloading; marginally strengthening existing competences when it comes to operations; implementing better managerial capabilities, say, by more extensive use of IT in chartering, etc. In other words, "squeeze the margins out of the business!" Exhibit 2.3 illustrates how this translates into a Protect and Extend commodity-type strategy. Let us now discuss each of these two classes of factors in more detail.

UNDERSTAND THE MARKET BETTER

Let us move to several brief examples. Suisse Atlantique in Lausanne, Switzerland, has operated for more than 60 years as a ship management company and shipowner. It is a fully integrated management company working for different shipowners, including Swiss registered firms with Swiss flags on their ships, and bases its shipping strategy on the old trading expertise of the former André trading company. This is seen to be an asset. The company has seven conventional Panamax bulk carriers, as well as two Panamaxes on charter. It also has three Handy-size bulk carriers on charter. It has further taken delivery of three container ships (2,800 TEU). These ships are chartered out on three- and five-year contracts respectively. Suisse Atlantique has four more container ships of a similar type on order, for delivery in 2005 and 2006. These ships are, in effect, analogous to very large container feeder ships. According to Suisse Atlantique, there is an interesting market for these "super container feeders." This ship size can be relatively volatile when the ships are employed in liner services, but relatively *less* volatile when they are employed as feeders for liner operations, particularly with the basic liner ships getting bigger and bigger. To what extent remains to be seen. Anyhow, a good understanding of the underlying markets is needed—for both bulkers and container ships.

SKS OBO is registered in Bermuda; it is 60% owned by Jebsen Gearbulk (which has 67 bulk carriers of its own) and 40% by a Chilean partner, Companhia Sud Americana de Vapores (CSAV). The company has 12 OBO (ore-bulk-oil) ships. The company's management asserts that a minimum fleet of at least, say, 10 OBOs is necessary to be able to establish an efficient trade pattern, which can then provide "tight" logistics for running the ships. The SKS OBO group focuses on cargo from shippers that appreciate that reliability and speed should be honored in the value chain, rather than only going for price. SKS OBO group focuses on the fast turnaround of its cargoes. This implies, for instance, that it does not freight grain, which would take too long to load and discharge, not to mention the time required for cleaning the holds. The building up of special ships and competences around this complex array of shippers cum customers—dry and oil—can perhaps be seen as a Build strategy. Still, the fundamental links to the commodity market are clear. SKS OBO must be on top of the basic bulk markets and act thereupon—succeeding in making the commodity-oriented strategy work.

The shipowner Arne Blystad seems to follow a highly opportunistic strategy with respect to exposure to freight markets and financial markets, but with a strong focus on a healthy risk profile—and a strong analytical focus also. He has made several good timing decisions, including the purchase of Team Shipping in 2002.

To shed more light on what might constitute an effective commodity-based Protect and Extend strategy, an interesting comparison would be between John Fredriksen's Frontline operation—running out of Oslo, with branches in Stockholm and Nicosia—and Teekay Shipping Corporation, which runs out of Vancouver. Both companies will be discussed in detail in sections 5.3 and 5.4 of this chapter, respectively. Fredriksen has concentrated on amassing a huge fleet of larger VLCC tankers, generally with relatively high exposure to the market. His fleet is rather heavily leveraged, and one might say that he is relatively highly exposed to the market risks of the oil freight market. Teekay, on the other hand, has focused more on the Aframax tanker segment and has tried to develop a more specific market dominance here, with initial focus on the Southeast Asian market, trading from Indonesia and Australia to Japan and China, in particular. More recently, its focus has also expanded to the Caribbean, Venezuela and the US East Coast. One might argue that Teekay, by dominating these more niche-oriented markets, has a somewhat lower market risk than Fredriksen. The VLCC market, on the other hand, in which Frontline is the world's largest player, would represent one of the most perfect atomistic markets in the shipping industry. Both Teekay and Fredriksen claim that they have very low operating costs, both running some of the largest tanker shipping fleets in the world.

The Marsoft Example

As indicated, the key to success for shipowners operating in the classic atomistic shipping markets is to better understand the importance of timing in their decisions, and above all, to learn to anticipate turning points in the freight rate market. Thus companies that provide forecasts for the freight rate markets, particularly when they have a focus on forecasting the turning points, would be in high demand. One such company, as noted, is Marsoft Inc. Others are Maritime Strategies International (MSI) and Drewry's. Marsoft, the world's biggest shipping forecasting consulting firm, will be our concern here.

Marsoft's main aim is to give its clients good, dispassionate information about discrete shipping transactions, thus allowing these clients to make better decisions on their own, i.e., with better insights into possible, realistic market developments. Marsoft thus focuses on each ship transaction and tries to come up with sophisticated analytical approaches for understanding the alternatives for every ship. The emphasis is on discipline, particularly a clear link between ship market decisions and finance decisions. Marsoft's aim, therefore, is to help its clients continue to be successful with their dual strategy of investments and chartering. Another key focal point for Marsoft is the composition of a shipping firm's entire portfolio of activities. This will, however, not be the topic here—see the further discussion in Chapter 4.

A starting point in Marsoft's analysis is thus, as noted in Chapter 1, to create market scenarios. They provide the firm's best possible outlook for a particular shipping market, taking a multitude of factors into account, which shape both the *supply* side and the *demand* side. A range of scenario outlooks are given—the so-called base case, high case and low case.

Why do we create market scenarios, such as the one given in Exhibits 1.11 and 1.12 (Cape 150,000 dwt, spot rates, Brazil/Rotterdam—Iron Ore)? The key is to get a better understanding of the rates we can obtain in various markets, with the turning points for these rate developments, thus also factoring in the risks involved.

Forecasting is, of course, always difficult. Not unexpectedly, Marsoft has thus also been off the mark several times in its market predictions. For instance, in retrospect, one might claim that during mid-2003 Marsoft was not bullish enough on its dry bulk forecasts. As noted in Chapter 1, this can, for instance, be seen from comparing Exhibits 1.11 and 1.12, where the actual rates and long-term freight trade levels turned out to be much higher than Marsoft's upper scenario forecast.

On ship values prediction, Marsoft might also in retrospect have been off the mark in mid-2003. For instance, the four Handimaxes that Oldendorff carriers bought were each worth $5 to $6 million more than purchase price six months later, several million higher than what Marsoft predicted. This can also be inferred by comparing Exhibits 1.11 and 1.12.

Acceptable risk depends on the risk taking propensities of the decision-maker. He can, for instance, respond to spot market exposure by more use of time charters. He can also hedge by using derivatives, buying insurance, etc. A realization is that these approaches require liquidity; playing the market requires a lot of funds and liquidity. With scenarios it is also important to try to understand the possible downside, which is important in communicating with the financial markets and banks. To raise equity capital from investors one should, on the other hand, of course, convince them of the potential upsides, another area where "objective" analysis of the sort provided by Marsoft can help.

Marsoft's inputs can thus also be useful for scenario planning as part of the process of budgeting and planning vis-à-vis one's banks. A key issue will be the downside or, posed as a question, Can we survive the potential downside? The answer will be found in the shipping company's liquidity pattern. Another important use of scenarios is to try to get the timing of ship purchase and sale decisions right, given that ships are always depreciating, and also fluctuating in value with the market, and thus, that the timing of the market turning points is crucial. In the end the questions are: What do you believe in? Can you survive a downside? What is the upside? And, how do you plan to handle the risk, including chartering actions.

During project financing, scenarios can help the shipowner understand the particular project better, particularly its timing in the cycle. It should also be noted that in corporate fleet financing, scenarios can help the firm to understand the "robustness" of the fleet's position, above all during a downturn. This will be discussed in Chapter 4. Scenarios must be part of the judgment of the individual decision-maker; they are not mechanical. Scenarios should be used to help the firm meet the *hard* targets concerning a ship, for example, that the *cash* situation is robust, and that the firm can also pay its dividends based on contributions from the deal, etc.

Scenarios might lead ultimately to the construction of probability distributions, with a high case, base case and low case. The decision-maker must not, however, treat the base case as the equivalent of a certainty, a fundamental "mistake" decision-makers often make. Stress testing the scenario is also key. Here a relevant question is: How can the firm operationalize the probability distribution so that it is easy to communicate, easy for decision-makers to understand, and easy to distribute internally and externally?

So, with all this said and done, the key decision parameters to consider in making a particular shipping decision are owned or chartered ship, newbuilding or second-hand ship, and whether to have it predominantly equity financed or predominantly debt financed. Marsoft's angle here would be based on developing computer-based forecasting scenarios, in the form of decision support systems, for explicit, systematically developed market and risk policy statistical inputs; specific decision rules for determining the overall strategy, tactical moves and implementation steps; and systematic benchmarking regarding one's performance and assessment of one's performance relative to internal budgets, as well as relative to external targets, including competitors. To "deliver," Marsoft offers several computer-based packages. (Marsoft, 2003, 2004).

The first is its *Timing and Risk Management System* (TRMS), a data platform that has been under continuous development and incrementally improved since 1985. TRMS provides a common market view as part of a clear strategy for the specific cycle-position given a particular shipping market. The focus is thus on understanding the turning points or, as mentioned earlier, the breakpoints. Marsoft focuses on the interaction between workstations and the more conventional data and management processes within the shipping firm, an attempt to build on and get better leverage from internal market expertise. Use of an often-impressive wealth of internal know-how and expertise on shipping markets and cargo runs is clearly important for achieving even better forecasts. Marsoft tries to develop more transparency regarding this *interplay* between the data provided by the firm and the know-how coming from the shipping organization itself.

The Marsoft approach also allows the setting of risk levels by specifying specific risk parameters, both for a single transaction and for the portfolio of ships/transactions (more in Chapter 4). The benchmarking and measurement of performance will hopefully also lead to improved learning in the organization. This quick reporting of results should highlight deviations and tracking of performance, thus also setting the stage for triggering ameliorating decisions, as needed.

Marsoft has two other complementary databased packages, which have an application at the level of specific ship decisions. The first is the *Marsoft Decision Support System* (MDSS), which tries to provide specific freight market monitoring, thus helping the decision-maker to time his chartering and purchasing/sales decisions. The specific focus of MDSS is on the freight rate cycle *timing*, i.e., trying to identify turning points or breakpoints. MDSS also allows the shipowner to undertake specific strategy analysis, doing simulations of the effects of various types of chartering or newbuilding decisions ("what if" analysis). The second forecasting package, *Shipping Risk Management* (SRM), helps the decision-maker manage risk more actively. It goes even further through the "what if" analysis, and thus gives the decision-maker a better feel for the potential payoffs of various risk exposures. This aim is further supported by the insistence on a standardized financial reporting system, so that the discipline toward risk taking can more easily be maintained—a key challenge when more than one decision-maker is involved in a given transaction.

An important challenge for Marsoft's researchers has been dealing with the cognitive limitations of decision-makers. Things tend to become very complicated rather easily. In practice, it is hard for a decision-maker to deal with more than one, or at most a few, critical decision factors at once. To enhance the ability to deal with complexities, Marsoft has developed the concept of "dashboards" to get all the relevant factors displayed together on one computer screen, to display in one screen frame all the relevant interrelated data and information for the decision-maker. As noted, most of the various market-related issues in shipping hang together, and the dashboard attempts to give a visual picture of this immense multiple equation set. Two such dashboards are particularly relevant for making today's ship decisions: the Market Evaluation Dashboard and the Voyage Simulation Dashboard. The two dashboards can be used actively together for, say, negotiating a deal for the shipowner with a particular freight demander.

The Market Evaluation Dashboard is particularly useful for chartering, since it comprises historical time charter rates, as well as vessel specific forecasts based, as noted above, on three scenarios: (1) the base case, (2) the high market rate case and (3) the low market rate case. These forecasts are further broken down for specific main trades. All in all, the Market Evaluation Dashboard is meant to provide a clear overview of the types of market conditions the decision-maker can expect, as well as a clear picture of recent and potential future market developments.

The Voyage Simulation Dashboard attempts to display all pertinent information relevant for evaluating a specific contract of affreightment. It tries to simulate how one can build up roundabout routes for each ship by putting together various legs, combining various contracts of affreightments.

Marsoft has had considerable success with its models for assisting shipowners to make better shipping decisions. This approach has clearly allowed shipowners to better understand the market, so that they can better execute a strategy that utilizes market imperfections through correct timing in the atomistic world of shipping markets.

DOING GOOD EVEN BETTER

The main area where "good can be done better" is on the cost side of operation. Shipping companies must aim for the lowest possible operating costs, while at the same time offering strong services. Operating costs can partly be a function of the configuration of the ship's engines, propeller, underwater design, etc., with the main objective being to get bunker costs down and the speed up. They can also be a function of operating routines—onboard and ashore—for practicing good operating competences. Often much more can be done to save on operating costs through better preventive maintenance, avoiding breakdowns, saving on spare parts by implementing preventive routines, saving on food and other operating costs, etc.

Information technology can also have an important cost-reducing effect. For instance, the interface with the customer can now be handled in a more cost efficient way, also adding a strengthened service component. For instance, both I. M. Skaugen ("Skaugen-online") and Norden have strong IT links with their customers, 24 hours a day, not least to get the costs of operations down, while maintaining superior service.

Ship designs and configurations themselves can have important cost elements associated with them. The size of the ships, for instance, can play an important role in reducing cost per ton freighted. A large VLCC tanker is, of course, much more cost efficient per ton freighted than a handy-size tanker. A large offshore supply ship is more cost efficient than a smaller one, in terms of cost per container freighted as well as cost per liquid unit freighted in its tank systems. Since turnaround time is important, more sophisticated unloading systems can also get the costs down, and more can be saved here. The new series of six liquid gas carriers just being built for I. M. Skaugen are of such modern design that the ships are expected to feature the lowest breakeven costs from operations of any ships of this type. Their ability to liquidify (cool down) the gases that are being freighted rapidly is particularly key.

All in all, shipping operations must pursue a relentlessly professional focus on "making good even better," of course complementing management focus on understanding the markets. In order to achieve success in the classic atomistic shipping markets, these two factors go hand in hand. The costs must be at a competitive level, and the "feel" for the market must be strong. Doing good even better thus involves coming up with better managerial practices and capabilities for operating the fleet more economically and dealing with the battery of interrelated complexities in shipping more consistently.

Risk

Let us now turn to another, increasingly important, aspect: How to handle financial risks. Handling financial *risk* is perhaps more critical today than ever. The Danish shipping company Norden has, for instance, developed a Value at Risk (VaR) approach that attempts to assess risks relative to expected returns for a given deal or, conversely, the expected return, given the risk level, acceptable for a specific deal. It has also tried to develop probability distributions for the returns expected at various risk levels. This has been inspired by best practices in investment banks, which use VaR to measure market risk. As Henry Paulson, CEO of Goldman Sachs stated: "No one likes trading losses, but they are a feature of our business. In fact, it is our willingness to tolerate such occasional, sizeable losses that enables us to earn attractive returns over time." (Goldman Sachs, Annual Report, 2003).

VaR measures the potential loss in value of trading positions as a result of adverse market movements over a defined time with a specified confidence level. If VaR were $1 million at a one-day, 99% confidence level, there is only one chance in 100, under normal conditions, for a loss greater than $1 million to occur.

As a predictor of trading results, VaR has historically worked well in stable markets and less well in volatile and illiquid markets. VaR has many other limitations: It is based on historical data; it often uses a one-day time horizon and so might miss the market risk of positions that cannot be liquidated or hedged in that time; confidence levels have to be chosen but limit potential losses beyond that figure; and because it is computed at the close of business, it misses intra-day exposures (Pretzlik et al., 2004).

A shipping firm faces many types of risks. Some have to do with developments in the shipping markets, and the given firm can, of course, not impact these types of risks. Managerial response can, however, affect the risk exposure, which must be handled with managerial competence and professionalism. Dealing with currency risks, for instance, is often of critical importance. It is, for example, becoming more and more important to build currency term options into many transactions. Interest risks are also important, even critical, particularly in ship financing. Interest rates represent an important cost element for ship newbuilding projects, particularly when the projects are large. Thus, interest rates are key for many successful shipping companies today. Interest rates have fallen dramatically over the last few years—an important cost advantage element, which has made fleet expansion more feasible. A stable, low level interest rate outlook has become an important critical success factor for many shipping firms. Increasingly often, interest rate swaps are being built into deals. Managing currency risks and interest risks underscores the importance of a shipping company's having a strong finance group. According to Henning Oldendorff, a strong dollar does not necessarily lead to lower freight rates. Also, higher interest rates may typically not be passed on to the shipper/charterer through higher freight rates. Thus, the shipowner typically carries the currency rate and the interest rate fluctuation risks.

One key area for the financial professionals to deal with is *credit risk*. This is the possibility of loss occurring due to the financial failure to meet one's contractual obligations. It would include the probability of default, as well as the size of the losses given the default. Credit risk in shipping companies has to do with the exposure arising out of chartering transactions. If the charter party agreement turns out to be insufficient to support the debt burden involved, there is a credit risk. This is particularly so in many cases when a ship is on the spot market and the income generated is insufficient to cover the financial obligations.

Other credit-related issues also need to be managed, such as the perception of credit worthiness of shipping companies, Basel II, anti-money laundering laws, the war on terror, etc. All of these risks would be part of a risk management approach and need to be systematically followed up by the company. This is the "discipline for living with the possibility that future events may have nasty effects; or risk management is the ongoing process of identifying, quantifying, planning for, tracking and controlling risks." (Bischofberger and Rybak, 2003).

Although we have discussed market risks already, suffice it to add that decision-makers can now deal with them in entirely new ways, with freight volume hedging, bunker hedging, freight rate hedging through long-term versus short-term time charter exposures, credit risk hedging when it comes to payment from major freighters, etc.

Hedging Instruments

Strategic positioning, as part of more dynamic freight rate cycle management, can provide increased operating flexibility, where one might take advantage of the opportunities from hedging and thus improve performance. Hedging instruments are thus becoming an important part of the professional management approach in shipping companies.

Basic bulk and crude oil shipping represent large global commodity markets. Both the tanker and dry cargo shipping markets are in transition toward becoming large financial derivatives markets. Shipping freight derivatives trading is now also an established market, which is showing strong annual growth. There is a great need for an exchange as this market matures. IMAREX was launched in November 2001 and has captured a position as the only viable exchange in this market. IMAREX provides an exchange for trading and freight derivatives. Its aim is to offer transparent online trading. It is based on the same principles for trading solutions that have been successfully launched in other commodity markets, such as electrical power, oil, etc. IMAREX provides a market broker desk to facilitate such trades and offers, above all, a clearing solution. It also makes trading data available, i.e., a forward data curve, which forecasts the markets. IMAREX's view is that the main segments of the shipping industry will grow into a highly liquid financial derivatives market, similar to what we have seen in other markets—oil, electrical power, several metal types, above all. Financial derivatives will become integrated in many of the trading and asset allocation decisions, just as in other commodity markets (oil, electricity, money markets, aluminum, etc). IMAREX aims to be the leading marketplace in this ship commodity derivatives market.

Derivatives are becoming integrated in the commercial management of many shipping companies. In line with this, it seems as if the commodity markets for the most part are becoming more spot oriented. Derivatives for hedging are becoming key in these commodity spot markets, often replacing physical contracts. Significant growth of derivatives trading is related to these commodity markets, certainly when it comes to oil, coal, grain, etc., but now also bulk and crude oil shipping. The derivatives for trading in basic commodities themselves also have spillover effects in the related shipping markets. Many of the larger shippers have developed risk management capabilities, which then also tend to set new standards for the management of shipping exposures. Further, industrialization of the shipowning community seems to be creating a shift in management practices in favor of modern risk management practices.

A common dilemma with such an approach would be whether the actual trading parties would live up to their commitments, or whether there would be a risk that one might "walk away," say, if the outcome turned out to be less favorable than anticipated. To attempt to ameliorate this credit risk, each transaction party might be okayed by the IMAREX exchange. It can further remove credit risks through a central clearing house for the trades, where the various parties come together, and where there will be daily off-setting settlements. These are based on established industry standard quotes, and thus the determination of the market levels.

Important players are active in this market, both in dry cargo freights and tanker freights, including coal importers, shipowners, financial institutions, energy traders and oil companies. This freight futures market does, indeed, hold significant potential, but it should be pointed out that derivatives are still in their infancy relative to more developed markets, such as the various stock markets. However, we have seen other commodity futures markets boom. The oil futures markets have been developing extensively for many years. The Nordic electric power market has also been developed for a while. Now it seems that the freight futures market is on its way, too.

As noted, one important task of an exchange like IMAREX is to provide *clearing solutions*, which are becoming more important. IMAREX provides facilities for such clearing. This means that, motivated by the pressure put on the performance of energy companies such as Enron and others, credit approval is now more strictly monitored and set. Due to lack of transparency, it can become increasingly difficult to judge whether shipping companies are bona fide counterparts in trades. Often, smaller companies enter the market with volatile earning patterns. Some of these firms would not even be qualified to get credits from the major oil companies. Hence, strong credit approval procedures and enforcement are key. The clearing possibility, however, increases the probability of matching deals, and thus increases liquidity for the derivatives business. In short, derivatives trading and arbitrage have become important elements of understanding risk management through a more dynamic cycle management approach toward the strategic positioning.

There are also a few clear disadvantages that firms trading on the IMAREX market can experience, particularly when one finds oneself with a "short" position in a rising market. One will then, of course, have to inject additional funds. One might thus have to have considerable liquidity reserves to stay in during such a rising market.

In total, all of these risks must now be managed. The approach to follow here is "good must always be done better." As indicated, a critical part of this managerial competence increasingly comes from one's own financing department. For leading shipping companies it is becoming indispensable to have the capabilities to undertake these many types of hedging, i.e., explicitly managing the risks that can be related to a hedging function, particularly, perhaps, interest rate developments and currency rate swap developments.

SOME SUCCESSFUL PROTECT AND EXTEND STRATEGIES

Let us now consider in some detail four particularly successful examples of executing Protect and Extend strategies in the commodity-based, atomistic shipping markets: Klaveness, Norden, Frontline and Teekay.

The Torvald Klaveness Group

Klaveness is attempting to win through a better understanding of the markets, and by managerially and operationally "making good even better." The company operates in the bulk transport segment, providing maritime services, mostly through relatively standard tonnage. A recipe for Klaveness is to go for reasonably large volumes, to get freight incomes from own tonnage and to get a management fee for tonnage operated on behalf of other owners through its pool. The fleet of ships provides flexibility and reliability for the customers, which many seem to value highly. It is key to operate this fleet of ships on a pattern of contracts of affreightment, so that the overall fleet ship pattern in terms of ton/mile costs are optimized. Here Klaveness has a strong track record (Klaveness, 2003).

On top of these efficient operations, Klaveness emphasizes optimal selling and purchasing strategies; in other words, it follows an asset play strategy to complement its operations strategy. A few factors seem to bolster Klaveness' success. First, the standard tonnage business is increasingly becoming a commodity business, with relatively small and seemingly shrinking margins. There may be a more and more short-term focus by the freight demanders; customers often demand shorter deals. This comes on top of the shorter macroeconomic cycles that seem to be emerging as well. Above all, the periods when the freight markets are relatively comfortable—the "window of opportunity" for entering into good contract of affreightment deals—tend to be shorter and shorter.

There seems to be almost total information transparency in this market. Shipping companies generally know what customers want. Klaveness, like all the other major players in the market, will tend to have a reasonable feel, more or less, for what their competitors will supply in terms of rates (all characteristics of an atomistic market). Risk management is becoming more and more critical, and so is clear management of the overall portfolio when it comes to risk management. Consistent risk profiling propensities in all Klaveness executives is thus key. Professionalism is also being taken to other levels. For instance, contracts are becoming increasingly standardized in order to avoid any unintended loopholes, derivatives for freight trade are becoming more common, and so on.

Klaveness' aim is to be a dominant pool actor in selective segments of the atomistic bulk markets. Its own ship investments are part of this pool. It is seen as critical for the credibility of the pool that Klaveness itself owns assets in the pool. The challenge is to come up with a satisfactory long-term result for all owners, including Klaveness. For such a pool to work, there can of course be no bias toward any particular owner.

So, clearly, improving the pool product itself is essential for further success, not only technologically, say, through innovative onloading/offloading gear, but also managerially, say, through more hedging as part of this strategy. Even the most innovative technological efforts can misfire, however. One example would be the so-called PROBO ships that can carry both liquid product cargoes and bulk cargoes, in fact, a smaller, more versatile, flexible version of the conventional OBO carriers. These ships, while technologically a great triumph, have not seen much commercial success.

Norden

Norden is active in two commodity business segments: dry cargo and tankers. In dry cargo, the concentration is on the Handimax deadweight segment (around 57,000 dwt), but also with some presence in the Cape-size segment (170,000 dwt) and the Panamax segment (70,000 dwt). Ships are owned and/or taken on short- or long-term time charters. Norden aims to develop an overall portfolio of contracts/charter deals, with both long-term and short-term time chartering and contract of affreightment elements. The trend seems, however, to be toward developing a stronger focus on relatively long-term charters (Norden, 2003).

Within the tanker segment, the concentration is on the Handimax product tanker area, in the size range of 30,000 to 32,000 tons. There are also activities in the Aframax crude carrier segment in Norden's portfolio. Again, the focus increasingly seems to be on more longer-term charter contracts, thus shifting the balance toward more in-depth relationships with the customers. Having long-term charter vessels is an alternative to owning vessels for Norden. The vessels are typically chartered in for five to eight years. They are painted in Norden's colors and bear Norden's name. Furthermore, Norden has the option to acquire the ship assets at prearranged prices. Hence, Norden is protecting its downside by securing assets to very competitive charter tonnage rates, while still being in a position to enjoy the asset market.

Norden has expanded its physical presence by establishing offices in the US, Singapore, Shanghai and Rio de Janeiro—above all, probably, in order to be closer to clients and to be active in the key bulk markets. These clients and markets are selected based on whether Norden can build and maintain barriers around their activities here, i.e., actively participate in the value chain of the customers. Developing an overseas organization has also been driven by the need to recruit and retain key people, again a prerequisite for becoming closer to each key customer's value chain. The company thus operates according to the principle of being *both* local *and* global.

The Singapore base was set up in 1997 as a tanker office and subsequently, in 2001, used as a bridgehead for an aggressive dry cargo expansion in Asia, with the Shanghai office commencing operations in 2002. The US office was opened in 1999 primarily to cater for American dry cargo clients. The office in Rio de Janeiro was opened in 2003 to cater for the potentially large dry cargo market in Brazil. The aim is probably to try to add a dimension of non-atomism to Norden's strategy.

Norden has put a lot of emphasis on developing its business systems. As already noted, risk management is key. Further, it has developed an extensive human resource management system based on executive trainees. Information technology has also been "pushed hard" in order to develop a closer relationship with its freight shippers and to be better able to effectively serve longer-term contracts. This might also add an element of non-atomism to Norden's strategy.

As a brief digression, Andreas Sohmen-Pao, CEO of World-Wide Shipping, Hong Kong, says, "Shipping has always been global in a way that few other businesses are. The assets are built in diverse places, they trade to diverse countries, and they are operated by diverse nationalities. If we accept that shipping is a fully globalized industry, then what is the relevance of local shipping communities? Local communities provide a platform from which to attack global markets. They are a source of information and innovation that can give companies an edge. The combination of a local support network with global orientation can be very powerful." (Sohmen-Pao, 2003). Sohmen-Pao has also been a consolidator in the large tanker ship industry segment—World-Wide Shipping took over Nordström & Thulin Argonaut and, most recently, Bergesen.

Norden's strategic picture is given in Exhibit 2.5. We see that its two basic business platforms—tankers and bulkers—can both be seen as falling into the Protect and Extend category. Norden is, however, making strong attempts to "extend" these positions by a Leverage element through operating with its own marketing subsidiaries in key markets, as well as by pushing toward Build via aggressive use of IT and entering into longer-term contracts.

Exhibit 2.5: Norden

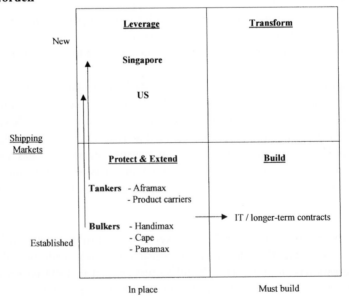

Source: Author

Frontline

Frontline is the world's largest shipowner in the VLCC oil tanker segment, with a fleet of 38 VLCCs, as well as 19 Suezmax tankers and 8 OBOs. It has 9.3% of the world's VLCC tanker fleet and 10.5% of the Suezmax fleet—No. 1 in the world in both categories. This totals a capacity of more than 16 million dwt.

John Fredriksen—the majority owner of Frontline—had a distinctive management style, characterized by:

- An assertive willingness and ability to take decisions.

- A strong base of knowledge regarding pertinent details of shipping markets, perhaps stemming from his initial background as a shipbroker.

- An impressive "feel" for the key driving forces of the tanker markets.

- A strong sense of memory, being able to relate back to specific transactions that might be relevant for a specific new business deal.

Exhibit 2.6 summarizes Frontline's strategic position, largely in the commodity market.

Exhibit 2.6: Frontline

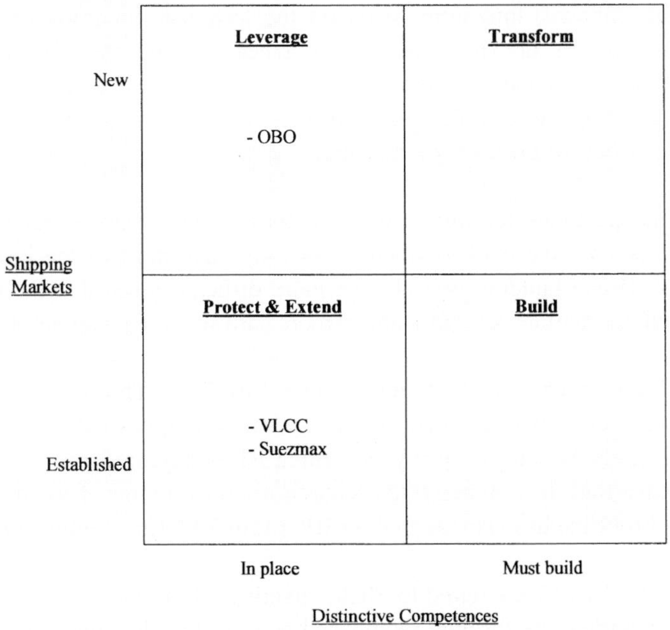

Source: Author

Frontline entered into a pool arrangement with OMI, a large operator of Suezmax tankers based in New York City, in 1998. It involves 14 Suezmaxes from OMI and the 19 Suezmaxes belonging to Frontline. Frontline takes care of the chartering for the alliance when it comes to Europe and all markets east of the Suez Canal; OMI takes care of all chartering for the US. The effect of the alliance is, therefore, a joint, coordinated marketing of a Suezmax fleet totaling 33 ships.

In 1999 a large pool of VLCC tankers—Tankers International—was established. It included all of Frontline's VLCC tankers, as well as those of A. P. Moller-Maersk, OSG, Bossimar/Exmar and Bergesen. Frontline withdrew from the alliance in 2002, when a large chartering arrangement with BP was under consideration, and Frontline felt that there was perhaps too much slow going in the decision-making process within the pool.

Frontline's operations are very much focused on each individual ship, with strong emphasis on the efficient running of the ships, including a heavy concern with safety and on delivering quality to the users of the ships. To keep its own organization small, entrepreneurial, focused on its key oil transportation business, and cost efficient is seen as key. Thus, when it comes to operations, the Frontline fleet is outsourced to four ship management companies: V. Ships (Glasgow and Oslo), International Tanker Management (ITM), Wallen, and Thome.

The company's management feels that this allows them to extract maximum performance from the subcontractors for operating the various ships. It is also able to benchmark one operations company against the others, and thus obtain even better performance. Frontline has its own in-house quality management group complementing this. Much emphasis here is put on overall staffing onboard, long-term focus on the technical condition of the vessels—including planning for dry docking—as well as a heavy focus on safety measures. The management feels that they can develop the most cost efficient operating structure in the industry through this approach, while simultaneously safeguarding safety and performance, all of which are so critical to the users of the ships.

With so much of its operations outsourced, the issue for Frontline is how to achieve a sufficient image of quality vis-à-vis the market, when it does not have most of the key management functions in-house. Brand building will also be more difficult, given that the human capital functions employed in Frontline will fall within a more narrow band of competences.

Frontline and BP have been working together since July 2002. Through their arrangement Frontline has a contract of affreightment for all the VLCC cargoes BP needs worldwide. It involves approximately 80 cargoes per year, which BP is paying for at market rates. For Frontline this means that the company has secured a large amount of steady work. Under the arrangement, Frontline has also taken over BP's four VLCCs on long-term charters.

Frontline also has six VLCCs chartered to Shell, covering all of Shell's VLCC requirements. There is a floating market rate formula established here, which also involves profit-splitting. Again, this ensures employment for a large part of Frontline's fleet.

The strategy shaping Frontline evolved into its present form in 1996 when Fredriksen, through his own private company Hemen, decided to establish a sizable public shipping company based on VLCCs and Suezmax tonnage. Several acquisitions followed, including acquiring a major share in the Swedish company Frontline. Since then a number of generally smaller entities have been integrated into Frontline, many of them paid for with shares. Another big acquisition was made in 2000, when Frontline took over 13 tankers from Golden Ocean Ltd, which then went out of the tanker segment.

Historically, Fredriksen's strategy might be characterized as "playing" on the freight markets, i.e., opportunistic. Frontline has taken all of its eight OBOs out of the oil transportation market and put them into the dry bulk market, where the dry cargo freight rates are now higher than for crude oil. Four of these ships are on long-term contracts, while the other four have relatively shorter contracts. This flexibility thus allows Fredriksen to take maximum opportunistic advantage of market developments.

Fredriksen's view was to act as a consolidator within a highly fragmented industry. He would provide charterers with a more flexible and reliable transport alternative through access to a large modern fleet. This should also be done so as to be cost minded with a flexible third-party ship management structure. The company's large modern tanker fleet should be professionally managed and operated in all respects—if any delays should happen, Frontline would be able to swap ships and also cooperate with the shippers regarding any short-term changes. It should thus have a flexible ship nomination procedure, coupled with competitive pricing.

Regarding operating philosophy, each vessel would be in the center. The ship manager would be responsible for the daily technical operation of the vessels. Frontline would, however, look after the management of the vessels more from a bird's-eye point of view, monitoring operating performance, dry docking, etc. It would also undertake to monitor the safety audit, on a bi-annual basis for the double U tankers and on an annual basis for the single U tankers. Thus, Frontline would guarantee uniform safety standards on all tankers, for all its customers.

Frontline has a market intelligence set-up for monitoring the freight markets that is quite similar to those of other leading firms in the tanker segment, such as Teekay. It specifically monitors each of the approximately 600 tankers operating in the VLCC and Cape-size segments, in terms of spot market employment, time charter, to whom (the name of the oil company), the historical patterns of employment, the specific position of each ship, etc. This allows Frontline to be quite aggressive in its chartering and often to achieve higher prices, given that it knows the supply picture from all of the other ships that might conceivably be able to bid for a job. Fredriksen has an extreme "broker" profile and an outstanding track record in judging the market.

A new corporate structure was developed in 2004. Operations activities and shipowning activities have been split into two separate companies. The operations company charters vessels from the shipowning company, allowing the operations company, Frontline Ltd., to be fully focused on market activities, with a relatively shorter-term focus. It also allows the shipowning companies to be financed on a long-term basis and to take longer-term points of view. Thus, a more consistent time horizon has been established for the various companies, which have also now been introduced to the stock market—with a good. Focus that is easy for the market to understand seems to be a key driver.

Teekay Shipping Corporation

Today Teekay Shipping Corporation is the world's No. 1 transporter of crude in the Aframax segment, No. 3 worldwide in Suezmaxes and No. 5 in Panamax tankers. It has more than 160 ships in operation, either owned or chartered. The company was started by Torben Karlshoej in 1973. The first phase of the history spans the time from the start until the death of Mr Karlshoej in 1992. During this period the company was a typical founder/owner enterprise. One of Mr Karlshoej's partners was originally an oil trader, and most of the initial efforts of Teekay were directed at the Indonesian oil trade, employing Aframax tankers to ship oil from Indonesia. Already, the company was focusing on having many ships of the same dimensions and specifications employed in the same geographical trade and area. Thus, it was possible for the company to have interchangeable ships, so that it could serve companies with the freight demand better, and probably also have a more effective way of coordinating back haul cargos. An important step for Teekay during this period was to charter, at a reasonable price, many Aframax ships from the defunct Japanese shipping company Sanko.

This brings us to the beginning of the second phase of the company's history, coinciding with Karlshoej's death. The financial situation was precarious then, and from 1992 to 1998 the company focused on cleaning up the financial difficulties and "repairing" the balance sheet. Axel Karlshoej, the founder's brother, was then the chairman of the board. This period saw a successful initial public offering (IPO) in 1995 and set the stage for the present and third phase of the company's history.

In 1998 Bjorn Moller was hired as Teekay's new CEO, and Sean Day joined the board. Subsequently Day took over as chairman of the board from Axel Karlshoej. A major strategic aim for Teekay at the beginning of this period was to move away from the huge spot market exposure that its fleet had, in order to dampen the effects of the freight market cycles. Teekay's vision changed to go from spot market heavy exposure to become an integrated logistics provider, with a larger part of the fleet on longer-term charters. Subsequently, this vision was restated to become a "mid-stream" logistics provider, meaning that while the oil companies are upstream, and the users of the oil are downstream, Teekay defines its role as developing a link between the two. This would involve all aspects of oil transport, offshore storage, lightering transportation, etc.

It was also felt that it was relatively hard to be a small publicly traded company. The need for growth was seen to be critical, both to be able to be more efficient in the capital market and to create a meaningful interest in and liquidity for the company's shares. This was further accentuated by the observation that the oil companies were consolidating fast, and it was necessary to have a sense of symmetry in size with the oil companies in order to match this. It was also felt that it was critical to have enough stock market muscle, and capital market muscle, to have access to the capital market during the low points of the freight market cycle as well, so that one could always make the strategic moves one would intend to pursue.

There is a "supercycle" which encompasses the convergence of four critical factors:

- The end of the technical life of the 1970s built single hull ships.

- The new IMO rules.

- The under-investment in large crude oil tankers over the last ten years.

- The exceptional demand issue for oil these days, and with very high crude oil prices.

The oil tanker business now seems to be in year four of this supercycle, and it is perhaps not likely that it will continue—after all, no upturn cycles continue forever! It is therefore important for Teekay *not* to make "big" mistakes at this point in time, say, by making the wrong timing decisions. The issue is one of discipline.

For instance, Bjorn Moller feels that the time for meaningfully ordering new ship assets destined for the spot tanker market has generally passed. A couple of years ago, an Aframax tanker newbuilding could be ordered for, say, $39 million per tanker. Now the price is around $50 million. The same general comment can be made about second-hand cyclical assets. It should still be noted that Teekay has 18 ships on order, and the orders were all placed during the earlier down cycle time. In addition, Teekay ordered four ships from Korean yards in January 2004, which it got at an exceptionally good price and which could be seen as abnormal relative to the general price picture as it relates to the cycles.

Teekay can be seen as pursuing two parallel employment strategies for its ships, i.e., being in two related businesses: Seeing the ships as cyclical assets—trading them on the spot market— and being in the long-term charter business. In terms of ships as cyclical assets, in the mid to late 1990s, the major oil companies came to focus relatively more on quality and reliability, etc. Before that, they had seen the shipping function more as a commodity. Long-term opportunities, based on the oil companies' gradually increasing willingness to pay for quality, then arose. Teekay, with its ability to achieve a scale effect—with many similar tankers in each specific segment affording a good operating cost effect—coupled with its reputation as a high quality ship operator and its strong balance sheet, was thus able to compete meaningfully in this emerging long-term charter business.

Torben Karlshoej, Teekay's founder, had a particularly good sense for the spot market and the "right" timing. His focus was also on developing similar types of ship assets, in order to achieve scale through a relatively high market share on key routes. This also gave Teekay more flexibility. He also chartered in a number of ships. At one point he became too optimistic, however, and Teekay went into a difficult financial situation.

The shift toward emphasizing the long-term charter business to complement the short-term focus on the spot market is relatively recent for Teekay. For instance, in 1998 the company received no cash from fixed long-term business; all was on the spot market. In contrast, in 2004 Teekay received a cash flow of approximately $400 million per year from the long-term charter business. This business now represents 50% to 60% of Teekay's cash flow, based on a typical mid-cycle tanker rate environment, and the return on equity is highly satisfactory—more than 20% of ROI. These long-term charters are on average seven years in length. They enable Teekay to become even more robust in the down part of the cycles, i.e., to become even stronger in a countercyclical sense. Importantly, the growth in Teekay's long-term business does not seem to have come at the expense of its large spot tanker business. Rather, it seems to have been built in addition to the spot tanker business. Both businesses have thus grown.

The strategy of being an integrated logistics provider has thus evolved. A major dimension became to develop a strong customer orientation. This was implemented through a heavy focus on measuring the customers' response and following up where signals from customers indicated that there were areas that could be improved on, i.e., "walking the talk."

The development of Teekay's organization was also evolving accordingly. For instance, 15 offices were gradually established around the world, so that the customer could be served locally, in a time efficient manner.

Teekay is thus attempting to have an organization that is *both* entrepreneurial, to take advantage of the opportunities to make good timing decisions based on a better understanding of the freight rate cycles, *and* process oriented, based on internal discipline. It is important that the latter is institutionalized. In line with this, Teekay is attempting to be "the world leader in marine service to the gas and oil industry by year 2010." The challenge now is to manage added complexity, since Teekay is getting into more trade segments, has acquired a number of businesses, which has taken it into new segments—including shuttle tankers and LNG—and has also entered into joint ventures, such as the one with Skaugen. The organization has been realigned accordingly into four units, and these implementation efforts seem to be working well. The four units are:

- Spot chartering.

- Upstream/shuttle tankers/offshore.

- Energy/LNG.

- Marine operations, including brand building and execution. This unit acts more as a service unit to the other three units.

The CEO, Bjorn Moller, does much of the market analysis himself, to signal his hands-on, pragmatic focus on the business. He has also written a booklet on Teekay's internal culture and strategy. It is important to note that he himself did it. This is similar to Tom E. Klaveness' delineation of his business strategy in his "little green book." In general, it seems critical that the CEO himself delineates and communicates the key strategy clearly, particularly when operating in such a competitive business as shipping.

There was almost no outsourcing, say, of ship management services. On the contrary, Teekay attempted to develop its own organization as much as possible, by controlling all elements of its delivery of logistics service, ashore and on board. This contrasts with other leading crude oil shippers, such as Frontline.

Teekay has thus always been ship product focused, namely primarily in the Aframax tanker size segment. In addition, it is also *customer* focused, i.e., vis-à-vis the big oil companies. The key is to be *both* product focused *and* customer focused. In order to do this, it must have *both* the physical size, i.e., be big enough to get the scale benefits, *and* enough legs and trade routes to offer meaningful diversity to customers, so that the customers feel they can get what they want.

It is thus critical that the company be large enough to have a minimum size in the segments in which it chooses to be active. A. P. Moller-Maersk has perhaps also done this well—but perhaps not entirely consistently—in that it does not operate its tankers to the US.

Teekay's strategy would then be one to *pull* customers in, and thereafter to *push* the tonnage on the customers. A complete logistics link is necessary in order to play this role as a link between the upstream and the downstream. Teekay sees itself as the "*mid-stream*" company.

Developing a global brand was seen as critical, with the same quality of service wherever one was, with whatever freighter one was dealing with. Another good example of this global branding approach would be A. P. Moller-Maersk. The focus on service, to develop both systems and people, involved more heavy investments, and the company might be seen as thus being geared up for even more growth. Continuous improvements, employee focus and a realization that the people are the most important asset also led to an increased level of spending on training and people development per ship.

Teekay can thus clearly be seen as building a brand strategy that is focused on delivering value to the customers via its own organization, its own people, its own "software." This includes a "project ability" where Teekay is able to bundle various services to deliver more fully fledged project support to its customers. Perhaps the other main proponent of this type of strategy would be A. P. Moller-Maersk. And, it might possibly be in contrast with companies such as Frontline, which perhaps focuses more squarely on its ships per se, in order to achieve low operating costs for each one. It runs each of these ship assets very efficiently, based on a lot of outsourcing—indeed more of a virtual organization compared with Teekay, which has all of the functions necessary to run a shipping company in-house. The customer-focused, service-driven brand building at Frontline would perhaps be less deliberate than at Teekay.

It was seen as important that no national identity seems to dominate Teekay. It is headquartered in Vancouver, Canada, but the executives come from all over the world, as so do the seafarers. The advantage is that anybody can feel comfortable in Teekay. There is no dominant nationality, which is so frequently the case in many other shipping companies. Teekay has the freedom to operate in the world without cultural impediments. In the best sense, it is therefore "stateless."

In order to further strengthen the organization after a number of large acquisitions—including Navion, Statoil's wholly owned shipping company—the company was reorganized into four operating groups, each with its own president reporting to the CEO:

- Tanker Services, consisting of all the conventional tankers predominantly, Aframax tankers. It also included Navion's conventional tankers, both crude oil and product tankers.

- Shuttle Tankers, built around the bulk of Navion's organization and headquartered in Stavanger, Norway, with a heavy emphasis on the North Sea.

- Gas and Offshore, which would include the LNG activity of the recently taken over Spanish company, Tapias, with its four LNG carriers.

- Marine Services, including ship management.

Except for Navion's shuttle tanker business, all of the other three groups were headquartered in Vancouver. Exhibit 2.7 summarizes Teekay's strategic positioning. As one can see, it is a mixed exposure, partly to the commodity market, partly to non-commodity niches.

Exhibit 2.7: Teekay Shipping Corporation

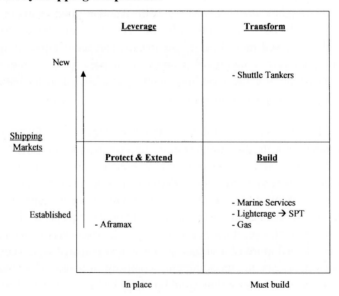

Source: Author

How does Teekay manage the market cycles? Discipline is key here, not "brilliance." It is key to understand the basics, i.e., that:

- A low market will always turn higher.

- A high market will always go down.

Teekay does a lot of analysis of data received from key research houses in the business, including Clarkson. The company tracks tonnage lists to understand historical patterns and get a better feeling for both the spot business and the medium-term cycles. This includes such details as specific fixtures for specific ships, the types of cargoes, the specific name of the ships, and in what market segments. This means that Teekay can have good execution regarding its specific chartering activities. It has a reputation for being relatively tough on the rates accordingly.

Teekay's management feels that one of its biggest challenges would be around having sufficient belief in its own analysis to take significant forward market actions in the direction indicated by the analysis. In a cyclical business one would never get a 100% clear reading about the future direction, not least because of the many variable involved. They feel that it is more a matter of weighing up probabilities and then acting on them—instead of waiting for "proof," by which time the opportunity would probably have gone. This was one of the strengths of the founder, Torben Karlshoej, who took definite views regarding the market's development and acted decisively on them. The company has had a fair amount of success in predicting the cycles since Mr Karlshoej's death, but management feels that it can do even more to develop a fundamental belief in a given market scenario. Such a scenario might even be quite dramatic. The key is then to be willing to actually *do* what this scenario implies.

A good example might be the problem that Teekay's management feels it faces today: Given the traditional wisdom of the regular tanker cycles of the past, one might expect the tanker market to go down—in fact, in a historical context this is perhaps already overdue, they feel. However, a number of market indicators point in the opposite direction. Could the market go up even higher—or at least remain at the present high level for some time to come? Teekay's management is wondering whether there might be too much of an opportunity loss by being too constrained by "conservative" discipline. Will one forgo such opportunities if the market should go even higher? Mr Moller sees it as a challenge for Teekay to maintain sufficient entrepreneurship to be able to meaningfully assess such questions, without defaulting to "conventional wisdom"—but at the same time not dismissing the lessons of the past.

Teekay is now also working on the derivatives markets. The issue here is to hedge, by buying "shelf space" vis-à-vis the consumers. This allows Teekay to lay off risks and to lengthen the long positions and shorten the short positions. Teekay uses IMAREX on this. With the tanker business being less of a commodity, it has been more challenging to develop an efficient derivatives trading market, according to Mr Moller. He feels, however, that there are signs that a market may finally be emerging. Sean Day, who used to be part owner and president of the dry bulk company Navios Corporation, did very well on his derivative strategies before he sold the company.

Another challenge associated with ultra high growth for Teekay is related to the further development of its people capabilities. While it may be relatively easy to develop the top layer, it is key also to cultivate the middle layer of management and particularly to identify the high-potential managers early. This applies to both the people at sea and those on shore; one attempts to create a common team spirit. Further, one attempts to keep "silos"/barriers to a minimum, and break them down whenever they appear. It is also important that everybody consistently understand the vision of the company.

Teekay has elected not to be in the bulk carrier business. Partly, this is justified through the argument that Teekay has done just fine in the tanker business segment, and a clear focus is important in order to provide true service in a particular segment: Strategy means choice. It is also felt that the strong upswing in the dry bulk freight market may perhaps be somewhat more short term.

Teekay has two OBOs which it may attempt to sell or put on a long-term charter to someone else. It has already sold the eight OBOs taken over from Bona Shipholding in 2003. It is realized that Teekay could have made more money on these ships now, but a policy decision was made that the company did not want to operate 21-year-old ships, since this would be inconsistent with its top quality policy.

This focus on "sticking to the knitting" can perhaps be contrasted with Frontline's strategy, which is less based on long-term values, and much more on an entrepreneurial, opportunistic focus. The heavy emphasis on the customer is much more accentuated in the long-term strategy of Teekay than in the short-term strategy of Frontline. Teekay is thus, as noted, long-term focused, with relatively little emphasis on in/out decisions and short-term market play on a more opportunistic basis, as long as they would be seen as inconsistent with the overall long-term strategy. This is thus true when it comes to Teekay's ownership of vessels and its building of long-term customer relationships. At the same time, Teekay attempts to maximize the benefits of shipping cycles, for example by chartering in short-term vessels at appropriate times to supplement its fleet. Further, it attempts to be disciplined over the timing of the purchase and disposal of owned assets and seems to have been successful in acquiring ships at or below mid-cycle prices and disposing of them at or above mid-cycle prices.

Acquisitions have played an important part in the company's development. Teekay has seen it as key to make acquisitions when the market goes on. In 1999, for instance, it took over Bona Shipholding from Leif Hoegh & Co. Teekay has the financial strength to take over other companies in any such situation. The most recent acquisitions include:

- Navion: It was more important for Statoil when it decided to sell that the acquiring company have a strong quality profile than that it be a Norwegian company. Teekay was checked out extensively by Statoil and found to be fully acceptable on all dimensions. There was a strong fit between Teekay and Navion—the oil storage loading ships were part of the service that Teekay's clients were demanding, i.e., a focus strategy.

- Tapias: This acquisition, which gives Teekay a platform in the LNG business, took place in 2004. Tapias has two existing LNGs on long-term charters; and another two are under construction and long-time charters for them have already been secured. Thus, Teekay is able to create immediate credibility in the LNG market, based on these safe, high quality, long-term charters.

Here, Teekay wanted to grow in this segment and was in fact prequalified to participate in several LNG projects. It again made sense, therefore, to buy into a company with an already established position. Teekay's own low cost of capital made this further feasible. Finally, the acquisition created stronger access for Teekay to the Spanish/Latin American shipping business sphere, i.e., a geographically driven acquisition move.

As further illustration of the important role of acquisitions when it comes to Teekay's geographic moves, in 1998 the company took over Caltex's Australian fleet of tankers. It thereby gained access to the Australian tanker market by extending its already established competences in Aframax tankers elsewhere. It also extended its Australian geographic focus to Perth and the Australian West Coast, where it had two Aframax tankers converted on long-term contracts. Finally, it entered into a joint venture for the management of BHP's fleet, largely out of Australia.

There were also several other examples of geographic spread, notably in Canada, the North Sea and, as noted, Spain/Latin America.

Although strategic alliances have been rare—wholly owned strategic moves have been the preferred route—there is one recent notable exception: the Skaugen PetroTrans (SPT) alliance. Teekay had concluded that it wanted to be in the lighterage business for three reasons:

- It is profitable.

- Teekay wanted to offer a full range of services to its main oil company customers, including lighterage.

- There would be a strong synergy with Teekay's Aframax tankers in the Caribbean, linking them up with lighterage on the major US rivers.

The question was then whether to go it alone or in a joint venture, and it was decided to attempt a joint venture with Skaugen PetroTrans for the following reasons:

- Strong cultural compatibility with SPT. Operational excellence.

- Market leader. SPT was seen as the first choice by the consumer.

- Avoid head to head competition, and thereby also a potential rate war. Further, it was important to save time and get instant ability to the top people who knew this particular business in SPT.

- SPT lacked a global presence. It was focused almost exclusively on the US. Teekay could add a global presence. A successful 50:50 joint venture was established in 2003—the key people running the joint venture are those who previously ran SPT.

Klaveness, Norden, Frontline and Teekay are all examples of shipping companies successfully following strategies that are essentially well suited to the classic atomistic shipping markets. And there are many more stories of success. Still, a recurrent question is: Would there be ways to avoid the commodity "trap"? Can one develop strategies that are more exclusive, less atomistic, less commodity oriented? Let us now start to consider trends in this direction—we will come back to this theme in more detail in Chapter 3.

BEYOND THIS—"LIVE WITH" COMMODITIZATION

There are several trends toward what might end up leading to less commoditization, less atomism in various segments of the shipping industry. Most of these are admittedly "weak" trends. Let us, however, review these exogenous factors here, since we intend in Chapter 3 to discuss how the shipping firms' own managerial actions might lead to more niche-oriented strategies.

As indicated earlier, the more or less free access to capital has, perhaps more than anything else, had the effect that main bulk shipping markets have remained highly competitive, highly atomistic. Nevertheless, it is worth looking at *some* trends toward more *restrictions* on the capital inflow to this industry.

The availability of risk capital, particularly for smaller firms, could become more costly and harder to get. At one time the existing capital accord agreement (Basel I) seemed to harmonize capital regulation very successfully. This regulation is, however, no longer in tune with current banking practice. The deficiency with Basel I is the fact that the framework it provides and the risk ratings are rather crude, and also risk management development is not considered. The new regulation, Basel II, seeks to regulate complex banking business, using generally acceptable rules in a banking world that is not simple and heterogeneous. Here, once again, the aim is to reinforce the stability of the financial system.

The importance of a stable financial system to national and global economies may justify the major expense imposed through this additional regulation. It was proposed in 1999 and will come into effect by the end of 2006. Commercial banks in countries that take on this accord under their national law will need to evaluate all credit for its individual risk within a rating system. This rating system is set out as indicated in Exhibit 2.8.

Exhibit 2.8: The New Basel Accord (Basel II)

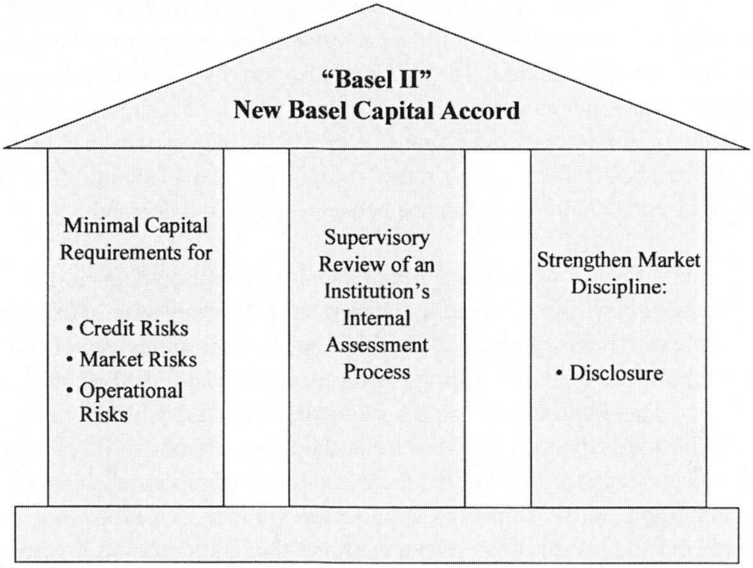

```
                          "Basel II"
                  New Basel Capital Accord


    Minimal Capital        Supervisory
    Requirements for       Review of an        Strengthen Market
                           Institution's       Discipline:
                           Internal
     • Credit Risks        Assessment
     • Market Risks        Process
     • Operational                             • Disclosure
       Risks
```

Source: Fueglistaller and Halter, 2003

For instance, the Basel II convention requires that all banks must more systematically assess the decision to give ship credits, in accordance with predetermined, more rigorous criteria. Their dealings with shipowner clients will thus become much more standardized. This regulation for lending within banks will involve all banks. All banks must set aside a certain reserve (i.e., de facto "dead" capital) for every lending amount it commits to a particular project as a loan. Top management in a bank will therefore typically "allocate" quotas to each business sector, and make sure that each sector then optimizes its sub-portfolio of projects within its area, in order to go for the best return for the bank. There is likely, thus, to be "competition" between sectors within the bank, so that the most lucrative projects are favored. This means that, in most banks in the future, shipping projects will probably have to yield higher returns and lower risks in order to successfully compete for capital. The net result: The cost of capital for shipowners is likely to go up. One can even question whether there will be enough availability of financing at all. Some smaller shipowners may be squeezed out of bank financing altogether, or at least be severely restricted. This might in the end lead to less overall capacity increase, although it cannot be expected to lead to significantly higher industry concentration.

Adoption of risk assessment procedures for banks and other lenders is becoming more and more standard. Outside data forecasting companies, such as Marsoft, play an important role here. Marsoft's emphasis is to provide a standardized approach for the banks to develop a credit rating matrix based on a risk profile customized for shipping lending—all, in turn, based on Marsoft's market outlook forecast. The net effect may be more prudence in ship financing, fewer excesses in making low cost capital available and, in the end, a better ship supply/market demand balance.

Another potentially difficult issue facing the shipping business has been shipyard subsidies. Traditionally, national governments in many countries have subsidized shipyards heavily to stimulate local employment by making the local yards more competitive. Shipyard subsidies are no longer allowed within the EU. The OECD is also heavily restricting shipyard subsidies, which is putting pressure on countries such as Korea to abandon its ship subsidies. China may also have to abide by this strategy over time. All in all, this may further lead to more realistic practices in newbuilding policies, i.e., more restraint on the availability of newbuilding capacity and, in the end, a more even balance between supply and demand.

Aging of the world's fleet of particular types of ships, and built-up demand for renewing the fleet due to infrequent new ships ordered in the past, is another key trend. For instance, within the offshore supply ship industry, one can consider the platform supply vessel (PSV) segment, which freights supplies to offshore drilling platforms and offshore drilling ships operating in deep ocean waters. There will always be a basic demand for this type of ship—after all, the platforms need constant support. It turns out that the demand tends to be particularly robust for the "Volkswagen" types in the PSV segment, namely medium-sized ships with good tank efficiency, exemplified by the ship type connotation UT755. The return on investment of these ships turns out to have been, on average, higher than the return on investment of more expensive PSV ships. The demand is more robust within this more versatile sub-segment of the PSV ship market on an average basis. The same argument can be made when it comes to large anchor handling tug supply vessels (AHTS). This can be seen from the world's fleet composition and corresponding possibilities for new ship investments, now perhaps with less commodity-oriented contexts, as illustrated in Exhibit 2.9.

Exhibit 2.9: World Offshore Fleet Composition

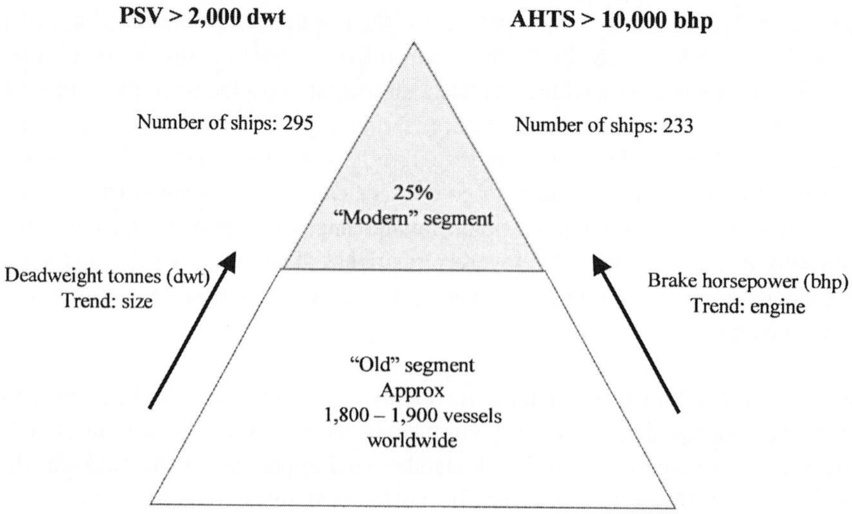

PSV > 2,000 dwt   AHTS > 10,000 bhp

Number of ships: 295   Number of ships: 233

25%
"Modern" segment

Deadweight tonnes (dwt)   Brake horsepower (bhp)
Trend: size   Trend: engine

"Old" segment
Approx
1,800 – 1,900 vessels
worldwide

Source: Andersen, 2003

Another example of such niches with higher demand might be RoRo ships for freighting automotive equipment, such as followed by companies like Leif Hoegh & Co. and Wilhelmsen/Wallenius. The demand for cars in the overseas export segment is relatively stable, which creates a relatively stable business. Traditionally, bulk carriers with extra temporary decks installed used to serve this segment. New technology has, however, created a less commodity-oriented segment.

Another example might be the large LNG ship business. Here, contracts will typically be based on long-term charters. Japanese companies, such as Mitsui OSK Lines, K Line and NYK, as well as Leif Hoegh and Bergesen have been particularly active here. The long-term financing element plays a strong component in these essentially stable "banking" deals. Perhaps this segment might thus be seen more as "banking" than as "shipping."

CONCLUSION

In this chapter, we have seen how modern shipping firms tend to be exposed to global market swings; they are competing in an atomistic context of more or less perfect competition. It is, of course, key to find ways for the shipping firms to come up with effective ways to compete in this context—using effective commodity strategies. Also, however, many leading shipping executives have been fascinated by the potential to move their companies away from this intense competition to find more specialized *niche* strategies. This will be the focus of the next chapter.

CHAPTER 3

THE DRIVE TOWARD NON-COMMODITY SEGMENTS

It is key to enter into niches where you get paid. —Shipping industry proverb

Many shipping segments have experienced large market swings, while the markets for Ro-Ro and LNG transportation remain on a stable level, with a good balance between supply and demand. [...] The Ro-Ro segment is based on long-term customer relationships and flexibility regarding phasing in services and products in the value chain. [...] The LNG activities will continue to be based on long-term engagements with solid contractual partners.

> *—Thor Jörgen Guttormsen, Managing Director, Leif Hoegh & Co.*
> *ASA Annual Report 2002, p. 1*

A high innovation pressure, being close to demanding customers, equals a high degree of innovation. We must keep an innovative culture.

> *—Simon Eidesvik, Offshore Supply Shipowner*

INDUSTRY STRUCTURE IMPACTING THE DEMAND SIDE

Several companies have withdrawn from, or are de-emphasizing, classic shipping segments. Leif Hoegh & Co. has withdrawn from, or is on its way out of, four of its businesses: Capesize dry bulk business, reefers, open hatch forest products bulkers, and liners business (sold in two parts, in 1998 and 2001). And we saw, summarized in Exhibit 1.4, that this has had a positive impact on its results. I. M. Skaugen was also involved in a number of shipping segments. Generally one could say that the company had relatively poor control over the various activities. The necessary cash flows were simply not there. Running costs were enormously high, and there was a lot of off-hire. Much of this was not even realized by the leadership of the company. In 1989/90 Skaugen diversified even further, and bought two VLCC (very large crude carrier) tankers at the top of the market, in addition to the two VLCCs it already had. This led to a loss of 1 billion Norwegian Kroner. The financial situation became acute, and the company was more or less bankrupt. Since 1992 Skaugen has refocused and is now in only two segments—gas and lighterage.

A. P. Moller-Maersk has withdrawn from the basic bulk business and also from some other commodity business segments. As noted, the group sold its portfolio of Panamax bulk contracts involving the Far East to Torvald Klaveness Group, including its marketing office in Beijing. Thus, an initial modification of a shipping company's overall portfolio to gain simplicity, focus and clarity may be advantageous. This may emphasize segments that are perhaps somewhat less volatile toward the atomistic markets. Withdrawing from the more volatile segments could also be a strategic choice. Choosing basic segments, which have an element of robustness in them, seems key. But these strategic moves are common-sense moves toward improving the classic strategic position through Protecting and Extending. Nevertheless, the classic shipping business remains highly dependent on the markets. One can perhaps move a little bit away from the most heavy commodity orientation by making choices, by focusing. A non-commodity strategy requires focus, and often an even more fundamentally radical approach, which is the theme of this chapter.

Three major trends have an impact on the industry structure and the demand side for ship services, and they may offer shipowners an opportunity to move away from "extreme commodity" business, by adding focus. We shall discuss these first. This means that the specific owners will be striving to find more niche opportunities "before they are obvious to everyone else": (1) the demand specifications of some major shippers that ask for entire fleets of ships, often taken on longer charters, aiming at a "one-stop relationship" with shipowners; (2) the trend toward broader coverage of the entire value chain by shipowners, again primarily as a consequence of the demands made by shippers such as major industrial companies; and (3) the investment size in particularly specialized ships, calling for a concentration in the shipowners' ranks, again primarily as a consequence of the need to invest in more sophisticated, more capital intensive ships, as demanded by some shipowners.

DEMANDS FOR LARGER "PACKAGES" OF SHIP SERVICES

Some companies that demand ship services may, in essence, be trying to simplify their relationships with shipowners. Essentially they are trying to streamline their supply chains. Rather than working with a number of shipowners, they prefer to have a one-stop contractual relationship with one owner, who administers a larger fleet of ships for the shipper. Consider the oil company ConocoPhillips and its demands for offshore supply ships worldwide. The company has issued a tender for 70 offshore supply ships to cover its needs worldwide, broken into several packages, each package to be bid on by one or more shipping companies, with each package being between 10 and 15 ships.

One package, for instance, deals with ConocoPhillips' needs for ocean supply ships in the Norwegian sector of the North Sea; another deals with its needs in the British sector of the North Sea; a third deals with its needs off Brazil, etc. Previously, the company dealt with many shipowners. Typically, each owner would bid for a particular time charter for a particular ship. Thus, ConocoPhillips' needs were covered through a complex web of relationships with many owners, ship by ship, on separate time charters. Its present intentions are to simplify all of this by offering entire "packages" to one firm, which would then provide all the required offshore supply ship services. In the Norwegian sector, for instance, there would be a requirement for ten ships, as noted, which the shipowner would need to offer en bloc.

Another interesting feature of ConocoPhillips' new approach would be that it seems to depend on the establishment of a computer-based bidding system to set the time charter rate for the entire block of ships. Each shipowning company that wants to participate would hand in an initial rate. Each could then elect to lower this rate during the computer-based auction, but no one could go up. They would know the rate levels that the other shipping companies were quoting, but not the names of these companies. Under this system, the role of the traditional shipbroker would indeed be different, or even eliminated.

Major industrial shipowners may increasingly insist on compliance with safety standards, environmental emission policies, more systematic crew training procedures, and "best in class" procedures for comparing operating performance between the various ships employed. While these initiatives, of course, often tend to be good in their own right, they also imply added costs in resources and funds. Some of these requirements can probably be met by administering a larger fleet of ships, perhaps offered to the shipper together, in a coordinated manner. Concentration on the shipowner side will clearly be on the cards.

All in all, there could well be a shift toward more power in the hands of the larger shippers, who would be able to increasingly apply their purchasing power muscle. The corollary of this would be a relative decrease in the power of the smaller shipowners. In the future, it is not hard to imagine that only larger shipowners will perhaps be able to match the needs of the large shippers.

What are the rate effects of all of this? The large shippers may believe that the rates will actually come down. A strong argument can be made to the contrary, however, in the sense that only a few shipowners will now de facto be able to bid. The atomistic nature of the supply side is therefore broken. It is much more likely that a sense of discipline will now prevail among the bidders, when only three or four of them will go after a specific deal. The net result may therefore be a move away from the classic commodity business in the direction of a long-term relationship business. This might seem to be fair, but it may also mean higher shipping rates in the long run, now that a market with less perfect competition has been established. The large shippers will often have large, complex—even compartmentalized and bureaucratic—organizations. A particular executive responsible for a logistics function may become more of a hero in his own company by simplifying the supply chain, rather than by practicing shipping "the old way." Technocrats rather than classic shipping executives may be on their way in, with the risk of loss of a true "feel" for shipping issues. Higher rates, at least on the average, may be the result, through the creation of a less atomistic supply structure by the major shippers.

INTEGRATION OF SEVERAL VALUE CHAIN SEGMENTS

Some industrial shippers may demand a more coordinated transportation service, not only sea transportation but also, perhaps, land transportation of containers that have been freighted by sea; warehousing; support with some of the paper work for the goods shipped—from the door of the shipper to the door of the final receiver of the shipped goods, which is essentially total outsourcing of the transportation function by the shipper.

Consider a few examples. The world's biggest liner corporation, Maersk Sealand, a division of A. P. Moller-Maersk, provides not only ship services but also extensive warehousing in its own port terminals, extensive trucking services over land, and also support for computer-based tracking of the containers and automated paper work on behalf of the shippers. Maersk Sealand has entered into several all-inclusive contracts to handle the logistical function of major industrial shippers worldwide.

DFDS, based in Copenhagen, Denmark, is another example. DFDS operates in the North European transportation segment, again not only with ships—primarily in the North Sea and inter-Scandinavian waters—but also with truck services, warehousing, etc. This is a similar concept to Maersk Sealand's, although more local.

The results of such shipping arrangements will be an all-inclusive "package" contract for shipping freight. The contract will be between an industrial shipper and the shipowner, which has now transformed itself into a total transportation provider. The freight rate levels in such a contract will be set based on one-to-one negotiations, not under market-based, atomistic perfect competition. Again, the result will probably be somewhat more stable, but probably at higher rates than under the conditions of perfect competition.

THE INVESTMENT SIZE PER SHIP AS A BARRIER TO ENTRY

As noted, in many segments of the shipping industry, there is a tendency toward increasingly specialized, highly capital intensive ships. In the offshore supply ship segment, for instance, there has been a shift toward demand for larger platform supply ships, which, however, require more extensive investments by the shipowner. Extensive add-ons would come on top: dead positioning (DP), firefighting equipment (FiFi), oil recovery equipment (Oil Rec), methanol tanks, tank-cleaning equipment, and so on.

Another new segment in the offshore ship area would be seismic ships, which are highly capital intensive in terms of investments needed. These ships are in increasing demand from shippers, oil companies, oil exploration companies, etc. It goes without saying that only a much smaller number of shipowners can afford to participate in these more capital-intensive niches. The effect will therefore again be less atomism, and therefore less perfect competition, which increases the likelihood of more negotiated—and in the end more balanced—freight rates. Still, we should have no illusions: Higher returns also tend to lead to more new shipbuilding contracting and, in turn, more capacity, which again will lead to record deliveries of new ships, and then lower rates and lower yields on return of capital.

There is indeed another snag in this development, which represents a "downside" for the shipowner. The markets for these highly specialized ships will, of course, be much "thinner" than for standard, normal ships. There will simply not be the same need for a large number of such specialized ships. Thus, in conditions where there would be no demand for these ships, or a large oversupply of such ships, a breakdown in specialized ship markets could occur, with extremely depressed rates and even the laying up of a number of ships and the obvious consequences. Thus, it might be advisable to build more standard, popular ships that will always be in relatively high demand. The tradeoff here is that the "Volkswagen" type ship will compete under more atomistic perfect conditions, with often lower freight rates, while the more specialized ships will compete in more "exclusive" niches, often with higher freight rates, but with perhaps higher downside potential. But the prerequisite for the latter is, of course, that a market exists at all.

NON-COMMODITY BUSINESS GROWTH

Chakravarthy and Lorange (2004) have, as noted, developed a model for growth in industrial companies (referred to in Exhibit 1.8) which emphasizes the need to develop new niches, based on the already established strengths that companies might have, pushing these into areas where there would be less commoditization and more growth potential. Chapter 1 provided a brief outline of this overall scheme for developing strategies in shipping firms; Chapter 2 dealt only with the part of the model that focuses on the strategies that utilize the basic established strengths in the commodity-shipping segment, Protect and Extend. Let us now expand on the model to include non-commodity niches for growth, i.e., the Leverage and/or Build strategic niche position in Exhibit 3.1 below.

Exhibit 3.1: A Framework for Niche-Based Internally Generated Growth

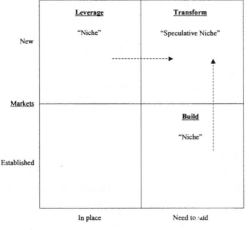

Source: Author

The starting point will be to consider the particular—hopefully unique—strengths of a company. Is there, for instance, one area of shipping where a company has a particularly strong track record, a concentration of ships with a supporting base of market know-how as well as a technological base to run these ships, etc.? This would be the Protect and Extend business segment. Here, one would have established competences in a given market, with proven distinctive technological and other competences in place. The challenge here would be to maintain one's position by continuously improving what one is offering in the market through natural product extensions—say, by offering more modern ships—as well as evolutionary, new product offerings like better cargo handling. Offering more efficiency, more service, adding more computer-based support, etc. can also strengthen existing competences further. The key will always be "to make good even better." We have discussed this extensively in Chapter 2. The question now is: Can this basis of strength—established in the context of rather atomistic, perfect competition—be the basis for expansion into other niches characterized by more growth, less atomistic competition, and higher freight rates?

The key is to be able to see the growth opportunities, and to go after the high potential niches, particularly those that might offer exceptional growth. One must see the opportunities *before* they are obvious to any one else. Timing is thus critical in developing niche-based creative business models. For a shipping company that wants to pursue niches, it must have the necessary resources available to be able to take the opportunities when they arise. Strategy is thus to *be prepared*. Key resources for being prepared would primarily be in the brains of the executives in the firm, i.e., organizational capabilities, rather than in the "steal" itself. Team-based eclectic resources are key, rather than relying on freestanding "prima donna" executives. The firm with the best team is probably the winner.

Build

One such step would be to add distinctive new competences to the present base business. We would call this a Build business. This can, for instance, consist of building new competences by, for example, including other segments of the value chain. We have already indicated how a company like Maersk Sealand, the container ship division of A. P. Moller-Maersk, has added competences in warehousing, harbor terminal handling, land transportation and computer-based support in order to possess the technology and competence base needed to offer a broader set of transportation services over a broader range of the value chain.

Other examples might be the development of highly specialized ships. One might, for instance, add cable laying technology capabilities for normal offshore supply ships. Or one might add conveyor belt offloading technology for Handy-size bulk carriers so that offloading can take place as a closed system, which would drastically decrease the amount of contamination and pollution. Companies such as Jebsens, Thunbolaget, and Canadian Steamship Lines have pioneered this self-unloading ship system (SUS).

Jebsens has the only sizable independent fleet of smaller SUS belt unloaders today, each ship with a capacity of up to 28,000 deadweight tonnes (dwt). Further Jebsens has pioneered the market for efficient self-unloading for "cheap" products, such as aggregates, ores of various types, China clay, coal and fertilizer. It can be said that Jebsens has indeed "revolutionized" the transportation of these types of products in Northern Europe, through its very efficient discharging system: up to 3,000 tones per hour. Jebsens' SUS ships have made the aggregate export business from Norway to the United Kingdom and the European continent, for instance, competitive relative to exports from other countries.

The SUS shipping business is clearly a niche business. It is also the foundation for the development of Jebsens' logistics, in both Europe and Australia. By using SUS as the most efficient means of transportation, also on short distances, the company has developed a distribution system right through to the customer. Jebsens also uses its Panamaxes and Handy-size ships to feed this distribution system.

Jebsens thus also has heavy exposure to the classic commodity-driven shipping businesses and has used this as the basis for developing several niche strategies. It has approximately 40 Panamax bulk carriers chartered in at each time. In addition, it owns approximately 15 Handimax bulk carriers, some of them in partnership with other owners. Jebsens' long time efforts to develop the SUS bulk carrier business have, however, led to a broadening of its focus to cover port handling in a wider sense. It has three large port handling facilities in South & East Australia where it does bagging and distribution to end users of fertilizers, grain and/or coal products. Further, it has the exclusive port handling activities at the Norwegian Arctic island Svalbard, where a considerable amount of coal is exported every year during a short summer period from July till November, when the harbor in Svea is ice free. Jebsens has its own tug facilities, and support to deal with all the port handling here. This is another good example of a Build strategy, first by pioneering the self-unloading concept to keep the cargo cleaner and avoid dust and pollution, etc., and then taking it one step further into port handling activities.

Seaspan Container Group, Vancouver, part of Washington Marine Group, is another example of a good Build strategy. The company is part of a larger group, the Washington Group of Companies, which has interests in a variety of areas: construction, local Canadian shipping, barges, tugs, rail services, real estate, mining, etc. The controlling owner, Dennis Washington, is a multibillionaire who lives in Missoula, Montana, US. (Miller et al., 2003, p. 57). As far as strategy goes, Seaspan has 12 ships on long-term charters (ten years) with China Shipping. These are container ships. Five 4,250 TEU vessels are in service; five more are under construction. Further, two huge 8,100 TEU container ships are being built. Similarly, it has nine ships on ten-year charters to Canadian Pacific. The fleet is thus all large container ships. The 8,100 TEU ships are in the very large class. The 4,250 TEU ships are the east/west "workhorses" of the container trade.

Seaspan's strategy is to fix its ships on very long-term charters, with strong charterers, and to finance the ships at high leverage with 80% to 90% long-term financing. The financing is done for the entire fleet. Seaspan views its strategy as providing long-term fixing of charters for sister vessels with very strong and reputable charters that allow it to finance efficiently. In addition, the similarity of its vessels allows its in-house technical and crew management operations to become very efficient in managing this class of vessel. All the 4,250 TEU vessels—all built at Samsung—are similar. Seaspan has used its repeat purchases from Samsung to allow it to achieve increasing economies of scale in the inputs for the vessels and their ongoing operations. In total, this is a Build strategy, with new competences applied to the technology of the ships, the financing, and the market relationships with the charterers. The result: economies of scale. Long-term charters further allow the company to have an exceptionally high debt rate on its balance sheet. As such, Seaspan contrasts starkly with many other container shipping companies.

Tschudi & Eitzen, Oslo, Norway, has several VLCC single hull tankers. It was able to upgrade them by strengthening the hull infrastructure around the tank areas, so that they can now be certified to operate in certain areas, including South African ports. The effective life of the ship has thereby been extended. This is an example of a Build strategy.

Viking Supply Ships, Oslo, Norway has traditionally operated a fleet of offshore supply ships. It used its technology to build combined icebreakers and supply ships, which were used as icebreakers in the Baltic during the winter on long-term contracts to the Swedish authorities, and then as platform supply ships in the North Sea during the summer. This is also a clear Build strategy.

Although it may generally not be all that easy to find new technologies and new competences to add to one's base in shipping, so as to in essence create a Build niche, it is still possible with determined effort and hard work. And the prize is that it offers less competition and normally higher rates.

Leverage

Another opportunity for niche strategy-building would be to use one's established strengths in other markets. We call this a Leverage strategy. One example would be entering new industries, where one would offer transport services, cover new product categories or focus on new geographies. Several shipping companies have established activities in mainland China, and I. M. Skaugen will serve later in this chapter as an example. Entering container ships in the so-called reefer shipping market, by offering reefer containers supported by reefer plugs installed in the container ships, is another example. Such container ships can now offer refrigerated containers, allowing for much more flexibility in the handling of products and taking away the market for classic reefer ships. The RoRo company Aug. Bolten, based in Hamburg, Germany, developed a strong link with Volkswagen for freighting cars. Later it used this acquired know-how to co-establish TT-Line, a RoRo service for cars, trucks and passengers in the Baltic—another clear Leverage strategy.

Transform

A fourth category of new niches would be the so-called Transform niche, which entails *both* entering new markets with new competences *and* applying new technological competences. Our experience calls for a word of caution here, however, based on our research in industrial companies. It will typically be difficult to go directly from one's established base to a Transform niche—a direct "leap" will normally be unrealistic. Rather, a more realistic case would entail *first* going into, say, a new market, in other words, developing a Leverage strategy. Once established in this new market, the company can *subsequently* look for new technologies and other know-how modifications to add, thereby eventually ending up in a Transform niche, via an indirect, two-step process. Analogously, a shipping firm could add new competences initially, ending up in a Build situation. When this niche has been established, the company could take this into new markets, again developing a Transform strategy.

Crédit Lyonnais has developed a strategy for serving the shipping sector where it goes from banking to insurance (Leverage). From there Crédit Lyonnais could go to direct selling (Transform), and also enjoy higher fees. It (and other banks, too) has acquired various retail businesses, with new competences for the shipping market (a Build strategy). Crédit Lyonnais is also focusing primarily on financing LNG and container ships. It has developed an advisory capability vis-à-vis shipping companies in these trade segments (a Build strategy). It also went into government financing in these areas in Japan (bonds with higher ratings), a Transform strategy. This Transform strategy has been extended, with Crédit Lyonnais now advising the government of Oman on its financing of an LNG fleet.

FedNav, Montreal, enjoyed a strong base in the Great Lakes, US/Canada. From there it diversified into land-based terminals, a Build strategy. From land-based terminals around the Great Lakes, it then went into land-based terminals on the US East Coast, a Transform strategy. Further, it created a strong concept of parcel service for its Great Lakes-based bulk carriers, to be more customer oriented, which happens to be a Build strategy. It could also be seen as a Leverage strategy, in the sense that new customer segments were approached. From there, FedNav acquired Panamax ships, but transferred the parcel concept to the Panamaxes, a Transform strategy: Panamaxes with parcel features!

Tschudi & Eitzen had a strong position in Handimax bulkers in trading with India, including the Bombay area, where it also developed a crewing activity, i.e., a broader local presence, a Leverage strategy. It then became apparent that it needed to handle heavier transportation. So it installed large grabs in various Indian ports, initially to handle its own ships, but then also for other shipowners to hire. This is a Transform strategy.

In 1985 Fairmont Shipping, with its crewing activities, was operating four schools to educate seafarers in the Philippines. During a downturn, Fairmont decided to go more broadly into human resource management, by Building a crewing organization to serve other firms as well. Today, it has 520 ships under management and 20,000 people in its crew organization, serving many other shipping companies. This can be seen as a Build strategy. Fairmont has now moved this crewing concept into other countries, such as India, Croatia and China—indeed a Leverage strategy. It is now developing uniforms, a mail order service for the families of the crews, etc., a Transform strategy.

Bergesen has developed a strategy to expand based on the same customer base, as it exemplified with its relationship with the oil company Total (now TotalFinaElf). Through this customer relationship, it has over a long time developed a strong position when it comes to crude tankers. It has also subsequently developed a strong position vis-à-vis Total with LPG ships, as well as LNGs. Most recently, it has introduced storage ships serving Total's offshore exploration activities. Thus, Bergesen has developed a growth platform based on a specific customer relationship: First by growing a Leverage position, then by introducing a number of new Build-type ship transportation solutions, thus ending up with a Transform business! Bergesen has thus been attempting to play a role of giving total service vis-à-vis Total. It was perhaps, however, too small in many of the segments it entered. In light of this, since Bergesen may not have had sufficient scale in each segment it went into, the diversification into all of these segments may, perhaps, have represented too much diversity.

DISTINCTIVE INNOVATIVE COMPETENCES

Let us look systematically at some of the more distinctive competences shipping companies might add. First, the option of developing distinctive *technical* competences. One well-known feature is the so-called double hull technological innovation in crude oil tankers. After a series of disasters with major oil spills, the law now requires crude oil carriers to have double hulls in most waters. This requirement was pioneered by the US, but has now also been adopted by the EU. Initially, this was a clear Build niche. A. P. Moller-Maersk, for instance, introduced double hull tankers some 15 years ago. While, as noted, the company lost a lot on these ships during the first several years, it is now well positioned to reap the market, which now calls for double hull ships much more broadly. Over time, this has increasingly become a "must," and double hulls are now de facto part of the more atomistic, perfectly competitive main niche for crude oil tanker supplies. Another technological advantage is the so-called shallow draft crude tankers that ply seas like the Baltic and other select areas. Again, this is a relatively small niche, where technology typically led to higher rates, until more ships of this type were delivered.

I have already mentioned the closed conveyor belt unloading systems (SUS) that have been developed for certain types of Handimax bulk carriers in order to diminish contamination of the cargo and dramatically cut down on pollution. As indicated, Jebsen, Thunbolaget and Canadian Steamship Lines were pioneers in developing this niche, followed later by Klaveness and others. I have also already mentioned the many technological innovations that have been developed for PSVs, such as DP, Fifi, Oil Rec, etc.

The so-called heavy lift ships, initially developed by Tschudi & Eitzen and Jan-Erik Dyvi, include a technology where the ship itself is largely filled with water, thus allowing for large infrastructures, such as offshore drilling jack-ups, to be floated on top of the ship. The heavy ship is then emptied of water—almost like a floating dock—and the infrastructure can then be transported on the "back" of the heavy lift ship. Others have further perfected this technology, with Dockwise—the Dutch transport company—now the leader. The development of this technology—in effect creating a brand new segment within the shipping industry—is so interesting that we shall discuss it in some more detail.

The semi-submersible deck carrier concept seems to have been initially developed by Tschudi & Eitzen (Lloyd's List, 1982), which had one of its bulkers converted to this purpose. This was the tanker *Venture Espana*, which was converted into what ultimately became a heavy lift ship, the *Sibig*—the world's first submersible heavy lift ship conversion. It was then further operationalized by John Nielsen, working as part of the shipping company, Jan-Erik Dyvi (Jeannet, 1985). This new ship was, as noted, to be semi-submersible so it could "ballast down" to place its deck underneath the floating rig, with legs jacked up. For the voyage, the ship would de-ballast to lift the cargo out of the water. Nielsen believed that the new ship design offered advantages over traditional tug/barge operations. Transportation time could be reduced by increased speed, and insurance rates could be cut due to improved safety (Jeannet, 1985, Case A, p. 3). This case is symptomatic of the development of niche businesses in shipping.

In 1985, Nielsen was looking back on almost two very successful years of operation following the company's introduction of the two semi-submersible deck carriers. Both ships had been fully employed during this time. However, several competitors had now entered the market with similar vessels, and this was resulting in lower freight revenues. Another five ships were to be delivered soon; Jan-Erik Dyvi ordered two of them. There were already nine ships in operation worldwide. Competition had reacted quickly, just as Nielsen had expected, and brought into service eight deck carriers. However, the tug/barge operators were not the only ones to order these carriers. Jan-Erik Dyvi ended up competing with several new firms: a Dutch company, a Danish shipping firm and two Norwegian operators (Jeannet, 1985, Case B, pp. 1 and 3).

All in all, one could see that this was a great shipping concept offering a unique service, with unique properties for the shippers, and also commanding a clear advantage in terms of setting strong freight rates. Interestingly, however, one can also observe how quickly and aggressively this niche was then pursued by a number of competitors, and thus grew from one supplier to five, and from two ships to fourteen. The niche market was quickly becoming commoditized. To develop sustainable advantages via purely technological features is normally difficult indeed—competitors can copy technological advances. However, discretionary, "softer" know-how—in the hands of lead experts in the shipping companies—will typically be more difficult to copy.

Let us look at the Dutch owner Heerema, which is a strong proponent of this type of niche strategy. The company is heavily exposed to the heavy lift ship market through its majority-held firm Dockwise (Wilhelm Wilhelmsen owns 21%), which now owns and operates around 19 such ships. Strong links, marketing wise, with key shippers is key to Dockwise's strategy.

It is this closeness to the particular market that seems to make a difference. Here it should be pointed out that Dockwise was awarded one of the highest fines ever given to a company in this industry by the EU regulatory authorities for price fixing, collaborating with another shipowner. This, perhaps, underscores the dilemma one can face when cooperating extensively with customers and with other industry players. Specialization calls for networking and cooperation. Current competition regulation does perhaps not reflect this sufficiently.

Heerema also has four huge crane ships. In this market segment there are only five such ships in the world, and Heerema operates three of them. These are unique ships for taking extremely heavy lifts, and they represent very heavy investments. They represent a significant part of the world's super heavy lifting capacity. As noted, the capital investment is considerable. The market is highly specialized, with strong links to the construction, harbor development and offshore oil exploration businesses. The strong links between this highly specialized firm and the appropriate construction contractors is critical for the successful marketing of this service—its organizational culture is focused on this accordingly.

Heerema also has two cable laying ships and has recently invested in one large oil pipeline laying ship, which can operate in water depths of up to 3,000-meters and is equipped with eight thrusters and dead positioning via satellite connection. This highly advanced ship represents a huge investment. There is only one other remotely comparable ship available, a highly specialized, but also highly capital intensive, segment driven by technological innovation. Once more, however, the dedicated marketing organization supporting this highly specialized niche is key.

More examples of technology-based innovations that lead to more or less effective Build strategies will come later in this chapter. Beyond technology innovations, shipping companies can also add intangible distinctive competences. Most prominent, perhaps, would be dedicated marketing support, computer technology that can be used to dramatically strengthen service to clients. For instance, IT is an essential part of Maersk Sealand's and DFDS's extension of their transportation services along a broader set of value chain elements, as previously discussed. Shipping companies that wish to qualify as effective logistic suppliers need to be able to track goods. I. M. Skaugen, Norden and others have followed a similar heavy emphasis on IT, all attempting to add distinctive, net-based competences to serve the customers better, perhaps with the aim of adding an ability to support the customers well worldwide and 24/7. Added closeness to the customer is the result, which also amounts to establishing a Build strategy. Without this distinctive competence, these firms could not have transformed themselves into what are, in effect, logistics suppliers.

But what about entering new markets, primarily through geographic expansion to create a Leverage niche? The Danish shipping company Norden, previously discussed, has done just that. In 1996 Norden established its Singapore office to be closer to the shippers in Southeast Asia. In 2000 Norden added its US office, initially to be able to better market its new series of 35,000 dwt double hull product tankers there. These had been ordered the year before and were tailor-made for the US market. In 2002 Norden established an office in Shanghai, again to be closer to the China-based shippers. A clear pattern emerged. Norden was establishing local offices to be closer to the local customers, in the spirit of acting locally but thinking globally. To establish a deeper relationship with the charterers, really *knowing* them seems important. One might, of course, say that this could be handled via modern telecommunications, but only up to a point. Ultimately, the face-to-face dimension of local presence through geographic expansion is often key.

I. M. Skaugen similarly has found that it is critical to have local offices to be able to serve the customers more intimately—being where the customer is, including working on the same time zone as the customer. Consequently, as of 1994 Skaugen had established its own offices in Houston, Singapore, Shanghai and Dubai. In 1996 it opened an office in St. Petersburg, primarily as a hedge against sole reliance on China when it came to providing a base for cost efficient crews.

Farstad has also pursued geographical expansion. From an initial base in Aalesund, Norway, it established an office in Aberdeen, Scotland, and then entered into joint ventures in Australia (1997), Brazil (1999) and most recently West Africa (2002). It is interesting to see that Farstad made use of local partners in these joint ventures, in order to gain more effective market contacts. This, above all, probably saved Farstad a lot of time, given that it takes time to develop one's own local market links from scratch.

INDUSTRY STRUCTURE

With the development of more know-how, as well as technical, commercial and IT-based geographical expansion, one would expect to see the possession of a larger resource base by the shipping companies to be viable, i.e., larger firms, more concentration in the industry, larger fleets controlled by fewer players, to leverage the added investment in prerequisite know-how. One trend would be toward developing pools, whereby many shipowners would band together to develop a joint set of capabilities and to spread the costs of covering these built-up marketing capabilities among the many shipowning pool participants. In the reefer business, for instance, four large pools basically cover most of the global reefer market today: Seatrade from the Netherlands, with close links with Green Reefer; J. Lauritzen from Copenhagen, with close links with Cool Carriers; Swan Reefers; and K-Line from Japan.

In addition, there are some smaller groupings, primarily spin-offs from the larger pools. The common feature of all these pools is their capability to develop a joint marketing effort, with more "investment" in specific customer relations. Another effect of this concentration is that the supply side now consists of four big suppliers, rather than a large, atomistic set of suppliers, thus shifting this niche away from a structure with more perfect competition. Here we can observe a tendency toward building up more full-blown competences in the larger shipping companies, primarily when it comes to adding service competences, not only in chartering but also in technical and financial areas. A more professionalized, formal management approach for the large shipping companies is thus emerging.

This, however, opens up a potentially interesting niche for the smaller, often privately held shipping company that can perhaps be more opportunistic, move faster, avoid the often inevitable slowdown of having to involve a board of directors and several management levels. The build-up of organizational "silos" and culture clashes between the so-called professional managers and the original "pit of the stomach" shipping executives can only add to this. The small firm thus has the speed advantage. The industry concentration might lead to *less* speed and *less* flexibility, as is the general trend. This would thus mean a potential competitive opportunity that smaller firms can utilize. Above all, we have seen this when it comes to the emergence of highly specialized shipping firms.

HIGHLY SPECIALIZED SHIPPING BUSINESSES

There are a number of examples of highly specialized shipping business segments in which shipping companies have been able to create niches with imperfect competition. We have already discussed the SUS self-unloaders and the heavy lift and crane ships. Other examples include industrial chemicals shipping, the wine business, the orange juice market, the heavy lift crane business (take out), the cruise business and LNG.

Industrial Chemicals Shipping

The industrial chemicals shipping business is characterized by having ships with a large number of so-called segregations, meaning that various types of chemicals—typically from different specialty chemicals procedures—can be transported in separate tanks and pipe systems on the same ship. These so-called parcel tankers thus serve several customers at once, each with its highly specialized products. The parcel tankers typically follow trading patterns between large terminals, also typically owned by the shipping company, where specialized tanker capacity is available to store the specialized chemicals on behalf of the various chemical companies. These can then be picked up by trucks, either organized by the shipper or the shipowner. For the shipping company there are thus huge investments in the parcel tankers—not least due to the unique needs for multiple systems of stainless steel tanks, excessive piping and pumping arrangements, instrumentation, etc.—as well as heavy investments in terminals to serve the specialized chemicals businesses.

Three Norway-rooted companies are among the four market leaders in this segment: Odfjell and Jo Tankers, both in Bergen, and Stolt-Nielsen in Greenwich. (Tokyo Tankers is the fourth.) The organizational culture in these firms reflects their extreme closeness to the chemical companies—almost part of their value chains. It should be pointed out that the "temptation" to collaborate on price fixing between such a small set of players might be high. Indeed, in this industry we have seen investigations by US auditors, executives from companies have gone to prison for price-fixing, and there is also an investigation by the EU regulatory authorities, to mention a few examples.

The Specialized Drinks Segment

The wine business has been pioneered by shipping companies such as Seatrans of Bergen, Norway, and Groupe Ermeva S.A. of Geneva, Switzerland. The business was initially started as wine transporting companies sent wine in railroad tanks. Then it was decided to put railroad cars on ships at the docks and transport the entire rolling stock. The next step was then obvious: Create special-purpose tankers to transport the wine. A key basis for this was large exports from the various Mediterranean countries to all over the world. Subsequently, however, several factors eventually created a downturn in this market:

- The emergence of bottles as a key sign of quality for wine and thus also the demise of bulk wine.

- The emergence of global producers in countries around the world, such as Australia, Chile, Argentina and the US West Coast, all with a strong focus on bottled wine and the relative demise of the bulk exporting Mediterranean area.

- The collapse of the former Communist markets, a big taker of bulk wines, calling subsequently for higher quality wines.

A niche market such as this was developed initially to grow. It then collapsed because of structural factors totally outside the supply and demand factors normally found in the shipping business.

The orange juice market goes primarily from Brazil to Florida. It is highly specialized, with one main operator, V. Pavesic, located in La Tour de Peilz, Switzerland. Again, this trade is characterized by heavy equipment in refrigeration, stainless steel tanks, piping and pumps.

The Cruise Business

The cruise business combines traditional shipping and the consumer business, with similarities to the hotel industry. It involves heavy consumer marketing. It is a booming business, with the bulk of the capacity highly concentrated among a few owners. The two dominant groups by far are Carnival (including Princess Cruises, Cunard, Costa and Holland America Line) and Royal Caribbean Cruise Lines (including Celebrity). The ultimate critical success factor and key know-how behind this business is consumer marketing, focusing on how to reach the vacation/leisure consumer business. In a sense, there are many similarities between this business and running vacation estates or even hotel chains. Brand building is critical. Much of the marketing involves direct advertising in several forms, telephone marketing and working through the travel agency channel.

As can be seen from Exhibit 3.2, the cruise industry is extremely concentrated, with three groups controlling 80% of the market. The barriers to entry—heavy investments needed for each new ship (more than US$1 billion to build a large cruise ship) and for marketing, operations, etc.—make it difficult for other players to enter this industry.

Exhibit 3.2: The Largest Cruise Ship Companies in the World: 2003

Company	No. of Ships in Fleet	No. of Berths	No. of Passengers per Year	Market Share
Carnival Corporation	73	118,000	5,422,500	44%
Royal Caribbean Cruises	27	58,300	2,990,600	25%
Star Group (incl. Norwegian Cruise Lines, NCL)	18	24,500	1,414,300	11%
Total	118	200,800	9,827,400	80%

Source: Aftenposten, 2003

The large cruise lines are continuously striving to develop cruising as more of a niche business, i.e., they are trying to distance themselves as much as they can from a conventional commodity business. They are, for instance, developing their product through innovations, particularly technical development—i.e., a Build strategy. Exhibit 3.3 illustrates this for Royal Caribbean. Innovations can be linked, at least in part, directly to each ship. Every ship in Royal Caribbean incorporates the incremental improvements from the previous ship. These innovations fall into four broader waves or classes, as can be seen from the exhibit, and one such class of general ship delineation typically spans a decade.

Exhibit 3.3: Continuous Product Innovation, Royal Caribbean International

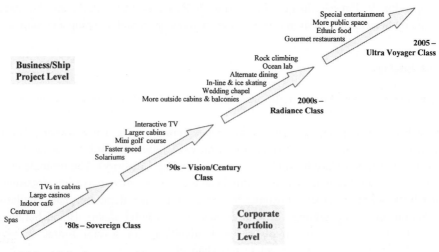

Source: Richard Fain, first reported in Lorange, 2001, revised 2004

Cruise lines are also now beginning to retrofit older ships with some of their most recent innovations in order to create greater brand consistency. For example, Royal Caribbean International is retrofitting all of its ships with rock climbing walls and is opening specialty restaurants on some of its ships that were originally constructed without them.

Although service- and product-based innovations may be somewhat more difficult for competitors to replicate than the hardware-based innovations in Exhibit 3.3, cruise lines have been investing heavily to distinguish service and product delivery as well. Princess and Norwegian Cruise Lines (NCL) led the industry in developing and promoting a deregimented cruise experience through more flexible dining and, to a lesser extent, entertainment. Celebrity launched a number of new product amenities under its brand rejuvenation and Concierge Class programs, and Holland America Line is on a similar path with its Signature of Excellence program. While many of these programs may not seem significant in isolation, collectively they may drive greater brand differentiation and create brand equity.

One may also see greater innovation through strategic partnerships. For example, Celebrity has formed an alliance with Cirque du Soleil to focus on better entertainment and is able to leverage Cirque's brand equity when promoting the Celebrity brand. Cirque gains greater exposure for its brand among Celebrity guests. Similarly, Cunard provides a Canyon Ranch branded spa experience aboard the Queen Mary 2 and has a partnership with Oxford University to provide enrichment programs. One might see a greater range of these brand partnerships in the future.

Innovation can also extend beyond the ship. For example, cruise lines are looking at ways of creating unique, exclusive excursions for their guests. Further, certain forms of innovation can create competitive advantage even if they do not directly touch the guests. For example, Royal Caribbean has launched Partner Insight, a new information tool for travel agents, which enables them to manage their booking information much more efficiently and effectively.

The geographical expansion dimension has been important in the cruise ship business. Initially, much of the cruise business concept was developed in the Caribbean market. Then the so-called Panama Canal market was added, leading to trips between the US East and West Coasts and vice versa. Subsequently, the so-called Alaska market was developed, typically initiating from the US West Coast or Western part of Canada. The Mediterranean market was also developed, as was the around-the-world market and various niche markets. All of these markets required their own marketing, their own consumer communication and their own land-based infrastructure—indeed a way of opening up new business opportunities, based on taking the same basic "technology" into different geographical areas—clear examples of a Leverage strategy.

Liquefied Natural Gas (LNG)

The LNG market has become an important niche market. Until now, it has not been dependent on the open market. The investment in such ships is huge, and traditionally they were ordered and built against very long-term charters, which also allowed for long-term competitive financing. Some say, indeed, that this business has had more similarities with investment banking than with shipping. However, some LNG ships are now being built on speculation, although long-term charter contracts, with corresponding long-term financing, generally still seem to be the rule. This business is thus becoming exposed to the spot market, too. A. P. Moller-Maersk Group, for instance, is reported to have ordered a large LNG ship in 2001, without a contract with a freighter. Only later was it possible for it to obtain a 25-year charter agreement for the ship, with Qatar's Ras Laffas Gas. A second LNG tanker was ordered in 2003 based on contract to the same charterer. Four LNG tankers were ordered in 2004; so far without charter contracts.

Japan is a major consumer of LNG, with 50% of the ocean-shipped world consumption. Stable supply is key for LNG consumption. Hence, long-term contracts have been the trend. Given Japan's power, this trade has been heavily dominated by Japanese owners. The value chain in the LNG shipping segment has four elements (with approximate costs in parentheses):

- Initial gas production at the oil/gas field ($1–$2/m^3)

- Liquefication plant, where the gas is cooled ($2–$3/m^3)

- LNG shipping ($1–$2/m^3)

- Receiving and regasification, at a terminal at the consumer end, linked to a consumer pipeline grid ($0.4–$1/m^3)

With a total cost of $4–$8/m^3, we can thus see that an overall "system" for LNG gas is expensive. It is important to consider the overall value chain in LNG shipping, not only the shipping portion. In general, there now seems to be a trend in LNG shipping toward relatively shorter contracts, with the financial risk shifting more to the owners. The spot market seems to be developing; the market may become increasingly commodity-oriented. This trend seems to be accelerated by the shipowners' being willing to take the risk and order new ships on speculation. Still, there will be high barriers to entry, primarily the price. A question will also be whether the banks will be willing to finance ships on speculation rather than on long-term contracts. Finally, the newbuilding price deflation may be an issue. A new LNG ship costs approximately $150 million today, in contrast to $250 million ten years ago.

The myth that LNG is a complicated and difficult shipping segment to be in, from an operating or technical/safety point of view, is perhaps overstated. The perpetuation of such a myth might have played a role, in effect, in creating a barrier to entry in this shipping segment.

These niche businesses—and undoubtedly many others—offer good examples of innovation through developing distinct competences and/or accessing distinct new market segments. The reward seems to have been the ability to move away from the classic case of perfect competition toward enjoying more exclusive niches, with accompanying higher freight rates. And, to a varying degree, it seems to have been relatively difficult to copy what has been offered. This may be particularly true when the core know-how is primarily in the heads of key people. A focused organization with a customer-oriented culture, combined with cutting-edge technological know-how adapted for a given specific niche, is advantageous.

FURTHER EXAMPLES OF NICHE STRATEGIES

Let us now look at four examples of shipping corporations that have done well in building niche strategies, all initially based on their basic strengths in the more commodity-oriented segments: I. M. Skaugen, Farstad Shipping, TMT, The Torvald Klaveness Group and Leif Hoegh & Co.

I. M. Skaugen

As noted, I. M. Skaugen has gone through a major restructuring since Morits Skaugen took over as CEO in 1992. It was a turnaround strategy, by necessity! Ships were sold and charter parties were terminated. All activities were reduced as much as possible. Much of this was done by negotiating with a large number of banks, so that the restructuring could take place. A key element in the restructuring strategy was to attempt to choose those strategic initiatives that would have a future. Only two strategic engagements were maintained:

- The gas business

- The US lighterage business

The lighterage business was rather small at that time, but Skaugen decided that it wanted to try to build the business, which was in fact a "diamond in the rough." The key was a *direct* customer relationship, which had been established vis-à-vis the oil companies. This could be developed further and was a major reason why the lighterage business was chosen as a strategic area of commitment. The same could be said of the gas business, i.e., it represented an area where there was a direct relationship with the customer.

During the 1990s a lot of focus remained on driving the financial side of the firm. There was an upturn in the gas business in 1995, which allowed the company to get more of its cash flow to be managed managerially, i.e., "kept away from the banks."

In order to develop the link with the customers even further, several offices were established, as noted, in the early 1990s, enhancing the direct contacts. Before this Skaugen had been too dependent on brokers and thus did not have the direct access to customers that it felt it needed. The ability to provide direct service to the customer was seen as key. At the same time, a strict focus on costs was initiated—aimed at technical operations and crewing.

Exhibit 3.4 gives a view of Skaugen's strategy, focusing on the need both to differentiate on the *service* side and to provide *lower costs*. The organization therefore had to perform on both dimensions. From Exhibit 3.4 we can see where Skaugen was positioned, and where it wanted to go.

Exhibit 3.4: I. M. Skaugen's Low Cost/High Service Positioning

Source: I. M. Skaugen, 2003, p. 5

Skaugen is pursuing several specialized shipping strategies, each based on offering reliability and flexibility vis-à-vis the customers, as well as on strict cost discipline, but without letting the service suffer. The company has a strict discipline of being *both* cost leaders *and* service leaders within its fields of operation. Skaugen was initially a highly diversified shipping company, with activities in classic bulk carriers, all sizes of crude carriers (VLCC to Aframax), crude tankers, the ferry business in Northern European waters (Color Line), and in the specialized smaller gas ship segments. This latter activity led to the development of the Norgas pool—one of the three areas in which Skaugen is active today. The company realized the need to focus its resources and to stay focused on a few areas of its key core competences. The classic LPG gas ship market is volatile and has been turned into a commodity business by the competitive environment. A low cost position *is* key! It is also critically important to have a strong service component vis-à-vis the customers.

It is equally important to have transportation solutions with ships that can achieve a low breakeven point, above all with the most efficient gas refrigeration plants. Skaugen has recently developed a series of six new gas carrier ships—all built in Shanghai and with state-of-the-art technology and also able to get operating costs down even further. This should allow the ships to operate at least at breakeven levels, even under the most difficult market conditions. With a weak balance sheet, Skaugen would have to pay more for the financing. Low operating costs and low ship acquisition costs have therefore also—lately—been critical. It was seen as critical to have ships that were efficient enough from a cost point of view that one would not go bust even in a poor market.

The newbuildings were key in getting the costs down. This created strong pressure on the competition also—perhaps one of the reasons why A. P. Moller-Maersk was willing to cooperate with Skaugen! As mentioned, in 2003, Skaugen formed an alliance with the A. P.

Moller-Maersk Group to enhance the semi-refrigerated gas carrier operations of the two companies by the creation of a new revenue sharing pool, Maersk Norgas Gas Carriers (MNGC). Skaugen has 19 ships in the pool and A. P. Moller-Maersk has 18. It specializes in serving the petrochemical and LPG industry, particularly freighting ethylene gas.

Skaugen is also active is in the so-called SPT (Skaugen PetroTrans) segment, which consists of several Aframax crude tankers supported by an extensive system of lighterage, i.e., with tug boats and support units. Here is the business model: The Aframax ships offload the freight of crude oil from larger vessels and into the refineries at the narrow point on rivers, such as the Mississippi Delta and other major US rivers. A total of 14% of the USA's crude oil imports are handled via this system. The key here, above all, is to provide a hassle-free, on-time performance system. It is thus run as an industrial service, with close contact with the customers. The customers are willing to pay a small premium for strong industrial service performance, including punctuality, safety and reliability. Exxon, Chevron, etc. are willing to outsource this service, based on Skaugen's focus on service leadership. Because of the volume that Skaugen built, it developed a scale advantage, thus keep ng the costs down and being able to deliver services at reasonable costs.

As previously discussed, in September 2003, Teekay of Vancouver purchased 50% of Skaugen's ownership in SPT. The company will continue to run as a freestanding business entity, as before, but now with two large owners. It was felt that SPT would be strengthened through Teekay's backing, above all since Teekay is the world's largest owner and operator of Aframax tankers. This is a highly specialized business, which offers more stable return on investment, say, than the gas business. It offers a system in which customers are prepared to pay a higher price for better service and where Skaugen, due to its efficiencies, can schedule the vessels and assets to achieve a margin that would otherwise only be available in an environment with less than perfect competition.

Skaugen's strategy when it emerged from its business and financial restructuring in 1993 was initially to cut overheads and to get the losses in the gas business sector under control. Then, in 1996, Skaugen entered China. Why China? It represented low running costs, using Chinese crews and operations; ships could be repaired at low cost; spare parts could be sourced at low cost. Thus, the move into China was initially more for cost saving than for exploiting China as a market in itself. This early move into China did, however, have a strong positive impact on Skaugen's ability to take advantage of the market later. Today, as we have seen, China's economic development represents immense business opportunities for shipping.

The third area in which Skaugen is active is in freighting liquefied gas via barges on the Yangtze River. This is a rare example of a Transform business strategy. At first Skaugen entered the Chinese market by running a number of liquefied gas carriers along coastal waters in China, based on an already established business base, the so-called Norgas pool. This was a clear Leverage niche extension. Later, Skaugen added the technology from its SPT lighterage business to its China business. This is coupled with a geographic base established in Shanghai through a 49:51 joint venture with a Chinese partner—Hubei Tian En, a local oil and gas distribution company in Hubei province.

The barge concept led to low variable costs, allowing Skaugen to compete well against its rivals, but the fixed costs were high. In November 2003 Skaugen obtained a permit to operate in oil and gas distribution, allowing for expansion of this business into other areas. Skaugen was in head-on competition with the government, and this was initially not approved by Beijing. However, the Hubei provincial government was always very supportive. The strategy to focus on the less "popular" parts of China, namely the interior, led Skaugen to develop its concession to be a general distributor of oil and gas products. Most of the other operators and the government had focused on costal areas. Skaugen is now building its competences in China to stay closer to the customers and to keep costs down, i.e., following the basic strategy that has worked so far. It sees keeping fixed costs to a minimum and trying to build the variable costs component as important.

Exhibit 3.5 depicts the development of I. M. Skaugen's growth strategies. The company's strategy was to stay away from the tops, i.e., a counter-cyclical strategy. We can find examples of all four strategic segments here: Protect and Extend (the basic Norgas business through the MNGC pool and the basic Aframax tankers, part of SPT); Leverage (the expansion of Norgas (MNGC) into China); Build (the North American lighterage support business, SPT); and finally, Transform (the river lighterage support transportation of liquefied gas on the Yangtze River, China, with Hubei Tian En. Thus, all of Skaugen's commercial activities are now executed via strategic alliances. The alliances in the MNGC pool and in SPT (with Teekay) have enabled Skaugen to enhance its two businesses into a "No. 1 position" as the market leader in both.

Exhibit 3.5: I. M. Skaugen's Growth Strategy

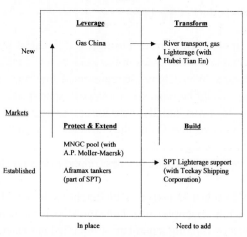

Source: Author

Farstad Shipping

Farstad, based in Aalesund, Norway, is active in two related offshore supply ship segments: large AHTSs (anchor handling tug supply vessels), with engine capacity of more than 10,000 horsepower, and the large PSVs (platform supply vessels), with more than 2,000 dwt carrying capacity. Both these segments represent rather specialized shipping niches, even though both have some degree of atomistic, perfect competition associated with them.

For both types of businesses the intent is to have direct contact with customers, as far as possible, and also to attempt to enter into longer-term freight contract arrangements when possible. This strategy for Farstad Shipping has been more or less clear since 1986. The company's few deviations—owning a product tanker and a few standby supply ships, etc.—did not have good results. Focus has thus become critical—"Strategy means choice!" Exhibit 2.9 gave an overview of the offshore supply fleet, pointing out that approximately 1,800 to 1,900 vessels are smaller than Farstad's. Many of them are also typically older. There is general pressure toward going after larger and stronger ships, and Farstad has been in the lead here. Even today, only approximately 25% of the world's fleet can be found within the size/power segments that Farstad operates in.

Farstad has not entered into other types of offshore segments, which often have highly specialized technical features, such as ships for seismic surveying, diving support ships, cable laying ships, etc. In Farstad's opinion these specialized ships may often find themselves without large markets, and the shipowners can thus find themselves squeezed by the operators—forced to become a supplier/subcontractor within a larger project. Farstad is not comfortable with subcontractor roles. Instead, it has developed strong technical and commercial competences in the two niches in which it operates.

Initially, until 1986, Farstad exploited the North Sea as a single market, for the Norwegian sector as well as the British one. Then the company established its own subsidiary in Aberdeen, initially based on a local joint venture. Here, the management is local, with only a few Norwegians employed. The UK operation runs its entire feet for the British sector, including market contacts.

In the offshore supply business, Farstad was initially part of a pool with several other Norwegian shipowners—Stad Seaforth Shipping. It became clear to Farstad that a pool arrangement meant that direct corporate contact with the users of the ships would not be developed. The market knowledge would rest with the pool organization, not with Farstad. It thus withdrew from the pool in the mid-1980s. The firm then made two key acquisitions to get into a viable size category to be on its own. It bought the offshore supply ship fleet owned by Wilhelmsen—10 ships—as well as a few supply ships from the banks. It also bought Loch Offshore Shipping in Aberdeen.

Farstad's strategy has therefore primarily been to go after new geographic markets—to try to identify growing markets and attempt to penetrate them. The demand for offshore supply ships has grown globally, and Farstad has taken advantage of this. The margins in various newer offshore markets have been better than in the traditional North Sea market, where Farstad started. The emphasis has been on adapting to each of these markets, without technological "overkill." There must always be an alternative use—a second-hand market—for the ships that the company orders.

To summarize, a strategy based on four elements was developed:

- To focus on the top segment of the industry, as indicated in Exhibit 2.9.

- To be international, going after the growth segments where they could best be identified, such as Australia/Asia, Brazil, West Africa, etc.

- To be publicly traded—it was felt that this would add transparency and discipline.

- To have the necessary focus on R&D in the two ship segments that the company had decided to pursue.

The ownership side within the company was consolidated into a publicly listed company in 1988. Previously there were several KS firms (*komandittselskap*). Here, separate ships are typically owned by separate KS firms. The investors own specific parts of each given ship. They are jointly responsible for the commercial results of the ship. The Farstad family presently controls about 52% of the shares.

The resource situation had been critical, sometimes making it necessary to say *no*. For instance, Farstad declined to participate in the highly capital intensive cable-laying segment. The realization that the relevant key human resources had been a limiting factor has been a guiding factor. The financial situation had also been critical. It was felt that the debt ratio relative to equity should be less than 50%. This had to do with the fact that since the offshore supply shipping business is highly cyclical, a reasonable debt/equity ratio and strong liquidity are key. One must have flexibility in order to go after the truly good opportunities when they come. One must, however, also be willing to take the time to consolidate. These considerations must be kept in mind when it comes to assessing two of Farstad's strategic moves—the acquisition of P&O's offshore shipping activities and the further global expansion in Africa.

The strategic alliance with P&O has developed well over a period of time. P&O, through its Australian office, has Australia/Asia-Pacific market contacts. In 2003 P&O agreed to sell its 50% share in the strategic alliance to Farstad. This represented a considerable investment for the Norwegian company—37% increase of its turnover and also taking over more than 400 new employees. There were nearly 20 ships in the former joint venture's fleet. For Farstad to evolve to wholly owned from the previous strategic alliance was important. It meant closer market contacts, better coordination between the parent and the (now) Australian subsidiary—a more coordinated focus within the entire group.

Regarding geographic expansion, the growth markets were increasingly seen to be in Brazil, the Far East and West Africa. Farstad has been active in the Brazilian market since 1985, when it opened a management office there. It has had several different joint ventures with local partners. It has also been out of the Brazilian market for a short period of time. The emphasis has above all been to focus on large AHTSs for the Brazilian offshore market. Brazilian staff carry out most aspects of the operation. The market development side, in particular, is critical, with strong links with Petrobras, The Brazilian state oil company. For Farstad it has been particularly important to find the most appropriate local partners to cooperate with in this regard.

Farstad developed a joint venture in Angola in 2002, with the aim of developing a base for further business expansion in the country. A similar approach has been taken in Nigeria, where the company is attempting to develop a business base with another local business partner. Farstad has assigned special managerial competences to building the African business. This is a high priority, but it is also recognized that it requires considerable resources.

Other potential geographic markets might be Sakhalin, in the eastern part of Russia on the Pacific Ocean rim, as well as in the Caspian Sea. But so far Farstad has not gone into any of these markets.

Farstad has also pushed the technological side. Many of its PSV ships now have larger deck areas and more tanker capacity, as well as more segregation between the various tank subsystems. The AHTS ships have greater winch capacity. Fifi, DP and Oil Rec are common. Thus, by upgrading the ships, Farstad can stay away from the more commodity-oriented markets. A special AHTS was developed for the Asian market, taking advantage if both its geographic and unique technical know-how, indeed, a Transform business.

Finally, a strong emphasis on safety and non-emission policies, coupled with building up a professional land-based organization, add up to an additional advantage for Farstad. Further advantage stems from Farstad's own market brokerage activities, dealing directly with the major customers, as well as a highly professional financial management organization. All in all, Farstad has been able to develop strong focused capabilities that tend to distance the company from the more commodity-oriented business segments by allowing it to pursue a more niche-oriented strategy, in both the Leverage strategy segment and the Build strategy segment—and even in the Transform strategy segment. Exhibit 3.6 gives an overview of Farstad's growth strategy.

Exhibit 3.6: Farstad Shipping's Growth Strategy

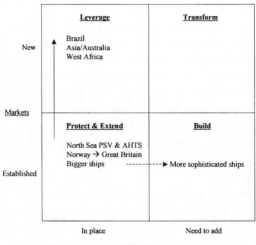

Source: Author

TMT

TMT is headquartered in Taipei and has small offices in Shanghai, Tokyo and Seoul. The company follows a general strategy of purchasing well-maintained second-hand ships and then adds organizational competence to operate these older ships effectively. Its shipping activities are concentrated in five areas:

- Wood chip carriers—five ships, with a tonnage of approximately 45,000 tons each. Marketwise, these carriers are conceptually quite similar to LNG ships—80% of the fleet is dedicated to long-term contracts with major pulp and paper manufacturers, and only a few are built and operated on speculation. This would be a Build niche business.

- Cement carriers—six ships. These form an integral part of the cement companies' long-term supply chains and operate in a niche between Taiwan, Korea, Japan and China. A cement carrier can last up to 50 years. This would be another Build niche.

- RoRo carriers for car transportation—five ships. This is also run as a niche business operating between Japan and China; it is also a Build business.

- Panamax—ten ships. This is a global commodity business.

- Cape-size bulk carrier—only one ship. This is a commodity business.

The central organization has around 40 people focusing on running older ships, maintaining their efficiency through preventive maintenance. Although this can be expensive, it is clearly feasible. All TMT ships are paid for in cash. The company has no debt. It does not deal with any banks. Some ships are 1970s vintage, others are 1980s, and still others 1990s. The company's strategy—to buy ships at low prices at the right time and upgrade them—seems to work. These ships can last for another 30 years or more with proper care.

Although successful, TMT still faces key challenges. One is regulation. How long will older ships be allowed to operate? Macroregulations do not make a distinction between a well-maintained ship and a poorly maintained one—they only stipulate an age limit. The same can be said of major industrial shippers. It is thus key to find niches in this respect, where the shippers appreciate that the older TMT ships are well maintained. Specialized markets are key here. Another challenge is keeping a good, *stable* operating organization, with experts actually running older ships. Exhibit 3.7 provides a summary of TMT's strategy.

Exhibit 3.7: TMT's Growth Strategy

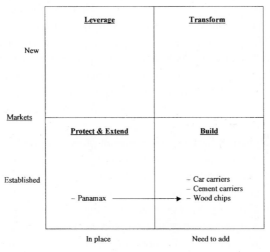

Source: Author

The Torvald Klaveness Group

Klaveness operates a large pool of bulk carrier ships. The company typically invites several independent owners and their various ship assets to take place in a co-investment arrangement with Klaveness. Klaveness has a policy of never owning more than 50% to 75% of any of the ship investments in its pool, but this is not always achievable. Strategically, this model would fall within the Protect and Extend area; Klaveness calls it "Maritime Services." A large part of the company's success here has stemmed from continuous, although in general marginal, productivity development efforts combined with achieving volume targets, thus gaining scale advantages. Managing the various backlogs efficiently is critical. The overall portfolio of contracts of affreightment is therefore optimized. It is thus important to have a mix of ships on contract and operating in the spot market.

The company presently enjoys a strong market, and China is playing a particularly important role too. Heavy emphasis is thus being put on analyzing the Chinese market, for instance, employing a senior Chinese macroeconomist to provide hands-on assessments of how that market is developing. As noted, Klaveness backs all of this up with a sophisticated hedging strategy, focusing on swaps and futures trading for parts of its cargoes.

Klaveness is, however, also pushing another business strategy hard, namely that of developing business activities in the Leverage and/or Build segments. It refers to these activities as "Maritime Logistics" and emphasizes developing new discretionary capabilities to set them apart from the more commodity-oriented business. The focus here, above all, is on innovative cargo handling, particularly self-unloaders. Know-how is focused on superior bulk cargo handling technology, as well as on broader logistics solutions. These often involve several steps in the value chain, backed up by extensive use of IT. There is more investment in the Maritime Logistics segment, which is more long term, than in the Maritime Services segment, which is more opportunistic. The overriding aim is to try to develop an in-depth understanding of customers' needs. And the driving force is to find solutions for customers that tend to reduce their costs. Klaveness measures its own performance in terms of return on capital, profit margins and outright fee levels. Following this maritime logistics strategic approach, Klaveness seems to be enjoying good margins for ship services with such specialized capabilities.

Projects are very much part of business development processes at Klaveness. The company has a project competence that has been developed over a period of 40 years. The Leverage/Build business, which has a long-term focus, is run by Trond Klaveness. The company was strong when it came to this type of business in the 1960s through the 1980s, but it had a weak period in the 1990s. It is now building up this Leverage/Build business again, but recognizes that it takes time. It is realized that it is necessary to have staying power—not only financially but also mentally—within the organization, i.e., not to become disappointed and to be able to take setbacks. The issue is very much how to marginally improve on projects as one goes along, never taking an apparent failure as a failure, but rather as a "license" to learn. This can of course be difficult, not least when it comes to an organization's ability to handle unfavorable news. The company's top managements' view is therefore that if there is more good news than bad news in a year, they are on the right track! The special projects *controller* is also critical here. He has an independent role within the organization and is mandated to ask critical questions. The CEO, Tom Erik Klaveness, also has the role of posing critical questions.

Klaveness appears to have been able to take advantage of several trends that characterize the way some of the major industrial shippers/industrial customers seem to want to move. The first trend is for major corporations to outsource major logistics functions, so that they can focus on their *own* core business activities. The second trend is developing door-to-door logistics approaches, which involves adding onshore activities such as warehousing, harbors and container transport, as well as taking a role in managing the information flow around the overall logistics chain. In this respect, Klaveness' strategic approach seems to have many similarities with that of companies such as Maersk Sealand.

In fact, Klaveness bought 13 Panamax bulk carriers from A. P. Moller-Maersk in 2002. The idea was to strengthen the pool, i.e., to make use of the ships in the Protect and Extend business area. Klaveness offered these ships to its various pool partners, but in the end they declined to commit to this new investment, even though they had initially signaled a positive interest. Klaveness was therefore left with the 13 ships. Even though the first year led to significant losses for the company, strong additional earnings resulted later because these ships were perfectly positioned to take advantage of the strong market that developed in 2003 and onward.

As already noted, part of the A. P. Moller-Maersk ship acquisition also involved taking over an office in Beijing, which has also become very attractive. In this connection, Klaveness has closed its offices in Hong Kong, Jakarta and Singapore to develop the Beijing office more fully. The Beijing office helped to foster the company's understanding of China, whose impact on sustaining global growth was indeed a new dimension for Klaveness.

In CEO Tom Erik Klaveness' opinion, the A. P. Moller-Maersk project was never ill timed. Top management had a clear conceptual vision regarding the need for such a project, namely to strengthen the pool with more tonnage. It was thus strategically prepared to make a move when the possibility of acquiring the A. P. Moller-Maersk fleet came along. Klaveness was mentally ready! However, by November 2002 "all brakes were on." The market was still depressed and very few new projects were being pursued. But the positive outlook from the China market led Klaveness to change to an offensive strategy. It saw the positive development of the China-based freight market sooner than most of its competitors. Thus, on the macro side, Klaveness saw the opportunity for China to become the "growth engine" very early on.

Klaveness at times even purchases standard shipping services from others, letting them run the more basic ship segment activities, thus lowering the overall costs of the total value chain logistics service it can offer. The cost efficiency of the entire value chain further depends on factors such as standardization of the technology (loading/unloading equipment, types of ships, managerial routines) and systems (above all IT). It is also key to have consolidation of volumes—so that each ship can run fully loaded, combining cargoes from many shippers. This requires capacity planning and advanced information handling. IT is thus becoming more and more important for Klaveness. It has entered into a strategic alliance with Cap Gemini to develop new IT solutions for its strategic needs. This alliance with Cap Gemini has led to even more momentum in the development of IT support. Note that the savings that are achieved commonly need to be "split" between the key customers and the key investment partners. Here, a partnership approach, rather than an adversarial competitive approach, seems to be a key driver. A mature perspective must be in place!

Klaveness has been actively expanding its geographic bases and introducing technological innovations to go with this. As early as the 1960s, it played a major role in transporting cement to the US East Coast, as well as to the Arabian Gulf (Abu Dhabi) and the west coast of Africa (Ghana)—in the latter two cases through the transport of half finished products (clinker for the cement industry).

In 1966 Klaveness started shipping caustic soda to Africa for Pechiney, in connection with its alumina operations. The return freight was refined alumina. Thus, it became clear that there was a need for ships that needed to carry both—wet cargo one way and dry cargo the other. The Probo ship project was developed based on this insight. The Probos were delivered in the late 1980s, having been ordered earlier in the decade. They ran into a large number of technical problems, which led to a relatively poor return on investment for the projects. However, looking at the returns *after* the technical problems had been resolved shows that the Probo ships had a satisfactory turn. The so-called CABU (caustic soda bulk) ships followed the Probos. They have been highly successful. Thus, the strong technological development that was put into the Probos was further refined when it came to developing the CABUs—indeed, an example of a Build strategy.

Klaveness also developed a business with self-unloading ships operating on the US East Coast. It took this technology to the Persian Gulf, where it had Cape-size bulk carriers arriving with iron ore. The Cape-size size bulk carriers could not, however, enter the Persian Gulf harbors. They were therefore emptied via self-unloaders, which were then sent into the appropriate harbor. Thus, the technological insight of self-unloaders was utilized to develop a business in another geographic area, migrating from the US East Coast to the Persian Gulf.

As we can see from Exhibit 3.8, the Klaveness strategy, with its customer-focused organization and its industrial marketing culture, is becoming relatively more focused on the brain dimension than on owning ships.

Exhibit 3.8: The Torvald Klaveness Group's Growth Strategy

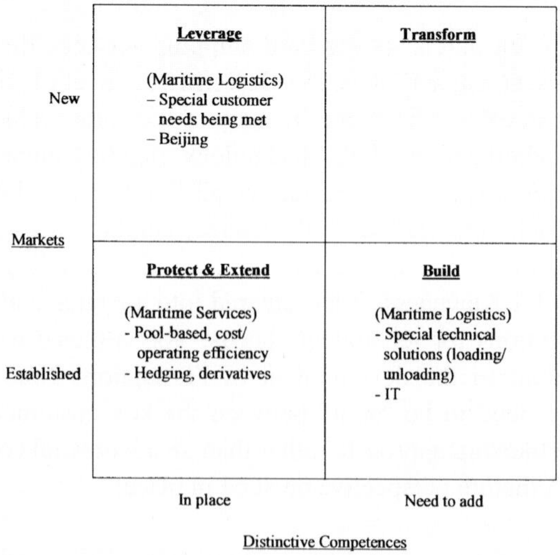

	Leverage	Transform
New	(Maritime Logistics) – Special customer needs being met – Beijing	
Markets		
	Protect & Extend	**Build**
Established	(Maritime Services) - Pool-based, cost/ operating efficiency - Hedging, derivatives	(Maritime Logistics) - Special technical solutions (loading/ unloading) - IT
	In place	Need to add
	Distinctive Competences	

Source: Author

Leif Hoegh & Co.

Leif Hoegh & Co. has traditionally been present in many bulk shipping business segments. For several decades it operated extensive liner operations (sold in 1998 and—to Oldendorff—in 2001). It has also had extensive activities in the crude oil carrier business, which it spun off to form the crude oil carrier company, Bona. This company was publicly listed, but Leif Hoegh retained a controlling interest in Bona from 1990 to 1999. All shares in Bona were then acquired by Teekay Shipping in Vancouver, Canada, paid for in part by new shares in Teekay. The main reason for spinning off the oil tanker business was the perceived reliability risk (potential oil spills) and the need therefore to isolate this business from the rest of the firm, particularly given the intention to operate effectively out of US territorial waters. The Leif Hoegh's response to the risk of operating tankers in the US was to operate double hull oil carriers, as well as to create a freestanding operating entity.

Leif Hoegh was a pioneer in developing the so-called open hatch forest product carriers through a long-term chartering agreement with Weyerhauser in Portland, Oregon. These ships are also now being sold. The company is also de-emphasizing basic bulk carriers, its investment in the reefer business. In 1995 Leif Hoegh took over the Swedish reefer shipping company, Cool Carriers, which was then subsequently sold to J. Lauritzen in 2001 (only the "software" side); the ships were still owned by Leif Hoegh but were run by J. Lauritzen and later sold). In 1996 Leif Hoegh also acquired Gorthon Lines, a Helsingborg-based specialty paper carrier company, which was, however, subsequently sold in 2001. The firm's management feels that when it comes to these last two deals, although the financial returns were ample, the transactions were erratically opportunistic. In retrospect a more fundamental strategic approach might have been pursued.

Leif Hoegh has been involved in a broad set of shipping activities, many in the classic commodity-type atomistic business segments. It has successfully developed market-based strategy implementation approaches over the years, but success has not come without hiccups. Leif Hoegh was in a deep financial crisis during the 1970s due to overextension in the classic business segments—with too much debt, coupled with heavy operating costs—in a market that was exceptionally depressed, and for an exceptionally long time (Bakka, 1997). For instance, it ordered a series of 10 large OBO carriers—without charters—and this nearly bankrupted the firm.

Today, however, the company does have a clear strategy, focused on two main segments: RoRo and LNG, as previously noted. According to the company, these segments depend less than others on atomistic market fluctuations, so they might provide better payoff for the high level of competences that Leif Hoegh is adding, and also allow for the in-depth development of competence-based systems and logistics solutions for each business platform. Finally, they allow for the linking of long-term transportation solutions with long-term customer relationships. A separate, disciplined organization is created, accordingly, for each of the businesses. All of this tends to take these business segments away from basic commodity businesses toward niche ones.

As far as RoRo goes, cars were initially transported via conventional liner ships. Then specialized bulk carriers were developed for the car transportation business. These ships had removable decks fitted in the cargo hulls and the cars were lifted aboard by cranes. Over time the roll on/roll off (RoRo) car carriers were developed. These ships had several fixed decks, which allowed the automobiles to be driven on board over the ships' ramps under their own power. These first-generation car carriers, so-called PCCs (pure car carriers), represented a huge technological improvement. A second generation of car carriers, the MPCCs (multipurpose car carriers), is now coming into service. They have several decks that can be adjusted for height hydraulically, and in general they have more height between the decks and can take heavier loads—trucks, earth-moving equipment, buses, locomotives, etc. in addition to the cars. They thus offer more flexibility in serving shippers. Above all, they offer a greater possibility to develop back-hole runs, so that the ships do not return empty.

Note that the car and automotive transport business is increasingly based on close communication with customers via IT, a desirable development given the high value per item transported. Transit time, seen as part of the overall logistics operations, must therefore be kept to a minimum.

The RoRo business has also gone into geographical market expansions in new segments. For instance, in 2002 Leif Hoegh acquired Kiwi Lines, specialized transporters of second-hand cars between Japan and New Zealand, a relatively protected market given that both have the steering wheel on the right-hand side. Leif Hoegh also entered into a contract with Airbus Industries in Toulouse, France, to transport airplane components between Airbus's various European sites, using so-called short sea special transportation. This has certainly added prestige. To stay out of the commodity segment, the RoRo business has evolved.

Now to the LNG shipping segment. This is based on long-term contracts with major LNG operators, and here, the financial dimension is critical in putting these types of deals together. We are talking about, say, 20- to 25-year long-time charters here, and the ships are specially built for these long-term services.

There are interesting technology developments in the LNG segment, too. Leif Hoegh has developed the so-called SRV (shuttle and regasification vessel) system. Ships are stationed offshore and regasification takes place on board while the ship is being loaded. When one ship is loaded, it moves the gas to the nearest port, where it can hook up with a gas carrying pipeline grid for the consumer market, while another ship takes over at the offshore gas source. Upon reaching port, the gas can be transported directly in available pipelines. There is no need for a land-based terminal for regasification. And there is no need for an underwater pipeline to take the gas onshore from the offshore field. This saves considerable amounts in capital costs and leads to less operating complexity for the gas operating companies. For this immense innovation, even a company the size of Leif Hoegh might have capital restraints— and there might also be problems with lack of free access to available pipeline hook-ups, which might be controlled by the oil company managers. Exhibit 3.9 gives an overview of Leif Hoegh's present growth strategies.

Exhibit 3.9: Leif Hoegh & Co.'s Growth Strategy

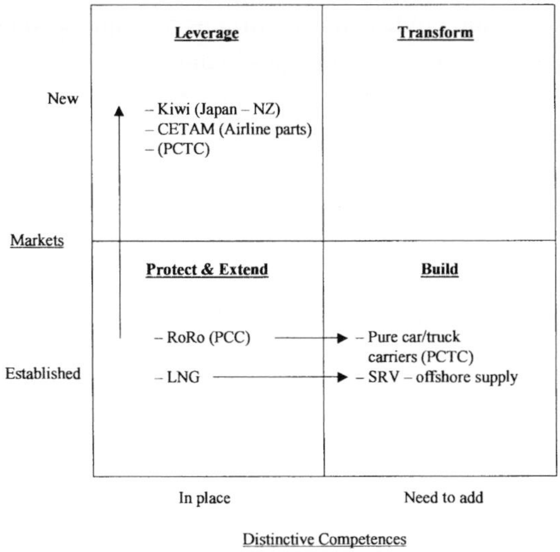

```
                    Leverage              Transform

        New      ↑  – Kiwi (Japan – NZ)
                 |  – CETAM (Airline parts)
                 |  – (PCTC)

 Markets

                    Protect & Extend         Build

                    – RoRo (PCC) ──────→  – Pure car/truck
     Established                              carriers (PCTC)
                    – LNG ─────────────→  – SRV – offshore supply


                    In place              Need to add
                         Distinctive Competences
```

Source: Author

CONCLUSION

There are many examples of successful niche strategies in shipping—developing Leverage niches, Build niches and even Transform niches. Such strategies, as we have seen, are often typically difficult to develop. A diligent effort to open up new markets, coupled with developing distinctive new competences, is key. Remember, however, that other companies can typically easily *copy* the shipping companies that have developed their own niches. A niche advantage is therefore not necessarily going to last for too long, particularly if the unique feature in question is based largely on physical technical properties—on the ship alone. Human-based know-how properties can, however, be more difficult to copy. To develop a focused, market-driven organization to serve the given customers in a particular niche is therefore key.

It is fair to say that one can hardly ever see real long-term barriers to competition. Commoditization takes place sooner or later. More entrants tend to be attracted to niches that have exclusivity associated with them, and the particular segment's structure tends to degenerate sooner or later, eventually becoming overcrowded. Even the most attractive niches eventually end up losing their charm. Obviously, the huge need for capital and new investment can create an effective barrier. A good example here is Maersk Sealand's development of the world's biggest integrated container shipping business—indeed, the world's preeminent container logistics business, with a worldwide scope. Another good example is Heerema's huge investment in four large crane ships, which gives it close to a virtual monopoly. But even in these two examples, there are critical human resource-based know-how components that complement and support—and this adds to the Protection of each niche! People, not steel alone, make the key difference. So now, the question of a shipping firm seeing various growth niches—together with more commodity-oriented niches—in an overall portfolio context for the firm as a whole becomes critical. In the next chapter we shall discuss such portfolio strategies in more detail.

CHAPTER 4

PORTFOLIO STRATEGIES

Would you invest all your money [in one type of shipping asset]? Probably not; putting all of your eggs in one basket in such a manner would violate even the most basic notion of a diversification. But what is the optimal combination of...asset classes? And how will the opportunity to invest in other asset classes...affect your decision? In short, is there a "best" solution to your asset allocation problem?...[How do we] achieve the best tradeoff between portfolio risk and rewards...How should one measure the risk of an individual asset held as part of a diversified portfolio? Can [portfolio managers] outperform simple investment strategies...?

—Bodie et al., 2004, p. 129

THE CLASSIC PORTFOLIO MODEL APPLIED TO SHIPPING

Before we apply the classic portfolio theory from finance, note that many experts have argued that the *investor*, not the firm, should diversify. This argument is consistent with building a stock portfolio, analogous to investment theory. Investors in principle will always have the right or privilege to diversify so that their portfolios carry the levels of risk that match their propensity for risk. They should thus also be able to pick various ship company shares with various risk profiles. It follows, then, that publicly traded shipping companies should try to be relatively focused, with clear risk profile characteristics. The investor himself should hedge, not the shipping company. The shipping companies should be efficient in their particular niches. However, publicly traded companies must aim for predictable cash flows and dividends; hence, there is an argument for some diversification.

If investors can diversify cheaply, there might be no reason at first for corporations to do so—a convincing concept of classic finance. Nonetheless, in some cases diversification may make sense. For example, it might allow for higher leverage with the same risks, such as when a corporation may be able to create extra tax shields that are valuable to investors without increasing its cost of debt financing. This might work particularly well when diversification does not create any negative managerial transaction cost value. For example, when managerial expertise is similar in the areas of diversification considered, one would not create any negative synergies. In shipping there are many examples of such diversification in order to take advantage of tax shelters.

The predictability of cash flows creates value for shareholders and investors in general. Financial analysts typically prefer predictable cash flows, but they are not shareholders and do not necessarily represent sophisticated investors' thinking. When predictable, cash flows could help create value, above all regarding management of tax shields through time, possibly through budgeting investments with financial market uncertainty. Further, however, we easily come into situations where management might prefer predictable cash flows (because it makes their lives easier), while shareholders may prefer risky cash flows, where the risk is clear. Hedging strategies of gold mines come to mind. Many mine executives hedge for gold prices, while investors tend to buy these stocks for gold price exposure. It was found that hedging was done more to satisfy management's own needs than investors' needs (Tufano, 1996).

But this is theory. The reality is, of course, that the discrete size of each ship investment is such that it may be difficult to apply the principle of portfolio diversity strictly.

Nevertheless, let's see what happens when we apply the classic portfolio selection challenge to shipping decisions. The broad portfolio planning questions relate "to the shipping company's choice of involvement between different types of shipping activities. To start with, a sequential approach is suggested for an overall planning and decision-making conceptual scheme within bulk shipping firms. The scheme is portrayed as a 'decision tree' with three major sets of acts [see Exhibit 4.1]." (Lorange and Norman, 1973).

Exhibit 4.1: The Portfolio Decision in Shipping Companies

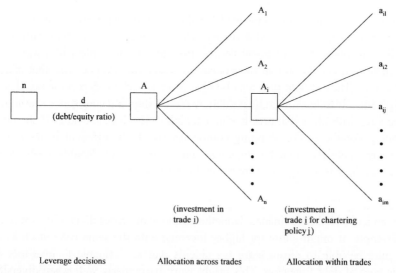

Source: Lorange and Norman, 1973

Looking at Exhibit 4.1, the three parts of the portfolio decision problem are: (1) deciding on the amount of Leverage (choosing the debt-equity ratio), (2) deciding on the distribution of capital across trades, and (3) determining a chartering strategy for each trade, to set guidelines for the capital allocation within the trades. In principle, the shipping company must make these three decisions simultaneously in order to reach a corporate *maximum maximorum* (from a strictly theoretical view, the problem is not "decomposable"). However, if we assume that there is a maximization of a utility function with rather specific properties, the most important of them being assumed risk aversion and the quadratic form (or, alternatively, a few other non-quadratic forms), the problem becomes decomposable. Working from this assumption will lead to an algorithm for setting "shadow prices" to operationalize the decomposition. Portfolio decisions deal with how to decide on financial structure (Leverage) and not only asset allocation. This interconnection is major. The problem is interconnected and is thus not decomposable, unless you assume some form of utility function, which of course simplifies the world—but it does create a basis for analysis!

For each of the separate businesses we need to know the expected future earnings, the variance of these earnings streams, and the co-variance with other earnings stream. This then helps set up the problem as a classic finance formulation, and we can then calculate the overall portfolio's expected earnings and variance. Recent works in finance recognize that expected values and variances do not define risk completely enough. Technically, normal distributions are fully defined by expected values and variances, and most modern finance, notably Markowitz's work (1991) on portfolio management, is based on normal distributions. But many assets today are *not* normally distributed, notably when it comes to hedge funds and credit risk. For example, in hedge funds, a key aspect of risk is what we may call *tail risk*: the risk of a rare but extreme event that will hurt the portfolio strongly. Even when it comes to equities, the normal distribution assumption might be challenged: The probability of a stock market crash, such as the one of October 19, 1987 (Black Monday), has been shown to be one in thousands of years, with a normal distribution assumption—something few people will accept as reasonable. When it comes to shipping markets, these arguments also seem to apply. The difficulty of dealing with tail risk, *kurtosis*—or with skewness, the idea that upside risk may differ from downside risk—is something that is not recognized by dealing with expectations and variances only. As the normal distribution is symmetric, it is hard to accept the general results on portfolio management, based on this assumption. We have a tool to help to deal with this: Value at risk is now used extensively in banking, and it can help us to address these issues.

Those with portfolio responsibility should undertake a systematic revision of the portfolio regularly, in light of the company's overall objectives. Due to the well-developed second-hand markets, it will, indeed, be possible to change a portfolio rather rapidly. However, the portfolio may also, often more easily, be adjusted through the Leverage decision rather than through the ship sales decision. Due to the imposition of the risk-aversion requirement, the actual search for the best portfolio can, in practice, be limited to a search for *efficient* portfolios. The number of alternatives to be considered thus drops significantly.

Lorange and Norman point out that the portfolio approach does not replace traditional planning for each ship and trade. Their claim assumes that we operate as efficiently as possible within each business, i.e., under the forces of profit maximization in the traditional shipping sense. The portfolio planning scheme, on the other hand, offers a way to "put it all together." (Lorange and Norman, 1973). The original portfolio selection problem comes from the field of investments in corporate finance, and these have been extensively researched over the past 45 years (Mossin, 1973).

Returning to the similarities and differences between portfolio management in classic stock markets and portfolio management in shipping markets, let us draw the following observations. In stock markets there seem to be two general approaches: the stock picking approach toward portfolio management and the index-based portfolio approach. These have analogies in shipping.

Stock picking is exemplified by investment managers like Warren Buffett, who would pick five to ten stocks, based on thorough analysis of the firms in which he takes a position, and then hold these stocks for a very long term. Typically, he buys more stock in these firms during market downturns. In the long run, he tends to outperform the market. Buffett is perhaps not a pure stock picker. He also influences management, for instance, by joining some of the boards of the firms he is investing in, rather than staying a pure outsider. Peter Lynch, for instance, may thus be a better example of a pure stock picker. The index-based approach, by contrast, tries to come up with a Pareto-optimal portfolio, based on risk/return considerations. Further, there will be a point of *maximum maximorum* on the Pareto-optimal curve, which indicates the optimal portfolio, given the particular investor's propensity toward risk. But how do these two approaches apply to shipping?

Stock Picking

Stock picking probably does not apply to commodity-type shipping per se (although it might be relevant to niche shipping). Remember: A ship is a ship, and you get more or less the same rates for any ship, depending, of course, on its size and configurations. There would be little to no premium associated with the shipowning company per se, or the claims that some owners make that they have "better" ships. Thus for investments in commodity-exposed ships, you probably cannot pick shipping companies the way Warren Buffett picks stocks and expect to get a better longer-term return. The shipowner can thus not develop a portfolio approach à la Warren Buffett, with the ship as the basic unit, in the sense that the "steel" is exposed to the commodity market, without any differentiation premium.

Further, ship values tend to stay stable, or even go down in the longer run. A major reason for this, as noted, is the fact that newbuilding prices on average tend to come down. A newbuilding LNG today can, for instance, be bought for, say, US$150 million, while eight to ten years ago, the same ship would have cost $250 million. Inflation can perhaps counterbalance this to some extent; still, a long-term, "stock picking" strategy applied to commodity shipping seems unreasonable. We have pointed out that ship newbuilding prices often go down in value and may have an analogue with regard to impact in classic financial portfolio management. The idea is that we have a similar issue with bonds, notably high coupon bonds. One would not agree with our earlier statement that inflation can perhaps counterbalance this to some extent. If prices go up with inflation, real values do not. Hence, this is not modified with inflation. That said, the inflation differential between types of shipping will certainly influence portfolio issues. This underscores the importance of what we might call the term structure in finance, i.e., the structure of values through time.

Index-based Portfolios

When we speak about index portfolios in the context of shipping, we are talking about finding a "best" portfolio, based on risk/return considerations. It is important here to look at *all* of the ship assets in one's commodity-based portfolio, in the sense that they are *all* exposed to market-driven risk/returns. This means that bulk carriers, tankers and container ships would be part of the portfolio. Marsoft has done an assessment of returns on portfolio strategies, based on these three types of ships, with various holding periods—two years, three years and five years. We can see the relevant return versus risk (measured in terms of standard deviation) given as examples in Exhibits 4.2, 4.3 and 4.4 respectively for the three holding periods.

In the short run, investments in bulk carriers and, to some extent, container ships seem to be more attractive than investments in tankers. In the longer-term, however, the relative attractiveness of investments in tankers seems to increase. The message here is that, given the volatility of shipping market outlooks and changes in returns, one needs to continuously re-configure one's portfolio. This approach to index-based portfolios thus differs from classic stock-based index-based portfolio management, where, for instance, the composition of indexes—such as the Dow Jones with its composition of firms—will not change very often. Shipping market portfolios will, however, be much more volatile, and the portfolio content will need to be reworked continuously, as opposed to index-based portfolios in the stock market, which tend to be relatively more robust.

Exhibit 4.2: Two-Year Holding Period

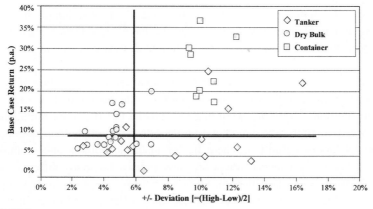

Source: Marsoft, 2003

Exhibit 4.3: Three-Year Holding Period

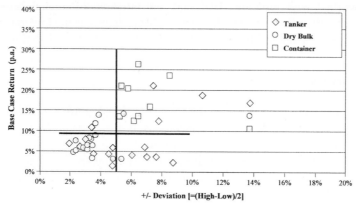

Source: Marsoft, 2003

Exhibit 4.4: Five-Year Holding Period

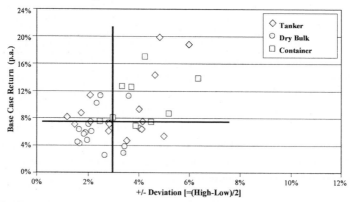

Source: Marsoft, 2003

Let us address the term structure of risk for tankers. In the longer term, the relative attractiveness of tankers seems to increase, as we have seen. Hence, there will also be a decreasing term structure of risk. This important point deserves our attention.

Index-based portfolios can be interesting, but with a caveat: Our definition of an index would not typically correspond with what a stock index is. An index might be seen as the "best" portfolio—an "optimal" portfolio, according to financial theory. In our mind, an index might be seen as a way to comprehend a market, to reflect its evolution, but this does not correspond with a financial theory definition. There is, for instance, nothing about optimality in our concept of an index. And indeed, there are now indices for many different sectors of the market (small caps, large caps, hi-tech, etc.). Of course, many investors see indices as an optimal way to trade in the markets because they offer a well-diversified approach to investing, typically not easy to manipulate by managers, and because they minimize the transaction costs that make many active management styles underperformers for the investor.

This is what we call passive investing and this might be preferred, notably for transaction cost reasons. The question is then whether passive investment should have a bearing on an index and which index. This relates also to where the value is created by investment management. We can differentiate between risk selection, asset selection and market timing. Risk selection (which comes not only from asset selection but also from leverage) defines the return one should expect to obtain if one performs normally. Asset selection consists of picking stocks that have positive alphas, meaning stocks that overperform. Many professionals spend most of their time doing this, but more and more doubt the value of such asset selection. It is indeed unproven academically. Hence, also the trend for passive investing. Finally, market timing refers to the major impact on portfolio performance of being in the right market at the right time, i.e., in small caps versus large caps, or in bonds versus equities. This can affect performance strongly. These issues are, of course, interesting if one considers specific ships as entities in one's portfolio. However, each finite ship would clearly represent too large a finite entity to represent a meaningful unit in a portfolio. Perhaps the above issues will take on a more practical meaning when we consider portfolios of stocks in shipping companies, however.

One implication is that if you intend to implement a portfolio management approach, you need to establish very clear performance criteria, with explicit and consistent articulation of the acceptable levels of risk, and the levels you require. Companies must apply this approach consistently across decision-makers. Also, the company must set clear "stop-loss" criteria for *exiting*. The problem here, however, is that, in practice, ships are after all less liquid than stocks, and it might be hard to exit when you wish, keeping in mind that even commodity-based shipping markets may be difficult bases for executing asset transactions when the markets are down.

The asset play in shipping, associated with shipping portfolio strategies, must be seen together with the operating strategy, which is in effect when one is holding the ship. In general, the financial costs for older ships relative to new ships will be lower, typically tending to generate higher operating income during the holding period, at least for ships that are in reasonably good shape and not excessively old, with running and maintenance costs that are not too high. New ships tend to have heavy financial holding costs associated with them, even though the strict cost of running and maintaining them might be relatively lower than the running and maintenance costs of older ships. However, the "amplitude" of the selling prices tends to be much larger for younger ships than for older ones. Thus, you can develop successful portfolio strategies, for both older and younger ships, as long as you go for consistency and apply a portfolio strategy that is sustainable from an economic risk/return point of view.

The delineation of a portfolio model with various types of ships, various types of charters, various types of debt-to-equity ownership considerations might be made according to a theory, a formula. It is, however, probably safe to say that in real life you can never determine an optimal strategy once you have set the parameters, not even in a deterministic, *passive* way. This is the theory!

I shall argue that a more *active* view of portfolio strategizing might be appropriate. Let us, however, conclude that it will nevertheless be important to have all the above information available, in order to assemble a rough approximation of a portfolio, i.e., in order to better understand what an optimal ship portfolio actually might mean. How we can actually push our understanding further in this regard is the subject of the next section.

A PORTFOLIO MANAGEMENT WORK STATION

Let us consider the Oslo-based firm Western Bulk. It was traditionally a combined shipowning and pool organization, operating a large contingent of own and chartered in bulk carriers. It ran into considerable financial problems around the turn of the millennium, and the various ship holdings were sold off. Today it thus operates solely as a pool, with chartered in tonnage. One can praise Western Bulk's focus on the "brain driven" side of the bulk shipping strategy, by splitting the management functions and ownership functions. It should, however, be pointed out that this strategic development was largely a function of the poor economic performance of the group in previous years. This was further accentuated by differences between two owner groups, which both held large positions in the group. Achieving a turnaround was not without difficulties. For instance, there has been a certain element of controversy over the fact that the firm defaulted on the contracts for four large bulk carriers on charter from Japanese freighters.

Over time, the marketing organization around the bulk carrier pool organization has evolved. In parallel, traditional shipowning has been de-emphasized, and in 2003, the last ownership positions in its own bulk carriers were sold. Western Bulk is thus now an entirely no-steel, all "brain-driven organization"—active in shipping without actually owning any ships. As such, it is perhaps particularly important for Western Bulk to have a clear understanding of its portfolio strategy. This would include an overview of the various types of business segments it is engaged in, as well as how the various types of ship contracts might fit together—potentially leading to aggregate cyclical or counter-cyclical behavior for the entire portfolio.

Interestingly, the senior management of Western Bulk, together with a financial consultant retained by the company, and also working with Marsoft for the market inputs, have developed a comprehensive set of analytical tools and information displays that provide an aggregate picture of how the portfolio strategy of a shipping company can be formulated and improved on. The market forecasts from Marsoft form the basic elements in this. The development process has, however, been highly interactive, with many resource people and executives being in dialogue, on an iterative basis. The result is that the approach has become unique to Western Bulk—it "owns" it! For a firm that provides decision support, such as Marsoft, this will thus probably represent a case where its inputs become particularly effective—through interaction and iterations its role becomes less visible, and the approach itself becomes internalized at the user organization, in this case Western Bulk.

The entire fleet is part of this modeling approach, including the overall set of contracts of affreightment (COA) held, as well as the set of all charters that have entered into time charters and bare boat charters. The firm's open tonnage is part of the model as well. Expected revenues and expected costs are aggregated to the portfolio level, i.e., building up the activities from each ship to a comprehensive overall picture of the firm as a whole. Several "dashboards" display the pertinent aspects of the overall portfolio. The dashboard concept was conceived by Western Bulk's top management, aided by Marsoft. They felt strongly that they needed a relatively simple comprehensive display of all the truly critical factors relating to the portfolio, seen in *one* frame on the computer screen—analogous to the way the driver of a car sees all of the critical factors relating to the car's performance on its dashboard.

Executive Dashboard

The *executive dashboard* can thus be seen as a visual tool that provides information on operations at several different levels in the organization. An executive dashboard helps structure the data, supports analysis of the data and its presentation in an inclusive manner to management, so that all of the required information is available, in one or a few frames on the computer (to get around the cognitive overload issue).

The executive dashboard tried to help steer the business according to established decision rules, to measure the impact of changes and to benchmark these against pre-set (budgetary) targets. Many companies manage their activities through historical results only, typically accounting data. With the executive dashboard, the intention is to allow more of a future orientation, giving the ability to look constantly at decision alternatives relative to pre-set standards, and to quickly benchmark the way things seem to be working out relative to these pre-set plans.

The Cash Flow Dashboard

The cash flow dashboard provides expected cash flows on an aggregate basis for the fleet as a whole. Needless to say, this must always be up to date in a firm such as Western Bulk and is thus provided on a weekly basis, as part of the portfolio management workstation. This is based on Marsoft's three forecasts—*base case, high case* and *low case*—for the relevant markets in which the firm is active (see Exhibits 1.11 and 1.12).

Portfolio Dashboard

The portfolio dashboard provides an overview of the tonnage in the fleet, categorized into "long period tonnage" and "short period tonnage." The dashboard also projects how the tonnage is divided between the Pacific and Atlantic basins. A further breakdown of main trades within each basin is also available.

Performance Dashboard

The performance dashboard reports on the expected financial performance of the current portfolio. Profitability is reported for both the long period tonnage subportfolio and the short period tonnage subportfolio. Expected profits are reported on each of the three forecast scenarios—the base case, the low case and the high case. The dashboard simulates profitability patterns by allowing decision-makers to change the composition of the portfolio incrementally.

Performance versus Budget Dashboard

This dashboard reports the performance dashboard information juxtaposed against pre-set, stated budgetary objectives. A manager can see how he is doing relative to the budget, at any moment. Specific deviations can be analyzed, and the composition of the portfolio can be adjusted when appropriate and, of course, when it is doable.

In general, the Western Bulk approach provides an overall database for a company's ship-related activities portfolio. It is a handy vehicle for simulating various options for the portfolio, with an interest in incrementally improving on this portfolio when feasible. The forecasts for the base, low and high cases project how the overall performance of the portfolio, including the profitability and cash flow, might be expected to develop.

The Western Bulk approach is thus intended to allow the decision-makers in the firm to develop a *consistent* view of *decisions* that have an impact on its portfolio. It allows decision-makers to apply their own relevant shipping business know-how so that they can improve the overall quality of the portfolio. Building on the in-depth market competences of Western Bulk's own team of shipbrokers, with their detailed market insights, is critical. The modeling approach is meant to support this, not to supplant it, i.e., to "make good even better." The computer-based portfolio approach can play a role as a vehicle to counterbalance potential individualistic, cognitive myths of individual traders.

As noted, it is particularly critical for a company such as Western Bulk to have a clear understanding of its overall portfolio. Owning no ship assets, and thus not being able to lean on large physical reserves to "bail it out" if necessary, the firm cannot support an overall poor portfolio implementation well. A detailed, comprehensive view of the business is necessary. It is not enough to manage each ship—the portfolio is key.

Let us recall that the specific business judgment around each ship-based commercial move will, of course, require a good understanding of the industry. In the end, it is the decision-maker, not the model, that will have to decide on the in/out, long/short and other related decisions—the models can only provide support. The decision-maker's point of view will now be discussed.

It is thus basically a "trial and error" approach, where you will be looking for ways to improve your strategy more or less via random "let's try it outs." Obviously, the overall strategy of the firm is thereby no more or no less than the result of this incremental trial and error simulation approach.

There are cognitive limits to using Marsoft's dashboard tool. For one, it is complicated—perhaps too complicated for the traders and decision-makers to use in their day-to-day work, in order to reach consistent decision-making and consistent corporate-wide risk profiles. Western Bulk therefore splits the dashboard into two autonomous components. This rather passive approach, while clearly very useful, may not be enough. Let's now discuss how we can further develop overall portfolio models even more proactively.

A "NEW" PORTFOLIO MODEL BASED ON DEVELOPING SEVERAL BUSINESS PLATFORMS PROACTIVELY

We have argued, particularly in Chapter 1, that a shipping company can develop various "growth platforms" to capitalize on its various business segments. I suggested that the shipping firm should take as a starting point a particular strength that it might have in a given business segment, building on its so-called Protect and Extend base. It could then expand on this by, say, projecting its established market strengths into new markets—a Leverage strategy—and/or by taking its distinctive competences and adding relevant new ones—a Build strategy. Indirectly, by first Leveraging and then Building or, alternatively, by first Building and then Leveraging, a shipping company can ultimately reach a Transform strategy.

A more proactive view of portfolio management might thus start out by stating that the amount of business emphasis we want to put on each of these business strategies—i.e., the relative mix, or balance, between the four archetypes in our model—would be an issue of *portfolio balancing*. In other words, we would consider a portfolio as the aggregation of the shipping business segment strategies that the company is engaged in. How much, for instance, would the relative emphasis be on the Protect and Extend strategic activities compared with the Leverage strategy part of the business? What would be the relative role of the Build part of the business? How much emphasis should be put on Transform? We can argue that a proactive, growth-oriented portfolio for a given shipping segment is one where we would have relatively more emphasis on the mix of capabilities, particularly new ones compared with established ones, i.e., Leverage, Build and Transform rather than the more mature Protect and Extend. Conversely, a more commodity-oriented portfolio for the firm would have a relatively heavy emphasis on simulating the various Protect and Extend options. This view of the shipping firm's portfolio gets to the competence factors, the know-how, that *shape* its strategy, i.e., a preamble to the Marsoft-type portfolio analysis that should subsequently be undertaken.

As implied, a shipping company can elect to pursue several business platforms. It can be actively involved in several business segments with different know-how bases. Examples might be bulk and tank segments, as in the case of Norden, or car carriers and LPG, as in the case of Leif Hoegh & Co. We can thus develop a portfolio overview dimension relating to the unique features of the portfolio by looking at the combined effects of the various growth platform strategies. Thus, the portfolio strategy would consist partly of having a clear picture of each growth platform, each major business segment, and then also having a portfolio picture of the overall mix of the various growth platforms. This picture would "show" how the various business segments fit together.

This approach would allow for a more active view of the developing growth in given business segments. It would allow senior executives to think through how they can Leverage the basic strengths of their firm to push for more growth by utilizing these basic strengths to develop a less commodity-oriented profile in each business segment and, as a result, for the whole firm. This approach would also afford a clearer understanding of how each business segment might complement another, more specifically, showing where the top-line growth is coming from, as opposed to where the bottom-line results are secured. Further, it would probably also allow for "a healthy respect for complexity." From a managerial and cognitive point of view, pursuing more than, say, three or four business platforms in one corporate portfolio would probably be very difficult. Rather, the trend seems to be for firms to focus on fewer and fewer portfolio elements—say, one, two or maximum three. Companies like Leif Hoegh and I. M. Skaugen, for instance, have dramatically narrowed their approaches to diversity by cutting out a number of their classic business shipping trades. Strategy means choice!

An active view of how to change one's portfolio strategy will be critical. Top management's attitude and willingness are, above all, critical here. Two brief examples can illustrate this. The large Ofer Brothers Group, based in Israel, owns and operates the country's largest privately owned shipping enterprise and has been active in shipping for almost 50 years. The group's fleet consists of more than 30 vessels, including containers, car carriers, reefers, bulk carriers, tankers and multi-purpose ships. The group, through Israel Corp., owns Zim Israel Navigation Ltd., the 12th largest container fleet in the world.

Ofer Brothers has shifted the point of gravity of its portfolio with remarkable smoothness from a more conventional bulker and tanker portfolio of ships to a relatively heavy commitment in containers. There has thus been heavy growth in the container ship market for Ofer Brothers, and they have Leveraged this position through long-term charters. The Ofer Group's container ship fleet, Zodiac Shipping, has grown rapidly, as a comparison of its size in November 2000 and in May 2004 shows. In 2000 it operated 17 container ships with a capacity of almost 22,000 TEU, while in 2004 it had 31 ships, with a capacity of almost 98,000 TEU. A further five large container ships are on order. (Fairplay Register, May 2004 and November 2000). The group's unique shift in portfolio seems above all to have been feasible because of strong inputs from the top. As part of this, the company has developed strong financial discipline for engaging in new shipping deals. It couples this discipline with a strong focus on maintaining the lowest possible operating costs. The group seems to be able to run ships at a profit for virtually any major type of ship, and in depressed market conditions. A clear fleet portfolio logic seems to be at play (Ofer Brothers Group, 2004).

The Teekay Shipping Corporation in Vancouver (discussed in more detail later in this chapter), under the able leadership of CEO Bjorn Moller and chairman Sean Day, has transformed what was primarily a ship-by-ship asset-based commodity business portfolio into one that is now much more based on scale and market power. Teekay acquired Bona Shipholding, Navion, and others, which were active in the VLCC and Aframax oil tanker segments. By concentrating on providing outstanding service to its clients, it created considerable market power for the company in this traditionally commodity-based segment. The focus has been on building critical mass—a unique strength—in the Aframax tanker segment, and trying to further build geographic strengths in this segment as it applies to the Venezuela–Caribbean–US trade, the Southeast Asia–China trade, etc. As an extension of this, Teekay bought 50% of I. M. Skaugen's US lighterage business in 2003 to consolidate its position in the trades of the US. Again we can detect a clear portfolio strategy—and with a customer focus! Teekay, with offices in 12 countries, now transports more than 10% of the world's seaborne oil.

The London-based owner John Angelicoussis has a relatively large exposure in VLCCs, organized under the name Kristen Navigation. It is ranked No. 6 in the world among VLCC operators, with a total of 13 vessels in its fleet, including a huge 360,000 dwt VLCC just delivered from Korean shipbuilders. Another three VLCCs are on order. (*TradeWinds*, 2004).

Angelicoussis has now, however, also entered the LNG market. Maran, his LNG carrier ship-owning unit, has three LNG newbuildings on order, all fixed to Qatar's LNG gas development authorities on long-term charters. Based on this, Angelicoussis ordered a fourth LNG carrier, also to be chartered to the Qataris. These large LNG carriers have a capacity of around 200,000 cubic meters of gas, and the newbuilding price, from Korean shipbuilders, is around US$210 to $220 million per ship. (*TradeWinds*, 2004).

What are the portfolio advantages here for Angelicoussis? First, he establishes two "growth platforms" that would not typically be perfectly coordinated, since the crude oil and LNG shipping markets tend to move in different cycles. Of course, there will be some overlaps, not least due to the general interrelationship between all ship freight markets and because of the newbuilding capacity effect and, in this case, also because both growth platforms are in the energy area. Second, the LNG platform allows Angelicoussis to enter a new area, where he can find opportunities for long-term contracts later, and long-term financing also, independent of the opportunities he would find in the VLCC segment. He thus finds another set of stakeholders that he can interact with as part of this second growth platform (*TradeWinds*, 2004).

How can major shifts in the portfolios take place? Clearly, several issues are at play here, all primarily driven from the top. Cognitive limitations will thus typically be real: How much complexity, for example, can top management critically handle? Here are some of the factors that a particular top management group can elect to "play" on:

- Purchase of second-hand tonnage.

- Newbuilding programs.

- Systematic trading in second-hand ships, selling and buying in order to evolve one's portfolio as desired.

- Systematic work with one's target customers, to develop relationships on which one can build the new portfolio.

- Development of internal systems of portfolio monitoring and control, to ensure that the new direction in the portfolio is actually implemented.

Very Long Term Time Horizons

Some shipping firms, typically privately held, are applying very long term time horizons to their activities. A good example is Knutsen OAS Shipping in Haugesund, Norway. It has built an important shipping company operating in the shuttle tanker segment, with 17 ships, LNG carriers (3 ships) and chemical tankers (10 ships). Typically there is relatively small equity capital per ship project, having received long-term time charters—often up to 10 years in length—as a basis for this. While the return on each project would generally not be very large, the firm puts heavy emphasis on the residual value of a ship, when the debt would be paid down or significantly reduced. Knutsen's growth is clearly linked to the Norwegian offshore oil industry. The company sees it as an advantage to be based in Haugesund, which offers a strong seafarers' competence base. Close attention to the operations of the ships is seen as key.

The small, privately held, offshore supply firm S. Ugelstad has also primarily attempted to follow a strategy of obtaining long-term employment, say, through time charters, securing a reasonable building contract, and then gearing the investment fairly heavily through long-term borrowing. At times the ships might have to be ordered before the long-term time charter contract could be achieved. Still a fairly heavy financial gearing could thereby be achieved.

Even for relatively small companies like S. Ugelstad, which—until recently—had a fleet of four PSVs (platform supply vessels) and one reefer ship, the issue of too much complexity in the portfolio comes in. The PSV business segment provides a good business platform, where the Protect and Extend strategy has offered a good basis for moving into new markets, such as the British sector of the North Sea and West Africa. The reefer ship, on the other hand, became more of a de facto distraction. To follow this market as well, in addition to trying to be on top of the PSV market, was difficult for S. Ugelstad's management, particularly in light of the firm's necessarily modest managerial staff. This thus did not turn out to be a good basis for developing a new growth platform, nor did it simplify S. Ugelstad's managerial tasks. Accordingly, the reefer was sold in 2004. This strategy, with two growth platforms, one of which did not really provide a basis for breaking out of the commodity cycle, was too complicated for this small firm. Exhibit 4.5 gives an overview of the S. Ugelstad's overall portfolio strategy.

Exhibit 4.5: S. Ugelstad's Portfolio Strategy

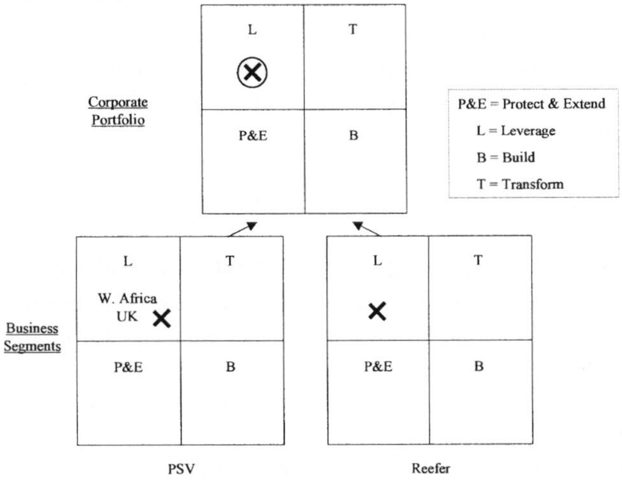

Source: Author

From Exhibit 4.5 we get a preliminary picture of the "portfolio" strategy by considering *both* the growth versus maturity tradeoff for each business segment *and* how these business segment "portfolio" elements fit together into an overall corporate portfolio. But it should be noted that this view of the "portfolio" is a rather limited one. It does not reveal much about either political risks or cash flow risks, for instance. In the next section we shall therefore develop a more full-fledged concept of a portfolio (see also Exhibit 4.6).

The decision to order a new ship will, of course, be part of the portfolio decision, i.e., often an important implementation step. Reflecting on the management challenges, when S. Ugelstad tried to decide on a newbuilding order, it followed several stages in its decision-making process. In March 2004 it then ordered a new large, modern PSV ship. Because there are so many steps, implementing a change in the portfolio strategy can often take a long time, or may not happen at all.

A Newbuilding Scenario

Japan was for a long time the most cost efficient place to build new ships. Then, Korea gradually developed its capacity and capabilities, typically becoming approximately 20% less expensive than Japan. More recently, China has developed its capacity and capabilities, again typically undercutting Korea by up to 20% on price. Most recently, however, the trend for newbuilding prices has been that they are stabilizing—or even going up, due to the generally tight freight market.

Investing in new ships is a must, but it needs to be done in a way that leads to the lowest breakeven costs. New ships must lead to lower breakevens. This also has a signaling effect vis-à-vis the competition. I. M. Skaugen's new gas carriers, as noted in Chapter 3, had better cooling technology and were thus able to cool the gas faster, thereby saving time for the customers. It was also able to operate these ships with fewer people. Skaugen made a calculation in terms of how much it felt it could pay for each ship. It was able to find a yard in China that was able to deliver to this price. It is critical to purchase new ships at a low price. If a ship is not bought at a low price, the result will be that it has a cost disadvantage throughout its lifetime!

Let us now go through a set of key steps regarding this critical decision:

Step 1: Why make a newbuilding order any way? Why live with more risk exposure? Why not take it relatively easy instead, and live with the less stressful, existing portfolio, with its financial ramifications, including among them, less financial Leverage? The counterpoint would be that ordering a new ship would mean another "card" to play actively, to be in a better position to do future deals, when the market will then be right.

Step 2: The timing of the newbuilding contracting will be particularly critical. In this respect, it is worth asking: What is the cost of the newbuilding? Have the costs come down, i.e., is the timing right vis-à-vis the yards? A difficult point for the owner is to realize that newbuilding prices often tend to fall in general, not least due to the higher productivity of the yards, thus implying a lower cost of capital for the newer ships, but leaving the shipowner with a relatively higher cost of capital for the old ships in the fleet. This can make ordering a newbuilding psychologically "painful."

Step 3: What is the market outlook? How long, say, will the market stay down? Is there a turnaround in sight? How can one avoid ordering overspecialized—and extremely expensive—ships, perhaps "pushed" by one's own technical organization, which generally wants rather sophisticated ships? Keep in mind: The market typically does not pay for such extra sophistication.

Step 4: How heavy can the financial gearing be? How can the financing be organized so that some of the marginal risk is taken up by, say, the shipyard? It could be that the yard will guarantee some of the debt, and it might also allow for a grace period when it comes to down payments—even interest payments on the last tranches of debt. It could also be that "cut the losses" tactics will have to be worked out for the newly ordered ship, so that the ship can be sold under the scenario of an extended depressed market, without major impact on the rest of the company's ship engagement portfolio, except for the loss of the equity capital put into the ship itself by the shipping company.

POLITICAL RISK AND THE PORTFOLIO STRATEGY

The previously discussed dashboard approach developed by Western Bulk can be very useful in portraying the financial consequences of a portfolio. The argument for developing a portfolio, however, is based on having a more proactive front-end view of how such a portfolio should be shaped, and *then* doing the necessary financial documentation of what the portfolio might look like, say, through using a dashboard-type approach.

Let us now look at the portfolios of several additional companies, returning to those we have already analyzed in Chapters 2 and 3: Norden, Farstad Shipping, The Torvald Klaveness Group, I. M. Skaugen, Leif Hoegh & Co., Frontline and Teekay Shipping Corporation. However, now we will add other types of risks that I will broadly label "political risks."

So far, I have argued that the portfolio strategy dimension is heavily based on the number of "business platforms" that the shipping company is engaged in, and the interdependence (or lack of it) between these platforms. There is, of course, another important dimension too, namely the *time dimension* embedded in the portfolio of shipping activities, and exemplified by how—as they expire—one's various bare boat charters/time charters and openness vis-à-vis the ship markets reflect the next set of business cycles. The time dimension will be key; the in/out, long/short balance, as already discussed, but also for the entire portfolio of ships as it will have to be managed. To recap from the discussion so far in this chapter, cycle management and risk management will thus be critical in developing a strong portfolio strategy, based on the fact that the real exposure of the portfolio will, of course, be a function of the underlying pattern of in/out, long/short positioning of each ship vis-à-vis the market, but now "adding them all up" into an overall portfolio pattern. Western Bulk's approach exemplifies how a shipping company might handle this.

We also pointed out that currency risks can play an important role in a shipping firm's risk exposure, and thus also in the portfolio exposure that a shipping firm takes. Some currencies are over- or undervalued relative to others. Often an overvalued currency will have a lower interest rate associated with it. Thus, a shipping company can decide to go for a lower operating cost of capital by going into more high-valued currencies, while, of course, also having to pay relatively more to get into a specific deal, say, the purchase of a ship. Running shipping transactions in, say, Swiss francs is an example of this—you pay more for the ships, but will face lower interest charges. If going for an undervalued currency, on the other hand, one will, at the same time, be taking the risk of having a substantial part of this initial benefit wiped out by a later appreciation in the value of this currency.

As noted, a shipping company's portfolio consists of the aggregation of the various business platforms that the shipping company is engaged in. The aggregation of the various ship segment activities will thus have a clear financial dimension. The degree of risk taking can be designed for the overall portfolio and can often be adjusted by modifying the specific activities in one or more of the specific business niches where the shipping company is active. Portfolio algorithmic support and analysis can help in this.

This is not all when it comes to risk in shipping, however. Political factors typically also play significant roles. In Chapter 1, we already made it clear that political factors have traditionally played an important role in the overall risk taking in a shipping company's portfolio. These factors can be directly linked to political issues, such as political instability, even war, change in political regimes, disruptions that such changes might cause in economic activities in a given country, etc. Further, the ramifications on economic growth can play an important role in determining, in effect, political risk. Some countries grow faster than others, which leads to more business opportunities. Clearly, due to the uncertainties of these growth outlooks, there are risk factors here. IMD – International Institute for Management Development in Lausanne, Switzerland, has assessed the world competitiveness of 60 countries and regional economies, which can hint at the attractiveness of each. Conversely, this ranking can be interpreted as a manifestation of political instability—and thus risk exposure—for countries that are not competitive (*World Competitiveness Yearbook*, 2004).

In the following we have tried to combine what we see as the most critical political risk factors into a notion of political stability assessment. The overall assessment of *political stability* can thus perhaps be rated subjectively—from unstable to stable. Let us take this to indicate one new dimension of a fleet portfolio model, as seen on the vertical axis of Exhibit 4.6. On the horizontal axis we have mapped financial stability.

Exhibit 4.6: Fleet Portfolio Model

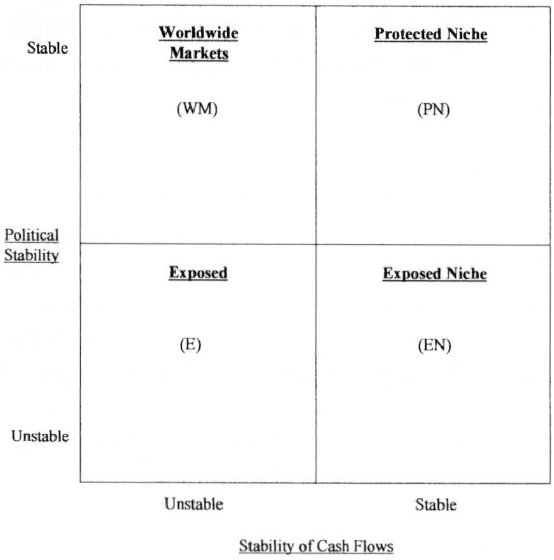

	Stable		
Stable	**Worldwide Markets** (WM)	**Protected Niche** (PN)	
Political Stability			
	Exposed (E)	**Exposed Niche** (EN)	
Unstable			
	Unstable	Stable	
	Stability of Cash Flows		

Source: Author

A *subjective*, judgmental assessment of *financial* stability is, as noted, captured on the horizontal axis, this being a function of the type of niches the shipping firm is in. The more commodity-oriented Protect and Extend position might typically lead to more unstable cash flows, while in contrast, a more niche-oriented position, such as Transform or Build, might typically lead to rather stable cash flows, as outlined in Chapters 2 and 3. The positions re "hedging" via chartering (long versus short), and thus currency position will play a role as well. Also, the interplay between the various platforms can lead to more stability if these platforms are exposed to counter-cyclical market cycles or—alternatively—to *less* stability if the platforms are exposed to the same market cycle. See also the discussion of how to estimate cash flows as part of the firm's risk management function at the beginning of this chapter.

In Exhibit 4.6, we have attempted to label various types of portfolio archetypes. "Worldwide Markets" would have a relatively stable political situation because the ships can easily be sailed away from an area of political turbulence, or be additionally insured, but it is combined with a more unstable cash flow situation characterized by worldwide Protect and Extend shipping activities. In an "Exposed" portfolio position, by contrast, political stability is low and the cash flow from the businesses is also relatively unstable, characterized by commodity-type shipping, often in particularly turbulent geographical areas, such as bulk shipping in the Middle East/Arabic Gulf area or in Chinese waters, in circumstances where one would not be able to withdraw the ships easily. In an "Exposed Niche" there would be a relatively stable cash flow from the businesses, say, due to long-term contracts or charters, but the political risk exposure remains unknown. The gas carrier barging activities of I. M. Skaugen on the Yangtze River in China would be an example. Finally, a "Protected Niche" portfolio position would be one in which *both* political stability *and* the stability of the cash flows are judged to be relatively high. An example of this could possibly be Leif Hoegh & Co.'s RoRo business.

How have these assessments specifically been made? We have *subjectively* calculated a political stability index and a stability of cash flow index in Exhibits 4.7 and 4.8, respectively, for the seven firms discussed in Chapters 2 through 4.

Exhibit 4.7: Political Type Risk/Stability

Geographic Unit	Political Risk	Economic Growth Risk	Currency Risk	Klaveness		Norden		Farstad		Leif Hoegh		I. M. Skaugen			Frontline		Teekay			
				Comm	Niche	Tank	Bulk	PSV	AHTS	Ro Ro	LPG	Gas/MNGC	US/SPT	Yangtze j.v.	Tank	OBO	Tank	Shuttle	LPG	SPT
USA	1	3	2		6	6				6			6		6		6			6
China	3	1	3	7								7		7	6	6	6			
Africa	3	3	3	9																
Middle East	3	1	2	6							6	6			9				6	
North Sea-UK	1	2	2					5	5								6	3		
North Sea-Norway	1	3	2					6	6	6							6			
Brazil	2	3	3					8	8											
Australia	1	2	2		5			5	5											
Singapore	1	1	1				3									6				
Japan	1	3	2	6			6			6					6	6	6			
Korea	2	2	2							6										
Algeria	3	3	3									9	9						9	
EU	1	3	2		6	6	6			6					6	6	6			
Worldwide	2	2	2	6	6	6	6					6				6		6		
Total				34	23	18	21	24	24	24	21	28	6	7	33	18	42	9	21	6
Grand Total				57		39		48		45		41			51		78			
Number of Entries				9		7		8		7		6					213			
Political Risk Score				6.33		5.57		6.0		6.42		6.83			6.63		6.0			
Political Risk Category				Medium		Low		Low		Medium		High			High		Low			
Company				Klaveness		Norden		Farstad		Hoegh		Skaugen			Frontline		Teekay			

Risk Levels : Low = 6.00 and below
Medium = 6.01 to 6.30
High = 6.31 and above

Source: Author

Regarding the political stability index (Exhibit 4.7), we have listed various geographic areas and assigned a macropolitical risk score, an economic growth risk score and a currency devaluation risk score to each one, with our subjective assessment of low risk as Weight 1, medium risk as Weight 2 and high risk as Weight 3. The author has thus assigned these rates subjectively. We could, of course, develop more sophisticated risk weight assignments, based on more systematic underlying research. For the purpose of illustration here, this is unnecessary. A given shipping company needs to develop its own understanding of which factors should be considered as part of its political stability assessment for its overall portfolio, and how it would assign these risks.

We have thus made a subjective assessment for each of the seven case companies we have studied:

- Klaveness: two business platforms (commodity and niche)

- Norden: two business platforms (tank and bulk)

- Farstad: two business platforms (PSV and AHTS)

- Leif Hoegh: two business platforms (RoRo and LPG)

- I. M. Skaugen: three business platforms (gas/MNGC, US/SPT, Yangtze River/Hubei Tian En)

- Frontline: two business platforms (tank and OBO)

- Teekay: four business platforms (Aframax, shuttle tanks, SPT and LPG).

We applied the risks assigned to each geographic area to each of these business platforms, depending on whether this particular business platform would be heavily exposed to a particular geographic area or not. Take note, however, that the author does not have full access to the actual geographic exposures for each of the business growth platforms; he has tried to make a subjective assessment based on information available in annual reports.

We have added the various subjective scores and divided the total by the number of entries, for all business segments of each firm, to normalize the political risk score for each. Accordingly, we have thus subjectively determined that Norden, Teekay and Farstad have a relatively low political exposure; Klaveness and Leif Hoegh a somewhat more medium-oriented position; and Frontline and I. M. Skaugen have the highest political exposure, i.e., might be facing the lowest political stability.

Three comments are in order here. The first deals with Norden, which is active in world tankers and world bulker operations. The fact that these business platforms are *both* relatively heavily exposed to the worldwide political situation is key. If a crisis should break out somewhere, then, as noted, there will always be other activities in the worldwide trading patterns where Norden might employ its ships. Unless a ship happened to be "stuck" in a war-stricken area, alternative—now less risky—employment activities can be activated. The fact that the ships are potentially constantly mobile is thus a good way to control the risk—any particular ship can be pulled away from a crisis area. Also, for Frontline, a huge exposure is toward the world's oil producing sector—not known for its political stability.

For I. M. Skaugen, the heavy exposure to specialized, dedicated markets, such as the river barges with liquefied gas in China and the crude oil lighterage in the US, represents a relatively large political instability. China, with its Communist leadership, may not be considered among the most stable countries politically, certainly not in the long run. The US, with its huge foreign debt and its potential problems with economic growth and stability, may also represent a somewhat larger risk exposure than traditionalists might favor.

Exhibit 4.8: Stability (Risk) of Cash Flow

	Klaveness		Norden		Farstad		Leif Hoegh		I. M. Skaugen			Frontline		Teekay			
	Comm	Niche	Tank	Bulk	PSV	AHTS	RoRo	LPG	Gas	US	Yangtze	Tank	OBO	Tank	Shuttle	LPG	SPT
Protect & Extend	3		3	3					3			3	3	3			
Leverage					2	2	2										
Build		2						2		2					2	2	2
Transform											1						
Diversification	2		2		2		1		1			1		3			
Score	7		8		6		5		7			7		12			
No. of businesses	2		2		2		2		3			2		4			
Cash flow risk	3.5		4.0		3.0		2.5		2.33			3.5		3.0			
Cash flow risk category	Medium		High		Medium		Low		Low			Medium		Medium			

Diversification effect and cash flow volatility: Low = 2.99 and below
Medium = 3.00 to 3.70
High = 3.71 and above

Source: Author

Let us move to the subjective calculation of an index for the stability of the cash flows, also key for the overall portfolio model of the shipping firm (see Exhibit 4.8). Here, we have listed the various types of business niche positions for each firm, as presented in Chapter 3. Protect and Extend is the position that represents a commodity-type situation, with—normally—a correspondingly relatively volatile cash flow. Leverage and Build represent somewhat more specialized niches, with correspondingly relatively more stable cash flows. Transform represents a rather stable niche, with—normally—a correspondingly relatively stable cash flow. We have further assessed the degree of correlation between the developments of cash flows from the various growth platforms of each company, for instance the relationship between Klaveness' commodity and niche businesses, where we felt that there was some element of correlation, although not total. In a company like Leif Hoegh, on the other hand, we felt that there was no correlation between the RoRo segment and the LPG segment. We thus assessed these cash flow volatility exposures—as well as the diversification effect exposures—as low, which we assigned the subjective rating 1. We then added these ratings up and divided by the number of businesses to reach a figure for cash flow risk. We here reached the subjective conclusion that Teekay, Farstad, I. M. Skaugen and Leif Hoegh seemed to enjoy a relatively low exposure to cash flow fluctuations, with rather stable cash flows on an overall portfolio basis. Klaveness and Frontline might be expected to have a medium type stability of cash flows on a portfolio basis. Norden, perhaps the most heavily exposed to the commodity markets, thus had relatively high instability of its cash flows on a portfolio basis. Exhibit 4.9 finally provides the combined corporate portfolio scores for our seven case companies.

Exhibit 4.9: Corporate Portfolio Scores

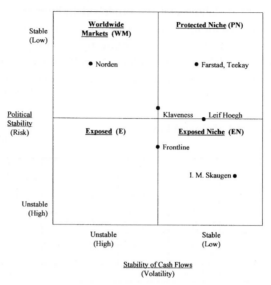

Source: Author

Norden would be positioned in the Worldwide Markets portfolio strategy segment, i.e., with a relatively stable political risk, but with relatively unstable cash flows. Farstad and Teekay would be positioned as being in a Protected Niche, with a relatively stable political situation and also with a relatively stable cash exposure in a portfolio sense—indeed an enviable portfolio strategy position. Klaveness would be focused in the middle, with both medium political stability and medium cash flow stability in its overall portfolio. Frontline would also be positioned in the middle when it comes to stability of cash flows, but with a higher degree of political exposure than Klaveness. I. M. Skaugen would have relatively high political exposure, while the cash flow stability would be scored in the medium category, again as seen as an overall portfolio. Finally, Leif Hoegh would be in a medium political position, with a stable cash flow position.

When we combine these assessments with the analysis done previously in this chapter, we discover that the various business growth platforms can lead to rather different corporate portfolio strategy delineations. This is the subject of the next section, in which we shall look further into the portfolio strategies of Norden, Farstad, Klaveness, I. M. Skaugen and Leif Hoegh in more detail, in each case seeing these as the aggregation of the business strategy platforms.

EXAMPLES OF PORTFOLIO STRATEGIES

Predominantly Commodity-Oriented: Norden

Exhibit 4.10 provides a picture of Norden's overall portfolio strategy. It consists, as noted, of two commodity-oriented business platforms, tankers and bulk carriers. The tankers are broken down into Aframax and product carriers. The bulk carriers are broken down into Cape-size, Panamax and Handimax.

The tankers were initially positioned for the US market, particularly the double hull product carriers. Today the tanker business is characterized as a worldwide trader, focusing on safety and being a customer-driven niche player. Still, we could probably characterize Norden's tanker business platform as rather commodity-oriented, although perhaps less so than we would find in a typical tanker company.

For the bulk carrier business platform, one can also see a geographic expansion, into North America, South America, Southeast Asia, China and Europe. Here too, Norden's extensive use of IT and its shift toward longer-term contracts has Transformed the bulk carrier segment into a less commodity-oriented one than what we would commonly find in a typical bulk carrier commodity operation. Norden sees itself as a customer-driven company. Further, Norden has intended its introduction of a comprehensive IT support system to stay in close contact with each shipper, combined with its emphasis on longer-term contracts, to develop the "tankerk" businesses—both tanker and bulk—into less commodity-oriented ones.

Exhibit 4.10: Norden's Portfolio Strategy

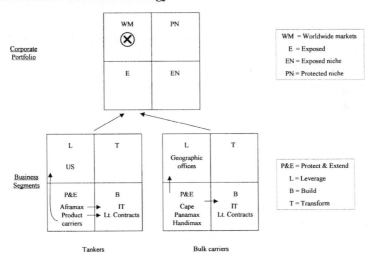

Source: Author

Looking at the overall portfolio, we can also see interplay between the two bulker and tanker growth platforms, both, however, being rather commodity-oriented. The overall portfolio will thus have to reflect these two relatively commodity-oriented sub-positions, which must be carefully monitored in terms of interrelationships between them—both when it comes to interrelationships regarding risks, i.e., the resulting overall portfolio risk, and particularly when it comes to the interplay between the market cyclicality of the tanker platform versus the bulk carrier platform. Norden was, as noted, one of the first owners/operators to introduce Value at Risk (VaR), a concept well known from the banking business. It consistently attempts to monitor the overall position of the company when it comes to the risk exposure of its portfolio. Here it is interesting to notice that Norden has decided to keep strong liquidity reserves, presumably precisely to be able to withstand an extended period with weakened cash flows.

Frontline

Exhibit 4.11 shows Frontline's portfolio strategy, which places heavy emphasis on crude oil carriers—the bulk of them VLCC carriers. A significant number of them are employed on a special arrangement with BP, which utilizes Frontline for all of its crude oil transportation requirements. Frontline also has a number of other long-term contracts, and a significant part of its fleet is also on short-term or spot market contracts. Frontline further has a somewhat smaller fleet of Aframax tankers, which are partly employed on long-term contracts, partly on short-term/spot market contracts.

Additionally, Frontline has eight OBO carriers. These have recently been shifted from employment in the crude oil trade to the dry bulk market. Four have been chartered out on long-term contracts, while the other four are open.

Overall, John Fredriksen's portfolio strategy is based on heavy focus on the commodity segments, particularly on large crude oil transportation. His strategy is opportunistic, with great emphasis on a strong sense of timing, in terms of in/out as well as long/short. Fredriksen is widely known for his keen understanding of the markets. In addition, Frontline has a strong emphasis on financial management, with a relatively low cost of capital and a healthy financial profile. Although Frontline's corporate portfolio can be seen as somewhat risky when it comes to exposure to political factors, it is, on the other hand, not particularly risky when it comes to the stability of its cash flows.

Exhibit 4.11: Frontline's Portfolio Strategy

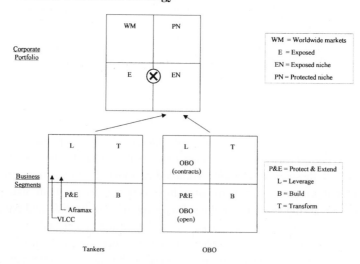

Source: Author

Mix of Commodity and Niche: The Torvald Klaveness Group

Klaveness' portfolio strategy, depicted in Exhibit 4.12, consists of two separate growth platform segments: Maritime Services and Maritime Logistics. The Maritime Services segment is relatively more commodity oriented, built up around a large number of more or less conventional bulk carriers, operating in a pool. Strong marketing, strong customer relationships, better know-how regarding unloading equipment, strong IT support, etc. represent the backbone of this business. Klaveness also employs extensive hedging and use of freight derivatives to dampen the potential effects of commodity exposure. All in all, therefore, the degree of commodity orientation of the maritime services business is probably less than we would find in conventional bulk shipping pools.

The Maritime Logistics business segment, on the other hand, is focused on developing new logistical capabilities—through Leveraging by entering new industries, product categories or geographies, such as Beijing, and/or by Building new competences through the value chain, such as moving onshore by adding more value chain activities to the overall logistics services offered (warehousing, trucks, etc.). Overall, the maritime logistics growth segment is therefore clearly non-commodity, probably more like a Transform type strategic business platform on an aggregate basis.

Exhibit 4.12: Klaveness' Portfolio Strategy

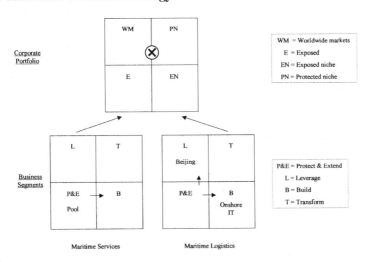

Source: Author

For Klaveness, the overall portfolio will emphasize the interplay in cyclicality of the more mature maritime services business against that of the much less mature maritime logistics business. The political risk exposure, based on the interplay of risks, is also key. The relative importance of the maritime services relative to the maritime logistics will also be part of the portfolio. As of today, the former plays a much more dominant role. One can expect that the cyclicalities of the maritime services business are more volatile than those in the maritime logistics area, which can be seen as much more stable and growth-oriented. The same is probably true of the risk exposures.

Farstad

Exhibit 4.13 gives a picture of Farstad's portfolio, which also, as noted, consists of two platforms—one for PSVs (platform supply vessels) and the other for AHTSs (anchor-handling tug supply vessels). For both types of platforms Farstad has made a geographical expansion, into the Brazilian and Australian markets. Farstad has also upgraded ships: larger size, greater power and more sophisticated equipment (FiFi, DP, Oil Rec, etc.) in general. Thus, the PSV and the AHTS segments are probably less commodity-oriented than we would otherwise expect. In addition, the firm has developed a special purpose AHTS by first going into new Asian geographic waters, then modifying the design—indeed, a Transform strategy.

Exhibit 4.13: Farstad's Portfolio Strategy

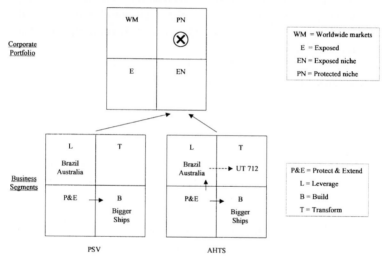

Source: Author

A key overall portfolio issue, again, has to do with the relationship between the two growth platforms, the two business segments. The PSV segment tends to be based more on long-term contracts, supporting the ongoing activities regarding offshore supply platforms and drilling ships that are producing oil. The AHTS platform, on the other hand, tends to support oil exploration activities, for example by moving the anchors of the drilling rigs that are being repositioned to drill hole after hole, searching for new oil. This segment tends to be more volatile, going up and down much more as a consequence of the drilling budgets of the oil companies, which again is largely determined by world oil prices, as well as expected oil price outlooks. Thus, the two segments only seem to be correlated relatively moderately. For Farstad, this means a relatively conservative portfolio strategy, when it comes to both cash flows and risk outlooks.

I. M. Skaugen

Exhibit 4.14 gives a picture of I. M. Skaugen's portfolio strategy. Note that the company bases its overall portfolio strategy on three business segment growth platforms previously identified.

Exhibit 4.14: I. M. Skaugen's Portfolio Strategy

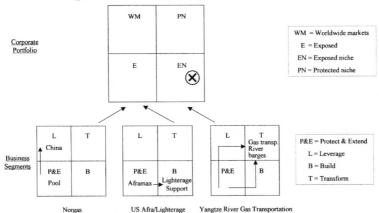

Source: Author

The first platform is the Norgas gas carrier pool. Here, the ships are employed in worldwide gas trade with the petroleum industry, some in fulfillment of longer-term freight contracts that the pool might have obtained, and some operating in the open market. Even with the pooled results of all this, I. M. Skaugen will be heavily exposed to the cyclicality in the world markets. An expansion into the Chinese-based gas trade business has taken place as noted, with the establishment of an office in Shanghai and also with the construction of six state-of-the-art newbuildings in China, all with high technical capabilities. All in all, the Norgas pool is a relatively mature business, although less so than if one would compare with freestanding independent operators of gas ships—in the Protect and Extend segment. As noted, A. P. Moller-Maersk Group has purchased 90% of this business from Skaugen—thus lessening, on a relative basis, the effect of this business on Skaugen's portfolio.

The system of Aframax crude tankers unloading crude oil cargoes (lighterage) off the coastal ports in Texas and Louisiana, which then can be transported up the Mississippi River as well as other large US rivers (Missouri, Ohio), represents a second growth platform for Skaugen. It is now 50:50 owned with Teekay. While the standalone Aframax crude oil carrying business would typically be a mature business, the technology behind the combined value chain and, in particular, the lighterage support is clearly unique. The overall focus of this business would be more of a Build strategy, more stable relative to the exposure to the world freight rate cycles than what we found in the Norgas business. The overall portfolio effect from this business has, of course, also been lessened due to the 50% dilution to Teekay.

The third growth platform would be gas transportation on the Yangtze River in China. Here the river transportation technologies from the US barging operation, as well as the gas transportation technology from the Norgas operation, are being combined with the know-how obtained through the geographical positioning already developed in China via Norgas. This thus provides for a new growth platform, which probably falls in the Transform business area. This would be largely independent of both the ocean freight rates that the Norgas pool is exposed to and of the market swings of the US lighterage business.

All in all, Skaugen's overall portfolio presents a rather diversified picture, with a relatively low likelihood of interconnectedness between the three business areas. Norgas would be the most volatile in market exposure, followed by the US barge business, with the Yangtze River gas business being the most stable. In terms of size, the Yangtze business is, of course, still relatively small, and Skaugen needs to build it up.

When it comes to political risk exposure in each business, we could perhaps argue that this "ranking" should be reversed, with the Yangtze business being the most risky. Indeed, the overall portfolio picture of Skaugen's businesses reflects an interesting view of the political exposure side. Clearly, here we can expect that the US barge business, which depends on the political context of the US, would be rather different from the Yangtze gas business, which depends on the political context of China. From a political risk point of view, these two businesses might therefore complement each other. The Norgas business would be exposed to world political conditions, including both China and the US. Overall, we can perhaps conclude that, from a political risk point of view, the Skaugen businesses seem to be rather well balanced.

Teekay

Teekay's portfolio strategy, summarized in Exhibit 4.15, is based on four business elements. As such, it is a relatively complex strategy. The major part of Teekay's portfolio consists of crude oil tankers, primarily in the Aframax segment, where the company is the biggest in the world. Many of these Aframax tankers go on long-term contracts, but others are shorter term. The Aframax fleet is employed worldwide to safeguard against too much political exposure in one particular area. The oil storage shuttle tankers operate primarily in the Norwegian sector of the North Sea, but some operate in the British sector also. They are employed on long-term contracts, typically ten years, by the oil companies and represent a very stable business. The LPG segment is relatively small within Teekay, and represents a new platform for growth. The company's intention is to make sure that the LPG ships will be put on long-term contracts, similar to the shuttle tankers, to secure a relatively risk free, stable business. Finally, SPT, the barge business on major US rivers, 50:50 jointly owned with I. M. Skaugen, is a relatively stable business. Many of the shipping activities are based on preferred relationships with key users of transportation services, such as the major oil companies.

Exhibit 4.15: Teekay's Portfolio Strategy

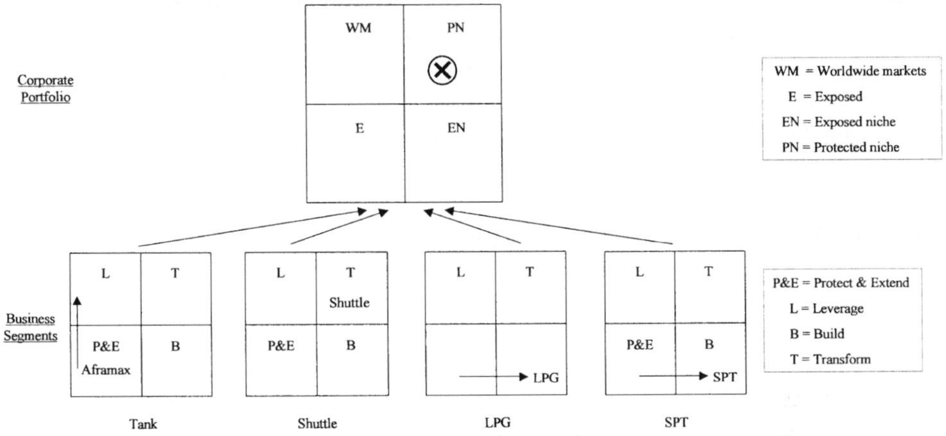

Source: Author

Teekay's overall portfolio is one of relatively little exposure, to both political risk and cash flow risk—the former due to the extreme diversification of activities within the Teekay group, and the latter to the conservative nature of Teekay's portfolio when it comes to financing. Teekay makes a point of being able to cover its entire debt payment servicing through the long-term charter proceeds it receives, i.e., it is able to operate the ships that go in the spot market independently of any financial exposure, as long as they cover their operating costs. Down payment of debt servicing for the ships in the open market is thus covered by those ships in the portfolio that are on long-term charters. All in all, Teekay has a somewhat complicated—but still focused—portfolio, which enjoys both political robustness and cash flow stability.

Niche: Leif Hoegh

Leif Hoegh's portfolio strategy, depicted in Exhibit 4.16, is based on two business growth platforms, the RoRo segment and the LNG gas carrier segment. Regarding the RoRo segment, the classic PCCs (pure car carriers) are typically chartered out to a relatively small number of car manufacturers. Typically, there would be a long-term relationship with them, which is certainly not a commodity strategy. But there are also interesting geographical developments here, both in terms of the acquisition of the Kiwi fleet (freighting used cars from Japan to New Zealand) and the CETAM strategic move (freighting aircraft components for Airbus Industries between its European locations). We also see a strong technical development, with the emergence of the so-called PCTC ships, which can take a variety of rolling cargo, thus not only further underscoring Hoegh's long-term relationships with a few automotive shippers but also allowing it to more actively develop back haul business.

Regarding the LNG growth platform, we have noticed that these ships are typically tied into very long term charters to major gas producers. These deals, with 20- to 25-year charters being the norm, thus tend to be highly finance oriented, with the freight streams being stable, non-commodity oriented. A technological development within this business—the innovative SRV concept—might further strengthen the long-term relationship with the gas producers. With SRV, natural gas can be deliquefied offshore and then transported to land stations *without* having to build extensive pipelines along the sea bottom or having to have land-based de-liquefication terminals. All in all, the LNG business clearly seems to be a Build business.

Exhibit 4.16: Leif Hoegh's Portfolio Strategy

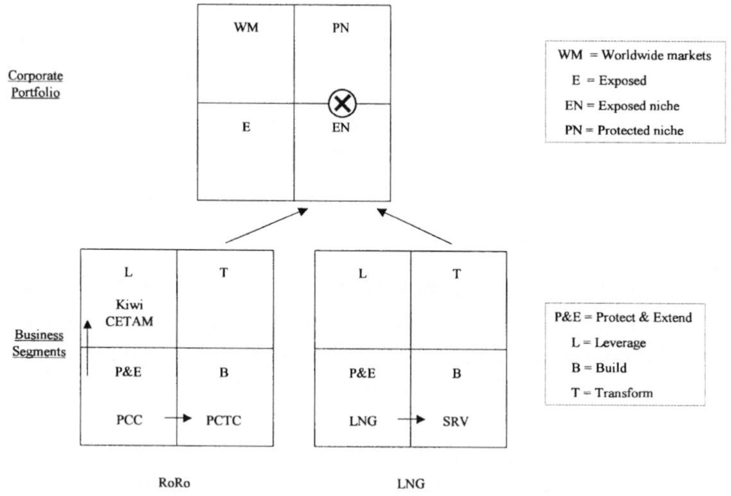

Source: Author

From an overall portfolio viewpoint, Leif Hoegh has a RoRo business that we can perhaps classify as a Transform segment, and an LNG business we can perhaps classify as a Build business. In many ways, we should not expect these two strategies to be related to each other: LNG is highly stable and long term, but RoRo is highly relationship-oriented and based on strong links with a few car manufacturers.

Leif Hoegh's portfolio strategy is perhaps the most niche-oriented we have seen (by corollary, the least commodity-oriented). It is important to keep in mind, however, that until very recently, Leif Hoegh was heavily committed to commodity-type niches, with heavy commitments in both the liner business and in tankers, in several bulk carrier business segments and in reefers. To some extent, the company is still exposed to some of these businesses, although it clearly states that it is on the way out of them, if not out already.

Exhibit 1.4 gave, as we recall, the financial results of Leif Hoegh's operations during 1999, as exemplified by the old strategy, and during 2002, as exemplified by the "new" more focused portfolio strategy. We can see from this that the results are dramatically improved by focusing, by concentrating and by practicing "strategy means choice."

CONCLUSION

In this chapter we have discussed the firm's portfolio strategies. We have seen that it makes sense to pursue a focused diversification for the shipping company. However, we have also seen that it is up to each shipping company to execute in a superb way whether it wants to focus on market-based shipping strategies (commodity) and/or whether it wants to focus on more customer-driven niche strategies. We saw that the political risk and the cash flow risk associated with a particular strategy do not necessarily have to do with whether a company chooses a commodity strategy or a niche strategy. Either can be combined with appropriate, modest risk exposure, politically as well as cash flow-wise. What it comes down to, therefore, is effective portfolio diversification, with an element of focus—not least from a managerial point of view—and also as much simplicity as possible. A well-run portfolio strategy implies less exposure to risks, whether it is based on a commodity focus, a niche focus or a combination of the two.

It is important to have a consistent overall portfolio strategy. Partly, the shipping company needs to develop the portfolio in such a way that it is likely to have at least some counter-cyclicality between the various cash flow and risk exposures, and that it might—given the aggregate risk exposure the company has taken—result in a reasonably robust overall economic outcome. Most portfolio strategy approaches tend to look at this issue as one of more or less mechanically undergoing "trial and error" simulations in order to heuristically come up with a better portfolio, perhaps even attempting to come up with an algorithm that would maximize the likelihood of a strong return relative to risk portfolio.

We have argued in this chapter, however, that it is probably relatively more useful to develop a prior view of what might lead to the true robustness of a portfolio strategy based on a deep understanding of each of the several separate business segments involved. Each of these segments needs to be developed in such a way that it represents a reasonable balance between mature and less mature growth-oriented subsegments. We have also argued that the overall portfolio then will depend on how the various cash flow and risk exposures of each business platform fit together, above all, when it comes to the counter-cyclicality of freight rate cycles and risk balancing.

A sound portfolio strategy will have to be based on developing a clear portfolio picture within each business platform, as well as an overall portfolio picture consisting of how the business platforms fit together. A Western Bulk-type data support algorithm will, of course, be highly beneficial here, because it can ensure a consistent, fully transparent set of dashboards of the relevant aggregate data and forecasts for the entire fleet portfolio. In addition, the political risk dimension needs to be complemented to this "market exposure only" view of the portfolio.

CHAPTER 5

ORGANIZATIONAL ISSUES

Organize People for Objectives and Customers. Objectives: What do we want? What are our goals? [To satisfy] customer needs/problems.
— *Tom Erik Klaveness, The Art of Business, 2003, p. 5*

It is not the strongest of the species that survive, nor the most intelligent, but the most responsive to change.
— *Charles Darwin*

Nothing is for ever, except change. — *Buddha*

RELEVANT PREREQUISITES FOR SHIPPING ORGANIZATIONS

In this chapter we will look at four prerequisites for any modern shipping organization to be competitively viable—to be a winner. But first, let's first briefly summarize what shipping companies need to have in place in order to improve their economic performance, from an organizational, strategy-independent point of view. Basically, shipping companies need:

- To put together a competent organization by attracting, keeping and developing the best possible team of executives that they can find. Although this sounds like a straightforward issue, it is in practice, of course, perhaps the most difficult challenge facing any top management, not only in shipping companies, but in corporations in general.

- More emphasis on corporate governance, i.e., effective roles of the board of directors, the management and the staff. (See also Chapter 6 for more on this in the context of family-dominated companies.)

- Effective processes for consistently setting and managing risk/return targets, seen as an organizational implementation issue. Here, it will be important to have a common view in the company regarding the market and scenarios. This view must be consistent among all key decision-makers. Reaching a common view can be a real issue when several decision-makers are involved, say, in managing a fleet of up to several hundred vessels (see Chapter 3).

- Tschudi & Eitzen, for example, has followed a strategy of acquiring a number of shipping companies over the last 15 years. Five of these companies were privately held and four were stock listed. The geographic spread of these acquisitions was relatively broad: four in Denmark, one in Estonia, one in Singapore, one in Holland, one in Sweden and one in Norway. An interesting effect of this is that Tschudi & Eitzen was able to develop a strong organization more or less from scratch, through these acquisitions. Interestingly, while the shipping companies were priced based on their ship assets, there was little or no price premium for the organizational "software." Thus, the company was able to assemble an effective international organization without huge expenses, and in a relatively short period of time. It should be further noted that the company felt that the best place to manage the bulk of its operations would be out of Denmark, but with strong subsidiary organizations in Estonia, Holland and Sweden. To maintain its organizational momentum(s) was a key factor in this decision. The headquarters of Tschudi & Eitzen, by contrast, is small and located in Oslo, Norway.

- Consistent rules and policies, etc., similar to those that credit lending banks use. This must be tailored to the particular shipping segment that the firm is in.

- Consistent measures, benchmarks and procedures for learning—in effect, to "make good even better." Wallenius Wilhelmsen, for instance, undertook a comprehensive internal program focusing on total quality management (TQM), a project that lasted several years. (Both of these two issues have also been discussed in Chapters 2 and 3.)

With these five sets of policies and processes in place, what are the prerequisites for success in a modern shipping company? Simply stated, the modern shipping firm needs to have its own top-notch organization in place. This means it needs to possess the relevant base of know-how, it needs to be able to change, it needs to have a penchant for keeping things simple and focused, and it needs to be the lowest possible cost provider. Let's consider these characteristics one by one.

The Know-How Base

The shipping organization needs to have the relevant know-how for pursuing a given strategy. Thus, it is strategy that determines the know-how requirements of the modern shipping company. The requirements of particular growth platforms determine the know-how requirements. If, for example, a shipping company pursues several growth platforms, it needs a multitude of know-how bases. Leif Hoegh & Co., for example, has developed entirely different business organizations for its car transportation and LNG business platforms. To state the obvious: With several growth platforms, the shipping firm may face great complications and find it almost impossible to mobilize the necessary know-how spectrum. For each platform, the strategy, the structure and the processes must be clear and consistent— the value drivers must be dominant.

It goes without saying that a shipping company can, or even must, meet its know-how needs by outsourcing. The general principle, as we shall see later in this chapter, will be that the firm may want to outsource the know-know that is not of key strategic importance. Whatever is absolutely necessary for success in supporting a given growth platform must, however, be kept in-house, or at least be part of a network organizational concept with reasonably high control over the relevant strategic know-how. Above all, the know-how necessary for supporting a given business platform has to do with the capabilities to execute the given strategy. An eclectic approach will typically be called for here. Thus, often it is an issue of combining several professional cultures within one shipping organization.

It is absolutely critical to maintain a clear market focus competence, often provided, on the one hand, via executives who have been trained in-house in the shipping industry from an early age, without necessarily having received much formal education. These executives— with their key market understanding—are critically important. On the other hand, alongside these experience-based executives there will often be highly professionally trained executives, say, from finance or technical areas, who may have a strong, formal university education, and who may provide equally important professional inputs to the shipping organization. How can these two cultures work together, symbiotically and positively? How can one avoid an "either or" culture, which perhaps ends up with too much weight on the "practitioner only" approach or, alternatively, a "too professionally oriented" approach. While cross-cultural organizational issues have been studied extensively, when it comes to differences between nationalities and their impact on organizational culture (DiStefano and Maznevski, 2003), relatively little has been done in terms of studying cultural differences based on different professional backgrounds (DiStefano and Ekelund, 2002).

Typically, there are four key know-how types—four cultures—that need to come together in the successful shipping firm:

- A *market* culture—the know-how necessary for pursuing a classic, market-based strategy, as delineated in Chapter 2. The body of this know-how will primarily be based on "understanding the market," i.e., a keen understanding of the relevant market(s), such as a particular segment of the bulk market or a particular segment of the tanker market, with a good feel for eventual turning points in the dynamics of these market(s).

- An *operations* culture—an ability to "make good even better." This means possessing the necessary know-how for executing the relevant aspects of the operations of a given ship, the relevant know-how for financing, for human resource management, etc., all focused on delivering the best possible transportation service at the lowest possible cost. Being able to deliver an integrated product will be key.

- A *business analysis* culture—the know-how necessary for pursuing various types of niche-based strategies, along the lines if what we discussed in Chapter 3, and moving away from commoditization, as described in Chapter 2. Here, the necessary know-how for executing each niche growth platform strategy will be key.

Some of this know-how may, for instance, have to do with geographical expansion. Often it can take time to build up the requisite know-how here, and alliances can represent a "short cut": we saw earlier in the book, for instance, how Farstad Shipping expanded into the Australian market, supporting offshore drilling activities in the Bass Strait. Farstad's approach to acquiring relevant know-how here was by going into a joint venture with P&O. This gave Farstad, above all, quick access to an already developed set of customers. Subsequently, Farstad was able to acquire P&O's part. Farstad also went into the Brazilian offshore market with a 50:50 joint venture, once more gaining fast access to the necessary local geographic market know-how. Torvald Klaveness Group bought the fleet of geared Handimax bulk carriers from the A. P. Moller-Maersk Group and inherited the latter's office in Beijing as part of the deal—a veritable flying start! For companies like I. M. Skaugen, it has taken a significant time to develop the relevant know-how bases necessary to operate out of Shanghai and Beijing. Skaugen built its gas barge transportation business in inland China with a 49:51 strategic alliance with Hubei Tian En, to ensure access to key stakeholders, above all political authorities.

- A *financial* culture—the ability to manage the financial flows and budgets, and to deal with currency issues, interest rate developments and, increasingly, new instruments and derivatives as they relate to futures freight market trading.

It is, of course, typically true that it will be necessary to develop new competences for expanding a particular growth platform into a Build mode. Know-how here might have to do more with acquiring IT, developing particular technical solutions, know-how for breaking into new segments of the value chain, such as warehousing and trucking. A few shipping companies, including Klaveness, A. P. Moller-Maersk and DFDS, have done this, successfully changing their entire know-how bases into logistics support delivery organizations. In total, the various specific know-how's to support a given growth platform in a shipping company's portfolio must be in place. This includes the required in-house chartering capabilities and customer relationship capabilities to pursue a realistic, growth-based, non-commodity strategy for each growth platform.

Finally, a shipping company often needs specific portfolio strategy know-how. This know-how will have to do partly with understanding the financial implications of the overall portfolio, as exemplified, for instance, by the "dashboard" analyses of portfolio management, like the approach developed by Western Bulk (outlined in Chapter 4). Overall cash flow and portfolio performance measures are particularly important here. Obviously, finance often plays an increasingly critical role. Active use if the futures markets, through hedging, derivatives and other financial instruments accentuates this trend. It is thus essential that in-house financial management is strong enough in modern shipping firms. Equally critical will be the know-how for understanding the various types of risk exposure that operate within a particular portfolio configuration, again calling for expertise in the corporate finance area.

Ability to Change

In most segments of the shipping industry today, the critical underlying success factors are evolving very fast. To some extent, this evolution is a function of macroeconomic turbulence; most segments are not becoming any less volatile. But above all, this evolution increasingly has to do with the speed of evolution in the shipping companies' *customers'* views on logistics; their requirements for transportation support are shifting continuously and rapidly. The configurations of their value chains are evolving, it seems, continuously. Technological factors add to this, and so do trends toward outsourcing and value chain management. On top of this, the drive to seek out new non-commodity niches never ends. It is therefore also critical that a shipping organization sees itself as truly dynamic; it must prove its ability to create value every day, and typically in rapidly changing contexts. Shipping organizations should, therefore, see themselves as going through a never-ending process of organizational change. Change must be seen as vital, never-ending and fun.

It goes without saying that network organizations might often be particularly appropriate for meeting the need for such dynamism and change. For instance, having a network organization might help avoid the emphasis on developing shipping activities more or less in order to maintain certain activity types and activity levels, in the end simply to keep the organization busy. In many traditional shipping companies it was, for instance, seen as important to run ships just to keep the operating organization intact, and simply to maintain a stable of officers and sailors. This heavy emphasis on human resource management stability, based on a set operating model, often led to strategies that, in the end, made little sense from an evolutionary commercial shipping view.

Keeping It Simple and Focused

In many shipping organizations, the respect for complexity seems to have increased. In the past, many shipping companies were active in rather large numbers of shipping trades. They often employed a diverse variety of ship types, but without necessarily having the requisite competences to effectively and realistically serve the dynamic growth platforms comprising each of these trades. In contrast, focusing on one or a few growth platforms seems to be the key to success today.

Leif Hoegh, for instance, has significantly reduced its organizational complexity by withdrawing from the liner business, by spinning off the tanker business (into Bona Shipholding, where it subsequently sold its 35% minority share to Teekay Shipping Corporation), by exiting (or being in the process of exiting) various "classic" segments of bulk shipping (Aframax and forest carrier open hatch ships, the liner business, including selling Hoegh Lines—with its trade from Indonesia/India to North America—to Oldendorff, etc.) in order to concentrate on car carrier (PCC) shipping and LPG gas. We have seen the financial results in Exhibit 1.4. Under these new conditions, Leif Hoegh now needs an organization that is dramatically different. The trend is toward having more in-depth capabilities in a relatively smaller number of niches. Accordingly, the firm has built up in-depth freestanding organizational competences in each of these two segments.

Lowest Possible Cost Provider

Shipping companies must keep their costs at a competitive level. After all, shipping is, to a large extent, a mature, commodity-like business. Costs must therefore be fully under control. A shipping firm cannot expect to be sustainable if it has a higher long-term cost level than the competition.

Costs will be partly related to the ships themselves. I. M. Skaugen, for instance, has just completed a newbuilding series of six new liquefied gas carriers, each with an extremely low breakeven point for operating cost. The refrigeration capabilities are particularly unique—allowing the gas to be liquefied through refrigeration exceptionally fast. Skaugen claims that its new ships have the lowest operating costs in the industry and that they should yield positive contributions even under rock-bottom freight market conditions. Keen attention to all aspects of costs is part of Skaugen's culture.

Crew costs are also very important. Here the country of nationality of the crew is key. Norway, for instance, has relatively high seafarer wages, and, on top of this, relatively high employee benefit costs, compared to neighboring countries such as Sweden and Denmark. Many of the more reasonably priced crews now come from former Yugoslavia, Russia, the former Eastern European countries, and the Philippines. A response by many traditional shipping countries has been to give their seafarers tax relief, even total freedom from taxes in some instances (Netherlands, Sweden, Denmark).

A virtual network organization may have a better opportunity to create lower costs. It allows the various operating entities in the network to minimize their own cost base by controlling the ships to minimize recurring costs and by registering them in a reasonably low-cost country. Also, of course, a network organization might allow the shipping company to maximize its advantages by cutting out duplication of effort for each business platform.

When it comes to white-collar labor it is interesting to see that a country like Norway still seems rather competitive. Much general shipping know-how resides in Norway. Basic white-collar salaries are reasonably competitive. Since shipping enjoys reasonably high prestige in Norwegian society, the shipping industry is reasonably successful in competing for talent. Also, by adopting a network-type organizational structure, many of the previous "silos" can be eliminated, which increases motivation in shipping organizations. It should come as no surprise, therefore, that Norwegian shipping executives seem to be comfortable. Above all, it is perhaps because of the relatively high competence levels in Norway that we see quite a number of shipping companies headquartered there and running on a network basis.

Studies have been done of the so-called Norwegian maritime cluster, using Michael Porter's methodology for assessing "the competitiveness of nations" where he claims that business clusters are critically important. Exhibits 1.6 and 1.7 gave a picture of the maritime cluster in Norway. The Norwegian maritime cluster is relatively "complete," which causes the author to conclude that Norway should be relatively well positioned to be competitive in the shipping industry. It is, however, pointed out that the cluster is still both mature and fragmented, and is thus under some sort of "disintegration pressure."

Perhaps the issue is much more one of each shipping company creating its own cluster, with its own links to the relevant environmental stakeholders for its particular strategy. This would involve the relevant suppliers in light of the types of ships, the specific ship trades, and particular customers, etc.; the relevant financial partners in light of a particular shipping company's strategy, etc. Thus, the Norwegian maritime cluster, for instance, could perhaps therefore better be redefined to come up with a headquarters culture in Norway, where the various headquarters of Norway-based shipping companies can benefit from all being located in a selectively small area with a common professional shipping culture, all within the same industry, and enjoying common respect in society. This must also allow individual executives to enjoy the necessary financial benefits from being located, say, in Norway, making individual tax burdens less harsh, etc. The rest of the cluster for each company, outside of the headquarters locations, would then be global and company-specific.

Like Norway, Singapore has a similarly favorable set-up for high-performing shipping headquarters, which are often parts of networked organizations. A. P. Moller-Maersk has a huge operating base in Singapore. Ofer Brothers Group runs the bulk of its operations from here. Westfal-Larsen has moved its bulk shipping operations to Singapore, too (consisting of 50% of the Star Bulk Shipping group, open hatch ships, particularly well suited for the transportation of paper). Areas such as New York, London and even Shanghai are becoming more expensive as headquarters bases and are perhaps not very competitive as bases for network-centered organizational activities either.

In a study of the European maritime industry, it has been pointed out that when comparing the share of revenue invested in competence development, i.e., in the human resources strategy for shipping companies, Norway scores the lowest out of five European industrial nations, while Germany scores the highest. This sophisticated outlook regarding human resource strategies is perhaps an indication that in a diverse labor market, high-cost country such as Germany, it is particularly important to have a strong human resources function, i.e., to create an approach where one can compete for the talents, and where the issue is one of "brain-driven value creation" above all. To attract the best people in the highly competitive German white-collar labor market, calls for an accentuated human resources strategy. For a small, less diversified labor market, such as Norway's, by contrast, the challenge for the shipping industry to be competitive may be less accentuated (see Exhibit 5.1).

Exhibit 5.1: Company Competence and Human Resources Strategy

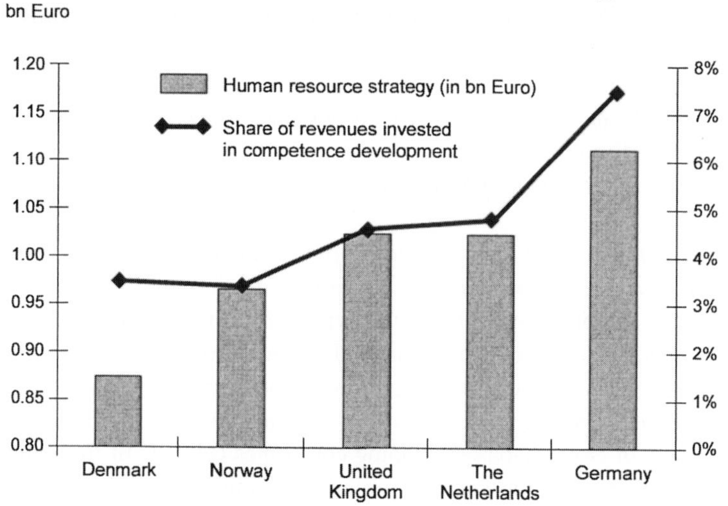

bn Euro

Source: Mortensen, 2003

NETWORK-TYPE ORGANIZATIONS

When it comes to performance, network-type organizations may be particularly well suited for meeting the four sets of requirements outlined at the beginning of the chapter. In the end, this is all about human capital issues. The organization must attract top talent, and that talent must be given highly demanding, meaningful jobs, calling for the highest degree of professionalism. Charterers, for instance, must be highly disciplined, in order to be consistent over time in dealing with key assumptions, such as risk taking.

At the same time, the network organization must be cost efficient—an efficient shipping organization outsources many of its less needed organizational tasks. Flexibility is, of course, also critical, and it is probably more easily attainable in a less permanently configured network-type organization. Above all, the shipping organization must avoid duplication of effort wherever and whenever possible. This has the valuable side effect of creating more interesting job challenges and more variety. Executives typically work in project teams and often have several assignments at the same time. In other words, they wear many hats. Responsibility is broader than formal authority.

As we shall see in a moment, there are many types of network organizations. One dimension the firm might need to determine would be how many core capabilities it needs to keep inside and how many it can outsource. A second dimension might have to do with what type of decision-making would be most effective, given the type of strategy that the network organization is supposed to execute. Here, the degree of complexity of the strategy is probably critical. Too much strategic complexity could imply too complex a network organization.

When the need to have more internalized capabilities is relatively strong—for example, when pursuing a non-commodity growth platform or several growth platforms, the firm may need to have more critical capabilities in-house. Take a look Exhibits 5.2 and 5.3, which contrast the organizational charts of two companies, both operating in the offshore supply sector: Farstad Shipping and S. Ugelstad. Farstad, with a fleet of almost 50 ships, and the largest shipping company in the offshore supply ship segment in Norway, as noted, operates two full-blown business growth platforms—PSV (platform supply vessels) and AHTS (anchor handling tug supply vessels)—and is also established in the UK, Australia and Brazil (through a strategic alliance).

Exhibit 5.2: Farstad: A Heavily Internalized Organization

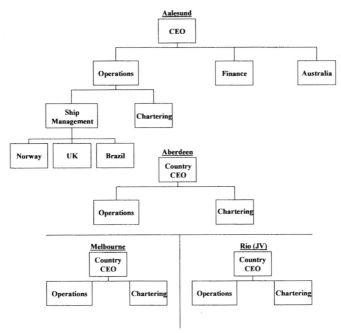

Source: Farstad Shipping, 2003

Quite a lot of Farstad's functions are heavily internalized. The company's size allows it to perform all the key functions of such a firm on its own. It is thus felt at Farstad that there must be a team that leads the company, based on two integrated functions—operations and the market focus. The chairman of the board, Sverre A. Farstad, is actively involved, but in a non-executive role. The operations and market focus is carried out by a four-person group consisting of Terje Andersen, as president/CEO, a CFO and two senior operating officers residing in Australia and Aalesund respectively. Developing an enthusiastic organization and avoiding bureaucracy are seen as critical. Many of the activities are therefore maintained in the various geographic areas, with as little as possible run out of Aalesund. No energy should be wasted—focus should be on key issues, not organizational politics, according to Terje Andersen.

In contrast, S. Ugelstad operates in only one growth platform, the PSV segment. Ugelstad—a small firm by any standards—has many fewer vessels than Farstad in this business segment (4 versus 24) and it is not geographically diversified, since it focuses on the Norwegian sector of the North Sea only. S. Ugelstad's organization is highly networked. The key reason, of course, is that it will not have the scale needed to internalize the many key tasks to be performed. To be cost efficient, networking is key.

Exhibit 5.3: S. Ugelstad: A Heavily Networked Organization

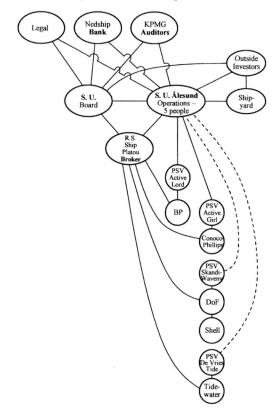

Source: Author

In general, we can argue that when a company is relatively small and focused, and pursuing a focused strategy of, say, a Protect and Extend type, then shipping firms can probably undertake relatively more external outsourcing and, hence, more networking. But the working mode in the two organizations differs. While there will be relatively more well defined, often more specialized, organizational tasks in Farstad, everyone must be prepared to perform a broad spectrum of tasks in S. Ugelstad.

Bringing this discussion together graphically, Exhibit 5.4 provides a classification of various types of network organizations, including portfolio, constellation, franchise and cooperative, with examples of the companies discussed in this book so far.

Exhibit 5.4: Network Models

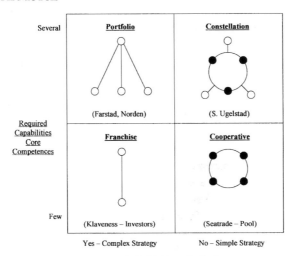

Source: Harbison et al., 2003, p. 12

On the horizontal axis, we have made the distinction between whether there is a strong need for one lead decision-maker or one dominant organizational entity, which would typically be the case when the firm is driving a more complex strategy to get the job done. If the strategy is simpler, on the other hand, we could expect that more decentralized decision-making and more organizational entities will do, opening up a more full-blown network, allowing a more wide-band involvement, while still getting things done.

On the vertical axis we have made the distinction between whether there would be a need for several core capabilities and competences to support the strategy, or whether there would be a need for only a few capabilities to support the strategy. The former would apply when a firm pursues several less commodity-oriented, more specialized niche strategies—several growth driver business platforms. The latter would apply when the firm focuses on Protect and Extend, i.e., one commodity-oriented business platform.

We can then identify four archetypes of strategies, each networked to a differing degree. The upper left quadrant typically has a "Portfolio" type strategic structure, and this would typically not be heavily networked in terms of outsourced activities. Examples might be Farstad (Exhibit 5.2) and Norden. The upper right quadrant has what we might call a "Constellation" organizational structure. This would typically be more heavily networked, and one example would be S. Ugelstad (Exhibit 5.3). The more central networked activities, such as a relationship between S. Ugelstad headquarters and operations, as well as a relationship with the bank(s) and the shipbroker(s), would be part of the so-called inner network. A number of other relationships, such as those with the ships, with the charterers, with the auditors, and with legal network entities would be part of an outer network.

The bottom right quadrant consists of a network one might call a "Cooperative." Here, virtually all the network relationships would be part of the inner network. There would be relatively few relationships. The Dutch Seatrade pool organization is perhaps an example; here, the (open and close) relationship between each pool participant and the center of the pool would be the same for all family members. Finally, the "Franchise" network organization is seen in the bottom left quadrant. The relationship that Klaveness has with each of its investors may be an example of this, with Klaveness treating each investor with some distance and in a more or less standard way, offering more or less similar service to each, indeed more of a similarity to a franchise-type operation.

Overall, the key to successfully running any of these networked organizations is for the firm to organize its people so it can best meet its objectives of serving customers. In most shipping organizations this typically means heavy emphasis on projects. Network organizations tend to be well suited to such project organizational work. It is also important to emphasize that for network organizations to function, a cultural maturity must have been established, where, as noted, the informal authority must be *larger* than the former hierarchical position-based responsibility. Network organizations tend to be flat, not hierarchical, and everyone must thus live up to the dictum "when in doubt do the right thing." Professionals tend to work best in such settings when inspired—it is *not* a "command and control" culture.

Focusing on the franchise-type organization in the bottom left quadrant of Exhibit 5.4, it is interesting to observe that a company like Klaveness has a policy not to hold more than 50% to 75% ownership in any specific ship venture partnership, although this may not always be achievable. It sees itself as having to *sell* its own ideas to others, and *not force* its own ideas on its investment partners via legal ownership clout. This is all in line with the true spirit of networking.

Focusing once more on the left-hand column of Exhibit 5.4 (Portfolio form and Franchise form), one can observe that one person, or a relatively small group of decision-makers, will typically make the final decision here. The relatively complex strategy that such organizations follow will call for this. It would probably be unrealistic to execute a complex strategy with too much of a diffuse, networked-based organization. Often in shipping one person does, indeed, make the final decisions. In classical shipping firms, which are diversified over a large number of trades, this "final decision by one person"—typically also the owner—is common. Considering the complexity of many shipping strategies, it will be key that final decision-making can take place fast and be centralized. In the past, Leif Hoegh was an example of such an organization. A. P. Moller-Maersk, Farstad, Norden, Klaveness, I. M. Skaugen, Frontline and Teekay seem to have vested final decision-making in the hands of one or very few people, such as: Maersk McKinney Moller, former chairman (who stepped down from this role at the end of 2003), and Jess Soderberg, CEO of A. P. Moller-Maersk; Terje Andersen, CEO of Farstad; Steen Krabbe, president of Norden; Tom Erik Klaveness, president and CEO of Klaveness; Morits Skaugen Jr., CEO of I. M. Skaugen; John Fredriksen, CEO of Frontline; and Bjorn Moller, president of Teekay.

Decisions often also come about by evolution, through extensive evaluation of a project's merits over time. This will often imply incremental moves, simulations of how to best evolve a strategy based on analysis of facts as they become available, i.e., through know-how-driven, not belief-driven decision-making. When it comes to the timing of decisions—so key in decision-making—the organization must live with the issues until it sees the decisions as natural. Of course, any good decision has to be accompanied by a basis of "feeling." After all, there is an element of "art" in practicing good shipping strategies. Perhaps this element of feeling is particularly important when it comes to network organizations, where all the networking entities must be expected to participate according to their professional capabilities, know-how and facts—not on loose beliefs. Again, a culture based on integrating multi-disciplines will be key, as just discussed (see DiStefano and Ekelund, 2002). This brings us to a more extensive discussion of what may perhaps be the most critical dimension—a *central focal point*—in all shipping organizations, namely how the customer must be handled.

CUSTOMER CENTRIC BUSINESS PRINCIPLES: HOW TO ACHIEVE CUSTOMER FOCUS

Oldendorff Carriers

Founded in 1921 and based in Lübeck, Germany, Oldendorff is managed by its principal owner, Henning Oldendorff, as chairman and Peter Twiss as president/CEO. The company follows a strategy focused on bulker ships that range in size from Panamax and down. It is ranked No. 4 in the world in Handy-size bulkers and No. 9 in Panamax bulk carriers. The group has approximately 215 ships, 75 of which are owned. The remaining 140 are chartered in from large Japanese, Korean, Chinese, Italian and Danish operators and/or owners. The fleet consists of bulk carriers, container belt self-unloaders, multipurpose ships and open hatch box-shaped vessels, but the majority is bulk carriers.

The company focuses heavily on building relationships with clients, trying to develop them over the longer term. The major competition seems to come primarily from large Japanese, Chinese and Korean shipowners. Oldendorff has an office with seven people in Shanghai. The company has an *integrated* chartering and purchase/sales strategy. For instance, the reasoning behind buying four five-year-old Panamax bulk carriers in mid-2003 was that it can do better by owning these ships than by chartering them. It then plans to sell these four ships. This thus calls for a close integration between the chartering and purchasing/sales organizations. In many shipping organizations, these entities are too separated. Cross-cultural integration will be key to making this operational (DiStefano and Ekelund, 2002).

It became obvious in the 1990s that a relatively small shipowner might not have enough critical mass to serve the large cargo clients as a one-stop service provider. The question was therefore: Could Oldendorff carriers grow by offering other owners pool participation? Or could it form itself into a larger integrated owner/operator organization, with a portfolio of owned assets, as well as medium- and long-term charter vessels?

The firm, under the leadership of Henning Oldendorff, chose the latter option. The group is today exercising the long-term strategy of becoming one of the leading bulk shipping operators, including focusing on offering bulk parcel and unitized cargo services. The philosophy is that shipping is all about patient, long-term positioning, combined with impatient quick decisive action when the turning points are there. The aim is to create a focused organization with no more complexity than necessary, not easily sidetracked by fringe activities relative to the strategy. Volume, market penetration and a strong position within the few strategic core trades chosen were seen as key.

How can one serve the larger cargo customers in the best possible way, especially in a strong market? The typical small operator, who might lack tonnage that would be available for longer-term periods, may be reluctant to offer freight services on a long-term contract of affreightment (CoA). He will not know what he will have to pay in charter party-wise for a ship that he will need to charter in to perform the CoA. Maybe he will also be too small to be regarded as a safe option by the shipper, who wants performance and security of supply. A large pool manager, in a similar way, might not really be in a much better position. The ships that he operates in a larger pool will also be working on fluctuating rate bases, which follow the market. Ships can also leave the pool on short notice. The large pool operator will thus have no fixed time charter costs as a base for his calculations regarding what would be acceptable freight levels. This will thus not help him to lock in a margin, while simultaneously enabling him to offer a necessary discount to the shipper for the long-term employment. It would only be the large owner/operator, with a large fleet at his disposal—bought or chartered in on a long-term basis—that can be a meaningful contract partner in this situation. A large owner can offer a reasonable long-term ship service package, which might also provide the shipper with a discount.

In addition to its bulker shipping activities, Oldendorff has also owned Flensburger Schiffbau-Gesellschaft yard since 1990, and it has shown a profit every year since then. The yard now focuses mostly on building RoRo ships and is run totally at arm's length from the shipping part of the group. It is rare for Flensburger to build ships for the group's shipping company.

Oldendorff feels that its organization must be open; there must be a fluid exchange between all decision-makers, and the organization must run on a non-hierarchical, flat basis. Accordingly also, Oldendorff's headquarters office is an open space, with "no walls." Management values the company's independence, as quick decision-making without having to ask "outsiders" may be vital in the cyclical shipping industry. This might mean more effective market cycle management. Oldendorff further believes that decision processes in shipping companies must be both top down and bottom up (macro and micro).

In micro terms, it is critically important that the various operating people, above all the charterers, have a good focus on the various micro issues, including trip assignments, single trip charters, clear understanding of positioning of one's own ship relative to the competition in various trades, etc. To complement this, as far as macro aspects go, Oldendorff expects its top management to have a firm grasp of the overall "map" of the broad development of the markets, including a good view of the turning points. At the micro level, this picture will typically look rather detailed, "nitty gritty," even confusing, with many conflicting inputs, at times even creating an almost "chaotic" picture. Clearly, it is essential that top management keep a more robust macro view of the market outlook—a *Leitbild*! Further, the top must "pump" energy into the micro activities, i.e., make sure that the operating organization does not get bogged down in too much detail, etc., operating in line with the top-down vision that the top management wants the firm to achieve.

In summary, top management must understand the macro picture of the industry, the dynamics and the major trigger points. Top management must be comfortable with the in/out, long/short decision pattern in the broader sense, and be ready to insist on execution. The organization's bottom up component will consist of experts who understand the specific markets, are very close to them and see their specific developments. They are, however, so close to the markets that they "might not see the wood for the trees." It is only dialogue between the two dimensions that creates a commercial success. Again, a multidisciplinary culture will be key—to add glue to the integration of the levels in the firm (DiStefano and Ekelund, 2002).

I. M. Skaugen

According to Morits Skaugen, it is critical to have a dual focus in the organization:

- On the one hand, the market focus must be there, with direct access to the customers, providing a service dimension to the customers that is real. To be the preferred supplier is key!

- On the other hand, it is equally important that a strong cost focus is there. One must be the lowest cost producer, with strong cost discipline. This means heavy emphasis on budgets and on performance monitoring relative to budgets, on both the revenue generating side and the cost side. With the focus on strategic alliances, with all of Skaugen's businesses now being in strategic alliances—with Teekay, A. P. Moller-Maersk and Hubei Tian En —budgetary control perhaps becomes more difficult. It is now an issue of reconciling processes and systems on both the partner side and the Skaugen side. A real problem is that this can lead to lack of transparency, lack of focus and delays.

Norden

Norden states that its key customers must see the company as having:

- Reliability: Norden must deliver on its promises. Here it is seen as key to think long term and never become too keen to "squeeze" the last dollar and cent out of the customer, say, during a period of freight market upturn.

- Flexibility: To satisfy the customer, Norden must match timing, location and handling. To come up with logistics solutions that are innovative and reliable is important—for example, in one instance, the company found a way to ship cement from Southeast Asia to the US during the Asian economy slump.

- Empathy: Norden must respect the local culture and traditions of the customer.

In total, the key customers will hopefully feel they want to work with Norden!

The Torvald Klaveness Group

To reinforce a customer-centric focus, Klaveness' principles for its organization are: To remain close to the customer, to be the customer's "first choice." This is quite analogous to what we found in Norden and is based on:

- Trust

- Quality

- Competence

- Longer-term commitment and relationships.

The Klaveness organization is thus built to leverage long-term relationships and partnerships with customers. To make this happen, Klaveness tries to build the future from today's strengths, with heavy emphasis on innovation benefiting the customer.

Tom Erik Klaveness is consensus-seeking, but in the end realizes that he will have to decide. He spends a lot of time talking with others, both within the organization and outside, before final decisions are made.

A. P. Moller-Maersk

A. P. Moller-Maersk's organization is built around a senior executive committee consisting of five people, including the CEO, Jess Soderberg. The former chairman, Maersk McKinney Moller, also used to be on this committee. One member is responsible for the oil and gas area, one for the liner shipping area, and one for tankers and tramp shipping, including crude products, gas and bulk. Each of the five members of the executive committee is responsible for several organizational responsibility centers that report to them. There are more than 40 such operating units.

With its enormous size, A. P. Moller-Maersk must clearly have a rather decentralized structure. This is achieved by having clarity of focus regarding the many operating units and how they each report to a member of the senior executive committee, with the operating activities clustered under each. The geographic dimension is also well reflected in this organizational form. For instance, there are large regional headquarters for the container liner business—in which Maersk Sealand is clearly No. 1 in the world—in both Singapore and New York, which are located in the center of the main markets. The overall portfolio issues are dealt with at the top, through the five-member senior executive committee, in which each member has the title "shipowner." A. P. Moller-Maersk draws its own organizational chart in an unusual way, as a circle (see Exhibit 5.5), to emphasize *both* clarity of responsibility through autonomous decentralized units *and* that it all is interrelated, through the five shipowners at the top of the firm, led by the CEO. A. P. Moller-Maersk is a highly professional organization, run in a clear, consistent, performance-driven mode. In many respects, it sets a benchmark within the shipping industry!

Exhibit 5.5: A.P. Moller-Maersk's Organization—Over 40 Operating Units & 5 Shipowners

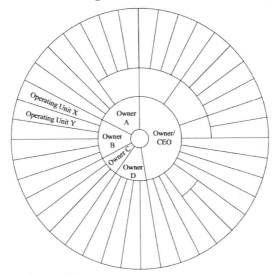

Source: A. P. Moller-Maersk Group, 2003

A HIGH PERFORMANCE BUSINESS CULTURE

It is interesting to observe how commercial success can also lead to organizational problems in companies in general, and in shipping companies in particular. This can be manifested in several ways:

- An increasing emphasis on "silos" or "kingdoms." Various departments within the organization can increasingly take on their own life, focusing on what is going on inside the silo and without enough cross-fertilization regarding interfaces with other functions, meeting new business opportunities, etc. The result can be business performance that is less than strong enough. It can also lead to a lack of overall portfolio management. Finally, an inconsistent implementation of risk management can also be the result. Success can thus lead to more sub-optimalization, through increased tendencies toward fragmentation—hardening of silos—within the organization.

- Bureaucracy and internal politics can also increase. They are related to the silo phenomenon. Individual executive status may become more important, to conform with the norms of the organization. Addressing the key question of how business can best be created may get lost—dealing with internal norms for performance, rather than the actual realities, can become the "norm"! For instance, in one instance we saw a shipping company which claimed to be managing its business according to tight professional financial control procedures. When this company entered into a joint venture, it turned out that the financial control was slow, fragmented and did not fully capture what went on in the business. It was, however, difficult for the management of the company to face up to this discrepancy between reality and its own perception of being a sophisticated financial entity. It was politically smarter for the shipping executives in this type of organization to "deny" the reality. To do things "the right way" for the given culture becomes less critical.

- In line with this, one can observe that in these types of organizations, although credit for success often tends to be taken at the top, blame for failures often tends to be directed at the bottom of the organizational hierarchy. This can easily create a risk averse culture, or even an uncommitted organizational culture, where nobody is really willing to stick out their neck to achieve extraordinary performance.

A general requirement for the management of any shipping firm, therefore, will be the ability to alleviate potential problems with success. One step might be to "translate" some general policies into practical decision rules. Although it may be quite easy to "declare" an intent to be customer-centric in principle, it will be much harder to actually have one's organization do this in practice. Above all, this implies managing the total portfolio in terms of a customer-centric focus. Every individual transaction must be evaluated this way, in the context of the overall portfolio, not as a freestanding project. Management must also ensure effective leverage and/or utilization of the firm's own resources vis-à-vis all middlemen to achieve customer-centricity. Above all, shipping companies should perhaps be aware of brokers' transaction biases, which might not necessarily be consistent with a customer-centric view. The shipping manager must have a strong ability to say "no"—the broker is often wrong, but never in doubt!

It is also important to differentiate between "winners" and "losers" among executives in shipping. The criterion of being able to effectively serve the customer will be key here. This means that executives' performance must be open to evaluation. All transactions must stand up to scrutiny and meet targets—also relative to this criterion. For this, all execution must be effective and efficient. A potential challenge in the shipping organization is the fact that key talents and key brains tend to be too mobile—it may be hard to keep them. And since customer-centricity typically requires continuity and a long-term focus, a dilemma can arise. Hence, fair performance assessment relating to customer satisfaction, as well as incentives, when justified, will be key.

See Business Opportunities Not Yet Obvious to Others

To be part of the marketplace and stay close to the customer, the shipping firm depends in the extreme on having at least several key executives who keep a broad, external focus. It probably also means that this part of the shipping organization must be eclectic, typically international, in order to maintain a broader perspective, to generate truly new ideas on how to see business opportunities. In short, the dynamic shipping organization must "lead the market," not "be led by the market" (Kotler, Kumar and Scheer, 2000). This can perhaps be particularly difficult in shipping, where the market mechanisms themselves play such an important role. It can be a trap for shipping organizations to say, "the market dictates it all," so there is nothing for us to do in terms of creating non-commodity niches. On the contrary, the customers are individuals also, and they do matter—a proactive vision, not a "me too" attitude is critical. The firm has to find new ways of thinking "out of the box." How can it do this? How can it better understand what customer-centricity truly means? There are several ways.

"Meeting Places" between "Problems" and "Solutions"

It is key to have extensive dialogues between executives in an organization who have "problems" with a customer, say, in finding a better logistical approach, and those who might have "solutions," say, new insights regarding innovative unloading equipment to better integrate a broader part of the value chain into transportation approaches. Non-obvious outside sources, such as shippers who might have particular transportation needs, might be brought into the discussion. And the dialogue could also involve the shipping company's technical experts, who might "see" solutions. The key here is to bring a broad set of people from both sides of the table together to listen to each other, to truly try to understand each other. Brainstorming without a set agenda is a good way. Clearly, this can best happen only where solid relations already exist, based on trust. Non-intuitive solutions can often then follow.

For the shipping company it is important to be able to argue for solutions that have clear *anticipated* value for the client. In order to maintain the trust, it seems critical to keep a level of sophistication that is "appropriate" for a given customer. Here, it is particularly important for the shipping organization to be humble, not arrogant—to work with the customer effectively, not in effect to belittle the customer. But how can the shipping company actually do this?

More Experimentation

It is important here to aim to try far-reaching solutions and to attempt to bring them to light far more rapidly, perhaps through more innovative prototyping—by trying faster, so that one can also learn faster, even from initial setbacks! The dynamic shipping firm must therefore make decisions based on creativity and personal interaction, so that *experience building* can also can take place faster. One must practice "fail early to succeed sooner." Or, as Tom Erik Klaveness says, "Put one toe in the water at a time—nothing is called failure." It is key here to create pressure on one's own team by *doing*, which is probably also going to mean trying to simplify—to be sure that the central, often more difficult, issues are grasped. Simplification probably also implies avoiding excessive data analysis and market tests *ad absurdum*. The excessive use of software support packages, with their strong analytical capabilities, can in fact become a barrier here, in the sense that it can induce a senseless "trial and error" attitude. Instead, how can more systematic true learning take place? Let's find out.

More Systematic Learning

As indicated, there should be nothing called failure—everything should be called learning. And—as also indicated—learning must be generally based on gaining experience through action. Top management must encourage the organization to actually *try*, to take action and to learn from it. Top management must avoid stigmatizing particular executives associated with occasional setbacks. Initiatives must be praised, not lead to punishments if they do not work out as intended. The style of the CEO will thus be central here for building a learning organization. As the head of the bulk shipping division of Norden says, he left a leading shipping firm to join Norden and finds his present tasks truly stimulating because he is given full support and "space" to be creative by the CEO. To give positive reinforcement—praise—will be vital (and very hard for many). This would also call for the development of curiosity and a willingness to try unconventional new approaches. The question is how.

Juxtapose Traditional and Radical Business Views

This is related to the "meeting place" approach, discussed earlier. Both are key for thinking "out of the box." Shipping is often traditional, some would even say largely non-intellectual. As we have said, the heavy emphasis on the "laws of the markets" can easily dry out unconventional thinking. Established truths of the industry must, however, be challenged. There can be no sacred cows. Unfortunately, in many shipping companies, the opposite is at times the case: "We are used to doing things our way here." In deriving inspiration from unconventional sources, it is above all key to come up with non-intuitive solutions that are inspired by lead customers. It is key to *listen* to these lead customers, not to treat them arrogantly, or as distant. Openness and willingness to try what they might suggest, based on humility, are important.

Fight "Not Invented Here"

As already noted, it is key to avoid a "we know best" attitude. The organization must avoid specialized silo thinking in organizational "kingdoms." Homegrown or home-biased organizational cultural structures and processes must not get in the way. In shipping companies it may be particularly crucial to make sure that the project-based nature of the value creation—linked to the customer—is preserved. This implies not isolating, say, the charterers from the operating organization. All key members of the organization should be part of the team that meets the customers. Leif Hoegh does this for each of its two business platforms, and so do others. Local information must not become a power base. For instance, the chartering department must not "own" the relevant information vis-à-vis the customers—it should belong to the entire organization. To find new ways to serve the customer depends on a broad sharing of information within each business area.

All in all, the above six principles should help to create customer-driven, commercially focused shipping organizations. One must learn to see shipping organizations in this light by actively developing a customer-centric, commercially focused culture. Nevertheless, a better organizational culture alone will not, of course, generate dramatically increased commercial results. For this, there will also be additional needs, particularly to ensure that key executives with decision-making initiatives are in place. This is the topic of the next section, first in terms of pointing out the importance of "internal entrepreneurs" in the shipping organization and then discussing the roles of the CEO and the board of directors as key initiative takers for creating economic value in the shipping organization.

THE NEED FOR "INTERNAL ENTREPRENEURS"

Shipping companies need people who possess a special initiative for commercial value creation—those who are willing to go the extra mile, beyond the customer-oriented and commercially oriented organizational culture. Culture is, of course, important, but not enough. Research from other contexts has shown that the internal entrepreneur needs to possess, above all, three interrelated characteristics (Chakravarthy and Lorange, 2004).

First, the internal entrepreneur needs to have the ability to see opportunities in the marketplace. As noted, he or she needs to have a close relationship with the customer and a well-developed network of outside market contacts. And he or she must be able to approach this with an analytic mind. This is in line with what we have discussed in the previous section.

Second, the internal entrepreneur needs to be able to identify the relevant competences that will have to be put together to pursue a particular business opportunity. These competences might come from inside the organization, as well as from outside sources. A clear network understanding of where various sources of competences can be found is therefore necessary. This implies a well-established set of relationships, not only inside one's own firm but also in the shipping industry, as well as knowledge of other relevant areas where competences can be found. This might include universities, technically driven classification organizations, consultants, the government side, etc. Curiosity characterizes the mind of the internal entrepreneur!

Third, the internal entrepreneur must be able to implement, by mobilizing the organization, and *lead* by providing inspiration and confidence building. The internal entrepreneur must, in particular, be comfortable with the project-based network approach. He must lead by "walking the talk," by inspiration, and not through hierarchy and formal titles.

The internal entrepreneur clearly needs to work closely with the CEO. But there is a dilemma here. On the one hand, the internal entrepreneur does not want to be so close to the CEO that he or she in fact loses the necessary freedom to create business actions. On the other hand, the internal entrepreneur needs to be close enough to the CEO to make sure that the CEO can maintain support for the initiatives that he or she raises, i.e., to back them up with resources. A workable top-down/bottom-up relationship would be needed, as discussed before. Let us now discuss the role of the CEO—and the board of directors—in the economic value creation process in some more detail.

THE CEO AND THE BOARD OF DIRECTORS

In the past, the CEO of the traditional shipping firm was often also the majority owner, and he would often have more or less all the say in the shipping organization. Many classical shipping companies were built up around strong owner-CEOs, who ran their organizations more or less dictatorially (Hoegh, 1970). Today, the CEO needs to be catalytic, less directive. It is important that he or she is able to unleash the creative thrust of the entire organization in a top-down/bottom-up dialogue. What are the key inputs from the CEO in such a dialogue?

First, the CEO needs to be a stimulator of visionary global thinking. As we have seen several times earlier in this book, this is perhaps best exemplified by Henning Oldendorff. This means that the CEO needs to demonstrate an open mind, true curiosity and an ability to get excited. Above all, the CEO must also take the time to be with the organization, to participate in potential new business projects. The CEO needs to "walk the talk" to demonstrate a readiness (and ability) to contribute—"let us sit down and think together." The CEO builds credibility with his own key talents in this way—and this adds to the decision-making resolve in the firm.

Second, the CEO needs to push the key people in the organization for more speedy action, and a good way is by allocating additional strategic resources to specific strategic project initiatives. The CEO thus acts as a "pumping station" by making sure that key people talents and funds are available. This is, for instance, what Thor Jörgen Guttormsen, the CEO of Leif Hoegh, did when it came to the development of the SRV liquefied gas carriers. Here, the key is to keep a keen eye on the timeline associated with the planned roll-out of a strategic project. The CEO needs to ask: Can these milestones be passed even faster? Can I allocate more resources to this project to speed it up and thereby increase its chances of success? It should be pointed out that all of this contrasts starkly with typical budget-based resource allocation—when the CEO tends to ask his organization to "do more with less." When it comes to these strategic programs, in contrast, it is important to recognize that innovations typically need resources.

Let us now turn more specifically to the board of directors of the shipping company. It seems important that the board in a shipping company be able to provide broad guidelines for the various risks that the company should be taking, based on a thorough discussion of which business platforms the shipping company should be in. Thus, the board must determine the overall rudiments of the company's portfolio strategy. In a shipping company, strategy—from the board's perspective—is prepared by mapping out the general direction that it would be desirable to follow. At the same time, it is important that the board does not hold up specific decisions. A shipping company can only thrive if decision-making is fast. The board must give management enough leverage to act aggressively and independently within the overall guidelines that the board has set, including which areas to be active in, which niche platforms to pursue, and the risk levels to take, financing, leverage-wise, chartering-wise, etc. The CEO and the top management can then appropriately "push" for decisions within this overall framework.

As Pearce and Zarha point out (1991), there has to be a balance between the power of the board and the power of the CEO. If one of the two entities dominates too much relative to the other, then there will be a dysfunctional relationship.

Let me illustrate this with two cases where I have been involved myself:

- Relatively too much power for the CEO. In this company, a large publicly traded corporation, the CEO fortunately had a very strong command of the business, understanding many of the details better than the board members, who all came from other professions and industries. It turned out that he came to dominate the board meetings, with long presentations and monologues, emphasizing that he felt things were going in the right direction and how the good momentum could continue. Because of his dominance, there was little dialogue on the board and consequently little sensitizing at board level to potentially negative developments that might hurt the company, and which would not be seen or recognized by the CEO.

- Another example demonstrates the opposite, i.e., too much dominance by the chairman. In this publicly traded company, primarily in the container business, the chairman became too associated with the specific business activities of the firm. The CEO was relatively weak and the chairman hence felt that he had to step in to make sure that decisions were executed. He came to associate himself more and more with the CEO as a result, and thus was increasingly tainted by the poor decisions made by the CEO, because he was seen as having been rather close to them. Again, there was not a good balance between the board and the CEO.

At Farstad the board is active when it comes to the strategy development of the firm. It meets once per year to review the strategy, and also on an ad hoc basis when it comes to all major investments, such as newbuilding contracts. The board also played an important role when it came to the investment in P&O, when the company took over the remaining 50% of the Australian operation. There seems to be a good balance at the top.

At Teekay, the board is composed of ten members, with strong, diverse competences and coming from various geographic areas. It is seen as a source of know-how, to be drawn on by top management for advice, perhaps particularly when it comes to key stakeholder issues relating to major business contract moves, major financial moves, etc. The board is attempting to implement strict governance practices. It is felt that the relatively strong stock price enjoyed by Teekay, as well as its ability to raise significant amounts of public funds for financing, are all positively related to the fact that the board is professional and follows strict governance practices.

It is recognized that many decisions will have to be taken fast within shipping. The board therefore focuses on the key strategic directions, allowing specific decisions to be taken fast when needed. Here there is a strong working relationship between the CEO, Bjorn Moller, and the chairman of the board, Sean Day. This strong relationship is seen as critical in making the broader interaction between the board and the professional management a positive reality. Needless to say, the close relationship here works due to the professionalism at all levels and positions, which is in contrast to what we saw in the rather "incestuous" relationship between the board chairman and the CEO of the container company, discussed above.

The board might, for instance, deal with the following agenda (Lorange, 2004):

- The delineation of which business platforms the firm should aim to be active in, and the risk/return target issues here. Are these particular business strategies realistic— and are the desired return targets realistic?

- The downside scenario: Can the company survive an extended low case scenario of the shipping markets when it operates cash-wise? What about the planned dividend issues under various market scenarios?

- The performance of the CEO and the upper management must be systematically addressed, and the administration of effective management incentives must be undertaken.

- There will always be weak owners and shy managers who might tend to say "yes," for example, to brokers. The board can play an important role here, to insist on professional handling and review of projects.

Getting the right composition of the board is also essential. Should it consist of the principal, the family, shipping experts and external experts? It is important here that the external experts are not seen or treated as "hostages," but as true additional resources. At Leif Hoegh, for instance, the board is clearly dominated by the family, which also has 100% ownership control, as discussed before. Still, there are several outside members on the board, including a former senior executive from a major oil company, with his expertise in gas and energy issues, and a former senior executive from another major shipping company, who can add a perspective on freight market developments and organizational issues, etc. Transparency, independent information, monitoring of target execution, etc. are essential for an effective board.

It goes without saying that the role of the board in shipping companies will be different than what one would find in many industrial companies or banks. In the latter cases, the board would be more directly involved in the specific asset commitment decisions, the specific projects. This would probably not work too well in shipping companies, however, because speed is of the essence. The board will therefore provide the overall guidelines, set the overall parameters, create "preparedness" and then allow management to carry them out. Top management must, of course, be totally loyal to the board. The fact that the board can be seen as rather hands-off is, of course, an illusion. The reality is that the board exercises its "power" by setting the frames within which the top management can operate, while not being directly involved in specific projects to the same extent as in many other companies.

DIVERSIFY OUT OF SHIPPING—OR NOT

Let us now discuss how the know-how base developed in a particular shipping company might be used by this organization to diversify into other industries. Some examples have been successful, while others have turned out to be less successful—even disastrous. It is important to keep in mind that a healthy respect for complexity is key here. Many companies have "diversified and died." Keep in mind, on the other hand, that many classical businesses have kept their traditional business focus for too long, and thereby eventually gone out of business. They have failed to see new opportunities in the market. It is therefore important to constantly redeploy one's relevant competences in a concerted effort to seek new business opportunities. The question, however, is how far one should go at any point (Levitt, 1975).

In the shipping industry, we certainly have many examples of large companies not adapting to new opportunities and eventually going out of business. We saw this a long time ago during the shift from sailing ships to steamers, and then later from steamers to diesel ships, as well as when it came to the switch to larger, more sophisticated ships. Companies that dominated particular areas typically more or less went out of business later on, often largely due to their inability to see how to redeploy their relevant competences in emerging new niches.

The Mallorys of Mystic, Connecticut, are a good example (Baughman, 1972). The Mallory family started out in the whaling business. Based on this competence, the company soon diversified into running commercial sailing ships operating worldwide. When the era of steam ships came, the Mallorys were quick to enter into various steam segments too. The company did not, however, follow up on the subsequent technological developments. It did not convert into diesel ships or larger ships, and it failed to run ships under more competitive flags than the US flag. All of this eventually led to the demise of this once very substantial company.

Let us return to the example of S. Ugelstad Shipping Co., which was founded in 1929, and was involved in various types of tramp shipping, both tankers and bulk. One of the earliest tankers was bought from British Petroleum the year the company was founded and became the basis for further growth and specialization within the tanker segment. At one point in time

(1951), the company owned the then biggest crude oil carrier tanker in the entire Norwegian commercial fleet. The company was, however, unable to expand into very large crude carriers, perhaps due to lack of capital. Eventually the company more or less faltered, through its focus on smaller, less and less competitive crude oil tankers. S. Ugelstad eventually utilized what remained of its relevant competences to diversify into the supply ship market, which emerged when oil was found in the North Sea, off Norway, in the mid-1970s. This led to an eventual withdrawal from the tanker business and expansion into the offshore supply ship business segment. The company was thus able to survive, but barely, due to a too slow rate of adaptive response.

Let us now take a look at some successful examples of shipping competences leading to diversification—impressive adaptive responses! Following these successful examples will be a few less successful ones.

Success Stories

District Offshore is active in both the offshore supply ship business and the trawler fishing business. The seafarer capabilities it pioneered in the fishing industry were subsequently utilized in the offshore supply business. Many of the offshore supply ship companies are in fact based in the western part of Norway. The availability of all seamen here, brought up with experience in the fishing fleet, is one of the key success factors. Clearly, there is a positive competence interchange between fishing ship activities and offshore supply ship activities. This is an example of so-called clusters, where, as already noticed, commercially viable competences are built up through a focus on several related areas— this would for instance also include shipbuilding and ship equipment (Reve and Jakobsen, 2002).

Fred Olsen and Smedvig were both active in the tanker business. Based on this, they diversified into the offshore oil platform business, above all semi-submersibles. They subsequently developed these offshore semi-submersible platform businesses into large organizations on their own, a successful diversification indeed. Smedvig eventually withdrew from the tanker business.

As pointed out earlier, several shipping companies have diversified into land-based activities, using their competences in logistics and their understanding of broader value chain issues. Maersk Sealand has, for instance, diversified into harbor terminals, warehouses and the transportation of containers via truck. Klaveness has also diversified into land-based activities for some of its specialized businesses and with the bulk carrier-based know-how at the core. Jebsen operates several harbors—with tugs, storage facilities, quays and all. When it comes to chemical tankers, companies such as Stolt-Nielsen, Oddfjell, Joe Tankers and Tokyo Tankers have diversified into land-based specialty chemicals storage terminals—also successful strategies. Broadening the value chain has been the driving force behind all of this—to serve the customer base even better!

Less Successful Diversifications

Several other shipping companies have diversified into land transportation, but without seemingly creating strong competence-based synergies here, and without much success. Initially, the Norwegian shipowner Ludvig Braathen ran a successful tanker shipping company. He then diversified into air transportation and eventually withdrew from shipping. The air transportation company—Braathens—was eventually taken over by SAS. It was never a huge success. Fred Olsen, a major Norwegian shipowning company, also diversified into the airline business. His company—Fred Olsen Airlines—was never successful either. He then bought Sterling Air, with which he has had some success. A. P. Moller-Maersk created the company Maersk Air. This company has never had the commercial success that most of the rest of the A. P. Moller-Maersk Group has enjoyed. All in all, the diversification into air transportation does not seem to have created long-lasting successes. The customer base that is being served here is indeed not the same as in shipping.

Many shipping companies have also diversified into shipyards. To cite the A. P. Moller-Maersk Group again, this company diversified into the Odense Steel Shipyard in 1917/18, which subsequently became the Lindoe Verft. This yard has developed a series of ships for A. P. Moller-Maersk. It has been claimed that this gave the company an initial time advantage over its competition, when it came to introducing new, innovative types of ships. For instance, as noted, a series of double hull crude oil tankers were developed in the late 1980s, creating a pioneering niche for A. P. Moller-Maersk. More recently, a series of more than 30 POST PANMAX container vessels were developed for Maersk Sealand. These ships gave its liner business an advantage over the competition of several years. All in all, the link with the yard has given the group a definite strategic advantage. Recently, however, the shipyard has run into large problems, due to the lack of profitability. As already noted, the Egon Oldendorff group has owned the Flensburger Schiffbau-Gesellschaft since 1990. It has turned a profit every year, but has largely *not* built ships for the parent group. It is thus *not* strategically related to the group's shipping activities, although successful.

There are many other examples of commercial, unsuccessful links between shipowners and shipyards: the J. Lauritzen Group and Danyard; Fred Olsen and Aker; Bergesen and Rosenberg; Broström and Eriksberg; etc. These links between shipping and shipyards have turned out over time to be unproductive commercially. Perhaps this reflects a lack of realization that, although for many years the capacity side was critical—i.e., the option to get new tonnage fast—and control over one's own yard capacity was an advantage, today there has been a shift toward more solution-oriented, door-to-door activities. The challenge now is perhaps not to extend the value chain much more into ship capacity, but to extend it into better understanding the customer via more tailored, door-to-door solutions.

There are many examples of non-related diversifications too. As we have seen, some of the Asia-based shipping companies have gone into other activities, such as real estate. The A. P. Moller-Maersk group in Copenhagen has diversified extensively into a number of industrial holdings, such as making plastic-based products (Rosti) and supermarkets (Dansk

Supermarket). Some of these diversifications seem to be going well. There are also many examples, however, of ill-advised non-related diversifications. S. Ugelstad, for instance, diversified into a yard spinning business (Dokka Bomuld Spinneri) with poor results.

CONCLUSION

In conclusion, as far as the core requirements of shipping organizations are concerned, we have emphasized the need to develop the necessary human resources to pursue a particular strategy, and where the focus to achieve this has been very much built around developing network organizations, reflecting the typical project-based, flat organizational reality associated with projects within the shipping industry today. Driving all of this is a clear customer orientation, a clear commercial focus in the organizational culture, and an emphasis on initiative takers, both from internal entrepreneurs and from the level of the CEO with the board of directors.

We have thus discussed several issues relating to a shipping company's organization. From an asset value point of view, the headquarters organization of a shipping company tends to be very small. Similarly, when looking at the number of employees in such a company, the bulk of them are employed on the ships, with only a few at the headquarters. We have also seen that many shipping companies are managed by strong, charismatic leaders, some of whom also have a significant ownership stake in the firms they lead. This all represents challenges when it comes to organizational design and achieving organizational effectiveness. We have given several guidelines for coping with this.

It seems key that a strong leader is particularly critical in the shipping firm. He or she must of course be entrepreneurial and business focused and must have a strong bent toward achieving consistency. We have repeatedly seen that focus and simplicity seem critical. Above all, this means that the organization can probably only effectively cope with a relatively small number of markets and similarly serve a relatively narrow group of customers.

CHAPTER 6

THE FUTURE OF THE INDUSTRY

Ownership in shipping is not so different from any other industry—you get some companies with strong individual owners running the business with strong personal control, others with private owners but relying on professional management teams, and still others with diverse public owners which includes money managers, pension funds, and grandmothers. I mention this because there seems to be a lot of focus on the traditional image of the ship owner rather than on the shipping company and its central role in this economic sector.

—Sohmen-Pao, 2003, p. 4

From old traditions to future innovations.

—Tom Erik Klaveness, Annual Partnership Speech, January 2003, p. 37

We think globally and act locally.

—Damskips Selskapet Norden AS, Annual Report, 2002, p. 22

UNATTRACTIVENESS FOR PUBLIC FIRMS

The decision-making structure in private shipping firms may differ significantly from that in public shipping firms. To secure proper valuation, public firms must be structured appropriately for the financial markets. There will be a heavy burden on management to comply with a number of reporting rules, which can delay decision-making significantly. Private firms, however, can take advantage of quick decision-making. But they must have a dynamic organizational structure to allow for this speed. Formality and reporting constraints can be less rigid, but the board of directors must then be dominated by the private owners. By contrast, if top management has relatively free hands, without clear, long-term targets set by the board, then it may not make that much of a difference whether a company is private or public.

There are, above all, five characteristics of the shipping business that tend to make the shipping industry, on average, less attractive for investors on the stock markets. (These characteristics can, however, represent opportunities for private shipowners who can effectively adapt to and tackle these rather difficult characteristics.)

- Insufficient liquidity, due to the typical capital intensity and long-term nature of this type of business.

- Family/owner combinations, often combined with minority shareholder conflicts, that create confusion on the ownership and management side, as well as a great deal of potential instability and discontent.

- Insufficient possibilities for creating economies of scale: "A ship is a ship" and "there is no economy in this."

- Accepting too low returns, often backed up by the availability of "subsidized capital," such as the German *Kommanditgesellschaft* (KG) market. This is similar to the Norwegian *komandittselskap* (KS), which was explained in Chapter 3. The German KG market continues to be strong. In the past, this was primarily driven by benefits due to depreciation and tax effects. Now it is linked to benefits investing in ship tonnage, again linked to tax effects.

- Persistent overinvestment, analogous to what can be found in the airline industry. Major airline carriers, such as Lufthansa, British Airways, etc., are not providing sufficient returns to their shareholders and investors. There are, however, examples of very lucrative airlines, such as Ryanair and Southwest Airlines. The key is to develop shipping companies that fall into the same high-performing category.

Many shipping business projects are inherently long term, lasting, say, five to ten years. The charters involved are typically longer term, and normally at relatively low rates, which allows for long-term financing and higher gearing. The value creation dimension in such projects is typically based on the residual value of the ship after the ten years. During these ten years, perhaps there would be no more dividend or surplus payout, i.e., effective return on equity, since all funds generated would be applied to paying the loan. For a publicly owned company, it may be difficult to participate in these types of deals, given that such a company will always want to maintain a relatively steady, more short-term oriented performance to allow it to keep its dividend payments and its stock price up. Entering into long-term, relatively low margin deals—not uncommon in shipping—will typically have the effect of lowering the short-term performance of a company and might thus be difficult for a publicly held firm. There is thus an opportunity niche for privately held firms to enter in a more long-term way. Privately held firms do not need to worry about steady dividend payments, thus financial long-term structures can make good sense. Several privately held firms have been built up based on longer-term charters, through long-term accumulation of equities. Bergesen, for example, based its initial growth on long-term charters from major oil companies. Short-term earnings dilution is thus a first factor that can give the privately held firm an advantage.

The typical shipping project deal can also seem rather risky to many investors. As Tom Erik Klaveness states, "Some people say that shipping is the same as any other business, but with a couple of extra zeros. The stakes and volatility in this business are very high." (Ward and Lief, 2002, p. 1). Thus, it might be easier to enter into such deals when the decision-making power and the ownership side are combined. In such cases, the decision-maker can assess whether the riskiness of the deal is in line with the risk propensity of the owner, which will now be the same as the decision-maker's. When ownership and decision-making are split, and when ownership is fragmented, it may be more difficult to reach consensus regarding propensity toward risk in decision-making. The privately held firm can probably be more effective in such business settings. The ability to follow the firm's risk profile more consistently might thus be a second factor that makes life for the private firm easier.

Shipping projects may also often need fast decision-making. For the publicly traded firm with professional leadership and a board of directors, all, of course, need to be involved. The result can be back-and-forth interactions and iterations. This can result in a longer-term, more cumbersome decision-making process than would be characteristic of the privately held firm, where—as noted—the owner and the senior decision-maker are often one and the same. Speed of decision-making is thus a third factor than can make the family firm more readily effective. For the family-owned firm this assumes that its board of directors—together with the owner/manager—actually exercise control, set clear, long-term targets, insist on professionalism, etc.

Finally, the potential problem of too much bureaucracy in the large, publicly held firm can be devastating for innovation and business-based value creation. A "lean and mean" family firm can have an advantage here (Hamel and Välikangas, 2003). Research carried out by Denison, Lief and Ward (2004) indicates that the well-managed family-owned firm can indeed outperform the publicly traded firm. Their data show that the culture in the family-owned firm can be more performance-oriented when the firm is run in a highly professional way.

Henning Oldendorff characterizes his father as having been conservative and bold at the same time, cost conscious down to the detail, but generous when he sensed a rewarding business opportunity: "He had the courage to go his own way and did not listen to the faint-hearted. But he was cautious enough to steer a prudent course for the long-term benefit of the Company and his employees. All of us, whether aboard or ashore, will continue to live up to the founder's standards of commitment and responsibility, which had always been high." (Oldendorff, 2004).

I. M. Skaugen is publicly traded and sees the benefits of being public by having transparency, a clearly articulated strategy and fast reporting to the markets. The fact that the company is public makes for additional discipline, which is seen as good for the business. At the same time, the family-owned part of the business provides a sense of stability. In Morits Skaugen's opinion, the company would never have been able to turn around in the 1990s if it were not for the family backing. In theory, the publicly traded firm would also allow family members to exit from the business. In practice, this has not been possible, in the sense that the values of the shares typically would be far less than the underlying value of the firm. All Skaugen family members have thus elected stay in.

Farstad Shipping also feels that it is beneficial for the company to be publicly traded. Again, this sharpens its ability to show transparency in all financial matters, as well as to be able to better communicate a financial strategy and the underlying basic strategies. The Farstad family owns approximately 52% of the shares; a large part of the remaining shares are in foreign hands. Farstad has not, however, used the stock market to raise additional capital for a long time. Presently it feels that this might lead to too much dilution, given the relatively low stock price compared to the underlying asset values. Debt financing, coupled with internally generated funds, has therefore been the basis of the firm's expansion.

FAMILY FIRMS: SUCCESSION PLANNING, PROFESSIONALISM

"What he [Torvald Klaveness, founder] feared the most was having children who would waste everything that he had built up. You can read that clearly in the shareholders' agreement. In his time, shipowners were 'Mr. Big,' but he saw the families [of many of them] disintegrate. He saw the values disintegrate. And that he did not want. He had a clear identity for his company." (Ward and Lief, 2002, p. 4).

To safeguard the proper evolution of the family-based company, there was a shareholder agreement at Klaveness that regulated management succession. Among other things, it stipulated that the aim was to preserve decision-making in the company, to promote individual professional growth of those active in the firm, and to protect the accumulation of assets and wealth in the firm as a going concern. Those family members who held the ownership also had to work actively in the company. And only one family member from each of the two owning branches of the family could be active in the firm. This meant that other family members from each branch had to be bought out. The issue of "watering down" and/or fragmenting the family ownership side is thereby addressed, maintaining a certain concentration of ownership in the hands of the active members of the family.

At Leif Hoegh & Co. the family ownership is held in a few hands—initially by the founder, and until recently by two brothers, and now by two sons, one from each side, i.e., two cousins. All other members of the family have been bought out. The owners had to borrow funds to do this—a clear sign of commitment. The "pruning of the family tree" thus seems to have the effect of adding focus and commitment on the part of the remaining owners. At Leif Hoegh the owners are not active in running the firm—a professional management team does this. The owners exercise their influence via an active board presence.

At Tschudi & Eitzen, founded in 1883, there has been one partner from each family side since the start. Today the fifth generation is working together. Interestingly, a decision has now been made to split the ownership between the two sides—perhaps to more fully allow each family side to follow its own strategy.

Many shipping companies go under because of bad succession planning. The next generation of the family may simply not have the talent needed to run a complex, modern shipping company.

They may thus end up taking the firm down. At the same time, one must of course allow talented family members to participate in the company. The question is how to allow such family talent to maintain a role in the family firm, while pursuing and maintaining professionalism.

As noted, in family-oriented companies, such as Leif Hoegh—as well as A. P. Moller-Maersk, Farstad and others—non-family members have taken over as president/CEO. The role of the family here shifted to that of playing roles on the board of directors, typically with a family member serving as chairman. This means that the family-owned firm will compensate the owners through dividends, rather than having the more active family members compensated via salary. In cases where the less active ones have to rely on dividends but the active ones are paid a salary, the possibility of friction and conflict can arise. Non-active family members might easily see the active family members as "milking the firm" (several examples exist). This underscores the importance of having a way to "prune the family tree," as seen at Klaveness, Leif Hoegh and Tschudi & Eitzen.

It goes without saying that the dynamics of families themselves often tend to lead to more and more family owners, with some owners taking up interests other than shipping in each generation. It therefore follows that it can be important to develop an exit structure for those who are not involved in shipping or, alternatively, to develop an ownership structure that a broader set of the family members—ideally all—can accept and be happy with.

One way to do this is through following a rather "liquid" strategy for the shipping company. An example is Fairmont Shipping, based in Hong Kong, which follows a strategy with an exclusive focus on Handy-size bulk carriers, where various ship assets can easily be sold without having a significant impact on the overall operations of the group. This means that non-interested family members can be bought out for cash. Unfortunately, there are many examples of shipping companies where this would be difficult, simply because the capital should be kept in the firm to maintain the firm's viability and competitiveness. In the liner business, for instance, there seems to be a tendency toward investing to win—or disappear. It will then be dangerous to take too much cash out of such firms, given the fact that size and the capital base will be critical for the firm's viability.

There may be two options here. The firm can develop a long-term dividend payment strategy. This, in turn, requires a shipping strategy that allows for the generation of enough free cash flows to allow for the dividend payments. Or the firm can diversify to afford the owners "risk/portfolio protection," normally undertaken by the individual owner-cum-investor himself. An example of a company in this category is the A. P. Moller-Maersk Group. It is the largest shipping company engaged in the worldwide liner shipping business, and is becoming excessively capital intensive. In addition, A. P. Moller-Maersk has diversified into a number of other shipping—and non-shipping—areas, such as oil, shipbuilding and industrial activities. The company has a multi-platform shipping business strategy and a diversified base that allows it to pay a steady dividend stream. The interests of the various owners should, therefore, be covered, even though none of the next generation is actively involved in the shipping company, except for on the board.

Another example would be Suisse Atlantique in Lausanne, Switzerland, which is dominated by the André family. This company is diversified, as noted, into the conventional Panamax bulk carrier segment and the 2,800 TEU container ship segment. It has three of the latter plus two on order. It turns out here, too, that it would be difficult to sell off ships to allow some owners to exit, since to be "viable" the company needs to have a certain minimum size, not least when it comes to its container ship fleet. Again, a steady dividend policy would be the solution.

It seems as if the succession in family firms works best when it is based on one or two principles: *Either* the ownership side is closely held, and typically combined with active management so that non-active family members in the firm are bought out by those who remain active in the firm, *or* the family members withdraw from active participation in the management of the company, and instead play their role as members of the board. Examples of the former are Klaveness, Tschudi & Eitzen and Oldendorff (Henning Oldendorff). At Tschudi & Eitzen, the fourth generation of family members is now managing the company, one from each side of the family. Other family members were bought out, and it is stipulated that only one active manager/owner should participate from each family. Examples of the latter are Leif Hoegh (Westye Hoegh, chairman; Thor Jörgen Guttormsen, president/CEO) and Farstad (Sverre Farstad, chairman; Terje Andersen, president & CEO).

FAMILY MEMBERS WITH DIFFERENT RISK PROFILES

We have already discussed the potential problem that can arise when owners and managers have different risk profiles. When there are several *family* members on the ownership side who have different personal risk profiles, it may also be difficult to reach decisions in the shipping area. For instance, the Lemos family of Greece had several bulk carriers, but the eight family members who owned the company were not able to agree on a long-term policy for operating the ships. It became clear that they had different attitudes toward risk. Marsoft was asked to manage the ships, with the mandate to sell them at the right time, rather than for the company to continue. For family-based companies, differences in propensities toward risk can be such a difficult issue that the only way out is to liquidate the firm. Or, as in the case of Tschudi & Eitzen, to split the firm into two autonomous parts, where the two families part company.

A study by Lorange and Norman (1971a) found that many independent shipowners indeed had a risk neutral—or even in some cases a risk-prone—propensity toward risk taking. We would normally not expect this to be rational behavior, in the sense that we would typically expect risk aversion or, at most, risk neutrality. Interestingly, most of the shipping companies reviewed in that study have since gone out of business—perhaps not surprising, given the risk propensity of the decision-makers. As noted, many Norwegian shipowners changed to more asset-play dominated strategies when their operating costs went up relative to those of owners in many other countries. Perhaps this turned out to be too risky for many!

THE NEED FOR CAPITAL

The need for capital is becoming greater and greater in the shipping industry. It may therefore be difficult for the privately held firm to raise sufficient capital to participate in many emerging shipping projects. The need for additional capital has led several shipping companies to go public to gain access to cheap capital on the capital market, and thus be able to continue to grow—hopefully at a faster rate. Several of these firms have, however, kept large blocks of stock in the hands of the founding family. In Farstad, for instance, the family owns more than 52%; and in District Offshore the dominant owner—Simon Mogster—owns more than 50%.

This heavy family influence in publicly held firms can lead to a substantial "discount" in the stock price, relative to the underlying values. This is due to a number of factors. First, everyone knows that these "quasi-family" publicly traded firms can probably never be taken over without the consent of the family. There is thus not so much upside in the stock price because a potential takeover raid or bid from an outside source is unlikely. Second, the volume of freely traded shares will often be rather limited, given the large family involvement and the resulting high fraction of illiquid stock. This may also limit the growth of the stock price. Third, external communication is key. This should be ample and clear. Many shipping companies, particularly when dominated by family owners, may be lax in their communication with the financial markets, which again, may lead to lower valuations. The Fred Olsen dominated publicly traded firms "Ganger Rolf" and "Bonheur" come to mind, which are known to be rather secretive, with only the sparsest information disclosed to non-family investors (*Aftenposten*, October, 29 2003).

If such a firm, therefore, wishes to tap the capital markets for capital through publicly floated stocks, it will be important to create a strong sense of *trust* vis-à-vis the financial markets—through full transparency, consistently applied over time. This implies that a shipping company must not, for instance, keep potentially more "interesting" deals private, for itself, while assigning the more risky shipping deals to the publicly traded part of the firm. Realistically, one cannot do private business in the context of a publicly traded company. All business opportunities must be placed in the same corporate entity. This is a prerequisite for a strong stock market-driven strategy.

Frontline, under the leadership of John Fredriksen, has succeeded in obtaining a far better pricing of its shares in the financial market than any other family-dominated firm. It has given the financial markets a clearly focused company, i.e., in VLCCs (very large crude carriers) and Aframax oil tankers. This is transparent and easy to understand. In addition, Fredriksen has three other publicly traded companies, all focused on a very specific industry:

- Golar NG: LNG

- Nordic Offshore

- Nordic Oil: oil production.

The stock market seems to appreciate this focus, as reflected in the pricing of the shares. This could perhaps be seen in contrast with companies, such as Bergesen (before it was sold to Worldwide Shipping) and Leif Hoegh (before it was taken private) and Fred Olsen's "Ganger Rolf" and "Bonheur."

Fourth, the shipping community—fairly or unfairly—is often perceived as providing a low return on investment, with an associated low stock valuation. The Oslo Stock Exchange, above all, tends to provide lower valuations than, say, New York. Fifth, it is important to have outside members on the board. In order to get a proper valuation for the stock, there must definitely be good outside board members and transparency. Sixth, it is preferable for managers to put in their own money, thus showing that they are committed. In this regard, managers must lead. And, finally, the strategies that the firms communicate must be clear. Such communication must include the strategy, the risks, the projected cash flows, etc., even quantitatively. A shipping company must prove to the capital market that it *does* have control, that it *is* well organized, that it *is* transparent, that it *has* a robust strategy, etc. However, managers can often miss the strategy and the big picture; owners can often miss the reality. For several firms that have ultimately gone private, the development of their stock price has been rather disappointing. There has thus been a discernible trend for the controlling families of several of these companies to take them private again—as evidenced by Leif Hoegh.

Exhibit 6.1 gives an overview of the development of the share price in Leif Hoegh & Co. from April 2000 until April 2003. Note that the share was generally rather depressed. The book value of the ships was, in fact, around 120 NOK per share. One might thus buy shares at a significant "discount."

Exhibit 6.1: Leif Hoegh & Co. Offer Price vs. Share Price (NOK)

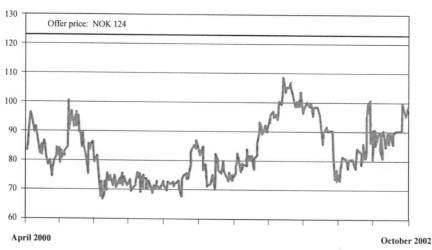

Source: DnB Markets, 2003

Leif Hoegh's decision to go private took place in several stages. One can expect that some shares, belonging to particularly "friendly" ownership groups, would be acquired immediately. In Leif Hoegh's case, this meant that the ownership share for the family increased by another 17%. We do not know the share price for this additional 17%, but it may have been less than the offer price for the remaining finally outstanding shares of 17%, which was set at NOK 124. Anyhow, the family acquired the remaining share, and now, as noted, it owns the company outright. The family enjoyed a "hidden arbitrage effect" in the sense that the valuation of the firm would now be, say, the equivalent of 125 NOK per share, while the stock market price was dramatically less. In addition to the more proper valuation, the company's being private also significantly simplifies the decision-making processes, as well as lessening the requirements of compliance with public governance requirements, reporting rules, etc.

In further examples, Awilco was also taken private by the Anders Wilhelmsen family. Bergesen was not taken private, but was sold, in 2002, by the controlling owners, Morten Bergesen and Petter Sundt, to Worldwide Shipping in Hong Kong, another privately controlled firm, with Helmut Sohmen-Pao—the son-in-law of the late Y. K. Pao—in charge. One probable reason might have been that the stock price for the owners could never be achieved by maintaining the "quasi- family" semi-public status, thus allowing the majority owners to realize the true underlying values more extensively by selling out to a group willing to pay for their firm's true value, not least due to the synergy between the seller's and the purchaser's firms.

Another contrast between the family firm and the publicly traded firm is the degree of long-term focus on developing relationships with key customers. The privately held firm can perhaps develop long-term "partnerships" with key customers more easily than the publicly traded company. The pressure toward consistent bottom-line results may mean that the latter simply cannot afford to "invest" in long-term customer development approaches. This "conflict" turned out to be one of the key drivers leading to the split between Leif Hoegh and Ugland, when the former bought out the latter from the HUAL car carrying business, which was previously held 50:50 by the two companies and involved the joint ownership of a large fleet of specialty car carriers. As long as Ugland was a private company, things seemed to develop smoothly; yet, when Ugland became publicly listed in London, a more financially driven strategic focus emerged. This led to a conflict between the two owning groups and made it more difficult to take a long-term customer-oriented "partner" view. By buying out Ugland, Leif Hoegh was thus able to maintain what it considers a more effective longer-term partnership strategy with key customers.

STRATEGIC ALLIANCES

Strategic alliances represent another way for the shipping firm to get access to more capital. There are many types of strategic alliances, as evidenced in Exhibit 6.2, ranging from—on the one hand—one-time, very short, arm's-length contracts, typically representing a shorter, smaller type of strategic alliance, to—on the other hand—a complete merger or acquisition, typically representing a longer-term "strategic alliance" (Contractor and Lorange, 2002).

Exhibit 6.2: A Spectrum of Cooperative Arrangements

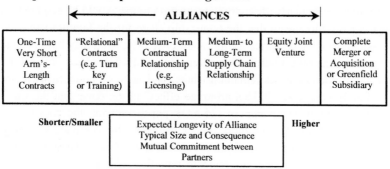

Source: Contractor and Lorange, 2002

One way to raise capital for the privately held firm can be through close partnership between a few private people around specific ship deals. The so-called *Kommanditgesellschaft*, as noted, is one way of raising such private capital, widely used in Germany—and in Denmark and Norway with its KS variation. Having outside investors in particular ships is also a rather common practice. Klaveness, for instance, takes the following approach: "We still avoid owning more than 50% to 75% in partnerships..." (Ward and Lief, 2002).

Following this exhibit, we can, on the one hand, look at alliances that are focused on joint ownership in one ship, such as co-investing in a particular ship asset. Alternatively, we can think about pools, where various shipowners cooperate with their ships during a joint commercial "regime." For instance, looking at The Torvald Klaveness Group, we can see examples of both! We have a split equity capital behind the ships under direct Klaveness control, as given in Exhibit 6.3.

Exhibit 6.3: Equity Capital—The Torvald Klaveness Group, Controlled Ships in 2002

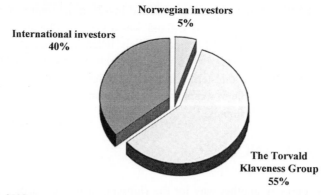

Source: Klaveness, 2003

Further, one can see from Exhibit 6.4 that the various pool participants come from a variety of countries, with 25 partners. It should be noted that Klaveness has typically invested in the ownership side of most of these ships too.

Exhibit 6.4: A Spectrum of Cooperative Arrangements in The Torvald Klaveness Pool

	Partners	Ships
Klaveness		9
Norway	2	7
Great Britain	2	3
Greece	7	14
Belgium	1	4
Italy	1	3
Turkey	1	1
Arabic Emirates	1	3
India	4	9
Japan	5	7
US	1	7
Total	25	67

Source: Klaveness, 2003

We can also think about joint ownership in a particular business platform, such as the 50:50 ownership in the US oil lighterage business that I. M. Skaugen developed and subsequently sold 50% to Teekay Shipping in Vancouver. Further, one can think about major shareholding positions in public companies. The Pritzker family of Chicago and the Anders Wilhelmsen family of Oslo each own approximately 25% of the shares in Royal Caribbean Cruise Lines. Indeed, this is a strategic alliance in the sense that the two families, through stockholder agreements, control the board of RCCL.

A second dimension of alliances has to do with the "psychology of stakeholders." Several factors are important here. The first is transparency. Everyone must feel that all data are available to each partner, and that each partner is being treated fairly relative to the others. This may be particularly important in cases of part ownership in one ship, pool arrangements, etc. Second, economic performance is critical. If economic performance falters, we would expect more adverse relationships between the partners. This may be ironic, but it seems as though strong economic performance is virtually a "precondition" for successful strategic alliances. And third, the chemistry between the partners, in terms of broad sets of friendships, say, between family members on both sides is important. A good example here is Jebsens' partnership with the Aboitiz group in Cebu, the Philippines, where a strategic alliance to operate shipping activities in Asia has been in effect for more than 25 years, with positive economic results for all but one of the years. The strong relationship, indeed, close friendships, between many family members on both sides is claimed to be a major reason for the stability of the alliance.

THE STOCK MARKET: "STEEL" VERSUS SHARES

A shipping company does of course not necessarily need to put all its investment into the ships or "steel" itself. It could also consider investing in other shipping companies' stocks and thus be a participant in the shipping industry via holdings of shipping company stocks. One example of this is Awilco, owned by the A. Wilhelmsen family of Oslo, Norway. Awilco today has two traditional business platforms—tankers and offshore supply platforms for the accommodation of crews, i.e., commodity and niche respectively.

In addition, it follows a more untraditional mode of investments in stock listed companies— all, however, within the shipping and offshore segments. For this, it utilizes its knowledge about the underlying shipping markets and decides where it can get the best return, i.e., steel (owned) or shares. Awilco has invested in several companies exposed to the container—and dry bulk—markets. Its experience has been that it can take positions in these companies before the majority of the institutional investors discover that the underlying markets are performing well. There are relatively few investors worldwide with in-depth knowledge of the shipping and offshore business. As result, the major investment banking houses have perhaps not dedicated their best analysts to follow this sector.

Each prospective publicly traded shipping company needs to be carefully analyzed, also taking into consideration the unsystematic risk. Awilco feels that this is a platform for the company, and also for other privately owned shipping companies with expertise in the financial markets. One important criterion for success is to combine this with being an owner of "steel" as well. One tends to get more information this way, for instance about movements and trends in the offshore markets through discussions with customers, etc.

CHANGE *AND* STABILITY

In thinking about the future of the shipping industry, we can safely assume that there will be a number of changes, and some of them are likely to be dramatic. We can probably expect a fast evolution that may even border on a revolution. At the same time, certain universal success factors and some universal dilemmas will remain in the shipping industry. Some of them have always been there, and many will remain.

What are the key critical success factors that seem to have universal validity? It goes without saying that this book has already taken a look at them most of them. But as a kind of brief recap, critical success factors for shipping companies are many and varied, but perhaps particularly salient—truisms—would be: To secure good positions for each ship within the portfolio; always to take advantage of markets; to have a clear market understanding, manifested through both each deal and a portfolio strategy.

More specifically, the shipping organization must develop a keen commercial cost and benefits culture. The needs of the business, not the need to maintain an organization itself, must drive the set-up of the organization. The board and other relevant stakeholders must reinforce this. Remember: The ignorance of some stakeholders can have a detrimental impact on the overall direction, the *Leitbild*. Bankers, brokers, major shareholders and family members must all pull in the same direction—any one of them can derail the firm. All of these parties can provide "advice" that can compromise and dislodge the overall strategy that, in the best case, should be driven by the CEO—either in the person of an active owner/manager or a professional.

The modern shipping organization needs to have the right type of organizational development principles. It needs to be a "flat" organization, with strong horizontal and lateral communication. These principles should include strong focus and commercial organizational values, including the definition of clear targets. The shipping company will need keen awareness of what it wants to achieve—the organization must be driven! This drive should include the push to create an organizational culture where "reasonable" mistakes are admitted and accepted and serve as opportunities for organizational learning. There must be a positive value-creating purpose!

But, as stated, there are also universal dilemmas that characterize the shipping industry, and shipping firms will need to reckon with them. Let us take a very brief look at three key evolutionary forces in the industry before covering four major dilemmas.

THREE KEY EVOLUTIONARY FORCES

Physical Assets

Traditionally, the ownership of ships lies at the center of what a shipping organization stands for. The very essence of successful shipping companies has been linked with the number of ships under management and the amount of tonnage that the company owns. However, there is now a marked trend away from owning the steel—to controlling the deal. We see a shift toward focusing on the commercial side of the deal making (and, of course, reaping the more wide-ranging benefits). This probably means more emphasis on managing the entire value chain, with heavy outsourcing of the more commodity-oriented aspects of the chain activities, including at times the ship transportation element itself.

We also expect a more finance-oriented focus, often again leading to a relative de-emphasis on owning the ships. Rather, a favored ownership structure for the future may include taking ships in on bare boat charters with a purchase option. This means that the organizational entity that controls the deal has the ship at its disposal—financed, however, by the owner. The controlling organization will typically have an option to purchase a ship at the end of the bare boat charter, and thereby reap the bulk of benefits from the value creation that may have taken place as the ship is being repaid and written down. The economic life of such a ship is often much longer than the financial write-down and repayment schedule; hence, in many instances there will often be a nice residual value for the controlling organization. For the owner the benefits will come from return on its invested equity capital and from the agreed-upon residual value of the ship.

An interesting question is whether one might simply invest in shipping company stock rather than directly in the ships cum physical assets themselves. In order to gain positive benefits from the fluctuations in the shipping markets, one might purchase shares when the shipping market is down and then sell the shares when the market is high. Again, there may be a trend away from actually owning the ship to owning stocks in shipping firms. The emerging tendency toward more "paper market" trade in shipping, in terms of derivatives and futures (IMAREX), falls into this evolutionary pattern. Clearly, it is easier to enter and exit the stock market and/or futures market than to purchase and sell actual ships. Further, the size of the deal can be smaller, and one can invest in many shipping companies, which spreads the risks further. With the evolution toward more highly focused shipping firms, discussed in Chapters 2, 3 and 4, we should now be able to find shipping company stocks that truly represent particular niches, allowing the investor to diversify the risk on his or her own, rather than investing in shipping company stocks where the risk diversification has already taken place in the firm. A counter point to investing in shipping stocks has to do with the fact that many shipping firms are family controlled, as noted, and thus do not necessarily yield maximum value in the stock price. As previously discussed, this may be further reflected in the rather limited open trading volume that many such stocks in family-controlled firms will have.

Let's look at examples of market-driven organizations that exclusively focus on using the markets for deal making by chartering in and chartering out. Western Bulk has 67 ships, all chartered in— and no ships owned. The company has worked extensively to develop state-of-the art know-how regarding certain markets within the bulk shipping area. The assets are thus the human capital— "brains, not steel." Trading and timing competences are key. Hedging and derivatives market competences are also key. Understanding efficient route patterns, including how to utilize the back hauls efficiently, is essential. Jebsen has around 40 Panamax bulk carriers, all on charter, none owned. J. Lauritzen's entire fleet of bulk carriers is chartered in, etc.

Coeclerici is an Italy-based company that owns no ships, but focuses exclusively on commercial management, in many ways similar to an industrial conglomerate. It has many contracts of affreightment to and from Italy, covering a large part of this country's imports and exports. Interestingly, but not central to the argument here, the ships that the Coeclerici Group uses are for the most part owned by Ceres.

The Dutch shipping organization Seatrade provides another example of an "asset free" shipping company. Seatrade operates approximately 125 reefers in a pool, with its major asset being its worldwide market organization. Marketing, strong relationships with shippers worldwide, and a good understanding of the logistical chains of shipping companies are at the heart of this company's operation. Contracts of affreightment play an important part in their strategy, together with conventional time charter and spot chartering. As pool operator, Seatrade gets a margin on its ships' results in the pool, as well as an upside if the pool's overall results are good. In a sense, Seatrade has taken over a major part of what would have been the individual owner's marketing-based activities. It would, of course, be difficult for an individual owner to have the same level of depth in marketing capacity as Seatrade.

In all of these cases, we are talking about a strong emphasis on being a "people make the difference" business, without owning any "steel" at all.

We have already discussed Awilco's successful diversification into a portfolio of ship stocks. A variation on individual investments in shipping company stocks would be establishing specific funds for investing in shipping, with asset play in mind. Marsoft, for instance, took the initiative to invest in the so-called Diogenes Fund in 1995, with Lehman Brothers being the key financial underwriter, and the Harvard Investments Trust being the major investor. With the aim of leveraging investors' desire to make money in a promising shipping market, the self-liquidating US$75 million Diogenes Fund was born. It targeted tankers as investment vehicles, and successful asset plays—executed between 1995 and 1998—led to a high degree of success for the fund. Marsoft withdrew in 1998 and most of the fund was liquidated then. To echo one of the mantras of this book, in order to successfully achieve the asset play objective, timing decisions are, of course, critical for both entering and exiting. A market outlook, with a particular focus on the market's turning points, can be particularly useful here.

One might ask whether the dry cargo bulk and oil businesses are going from "small" commodity businesses to "large" commodity businesses—as we have seen in the development of oil itself as a commodity and the emergence of global oil trading with a heavily developed derivatives market. It should be pointed out that oil was essentially becoming a "large" commodity between 1975 and 1980. At that time, major investment houses, under the leadership of companies such as Phillips Brothers, Salomon Smith Barney, Goldman Sachs and Morgan Stanley, significantly increased their interest in oil as a commodity. As part of this, oil, which had previously been traded in big shiploads, typically in volume units similar to that of a VLCC (very large crude carrier), was now broken into smaller units for easier trading. A critical success factor was to understand the commodity nature of oil, with cost and volatility being absolutely essential. (Eckbo, 1976; Verleger, 1999).

Today, the major financial houses seem to be developing a similar interest in the paper market for shipping, derivatives, hedging, etc. We can perhaps take this added activity as an indication that commodity-type shipping is going from a "smaller" commodity focus into a "truly" commodity orientation, i.e., "large" commodities, similar to what we saw in the oil industry in the late 1970s.

It should be pointed out that in the dry bulk markets there seems to be a similar, but perhaps not so accentuated, pattern. When it comes to the use of futures and derivatives, the big industrial charterers seem to be more dominant here. For instance, the big grain houses (Cargill, Dreyfus, Bunge and others) are all extremely active in futures trading in the dry bulk market. There are, however, relatively fewer players in this market, which is thus perhaps still more a situation of a "small" commodity not a "large" commodity.

Organization

As we have already discussed in Chapter 5, the classic hierarchical shipping organization—based on functions and major trade involvements—is probably not going to be as prominent as before, particularly when shipping firms pursue relatively simple and clearly focused shipping strategies. Here, the network organization will emerge instead. Increasingly, network organizations will probably be based around specific "brains and talents" that meet the key value-creating needs of the strategy the shipping organization is pursuing. The rest may be outsourced more and more, i.e., linked up with the core of the organization through a network. We already discussed the non-shipowning shipping firms as an example.

The network driven organization has become widely known already. Frontline, for instance, the world's largest tanker fleet owner, with 27 Suezmax tankers and 39 VLCCs under its control, has no operating organization. Operations are all outsourced. Frontline is small and networked, focusing on timing—through chartering, financing and asset play. Not only are the costs thus kept low but also, more importantly, the flexibility and speed of execution remain very high. We can increasingly expect to see the classic, often more internally focused, hierarchical shipping organizations disappear.

The use of middlemen has always been prominent in shipping, including regular shipbrokers, project brokers for specific initiatives, financial brokers focusing on fundraising, insurance brokers, etc. Experts now expect a trend away from the use of middlemen toward more direct contacts between the shipowners and the shippers as well as other principal actors. There are many reasons for this.

As noted earlier, "the broker is often wrong, but never in doubt." A key question therefore is: Why are some brokers successful, others not? A strong broker relationship can be very important, such as the relationship between R. S. Platou and S. Ugelstad, in the development and execution of the company's strategy. In the relationship with brokers, the shipping firm should try to avoid transaction volume biases, i.e., keep in mind that residual values might often be systematically overvalued by the broker, so that a project may look "too" good, according to his proposal. Further, back haul rates tend, at times, to be overestimated, so the project would again look better than it actually is. All of this is done so that the calculations for a particular project can work out well, thus paving the way for a transaction that is, in the end, perhaps unrealistic. Brokers can "sin" here. But, in the end, it is up to management not to fall into these traps.

Middlemen can be expensive too, at times levying rather heavy commissions. This represents funds that the owners themselves might benefit from, perhaps to be split with the shippers. Standard brokerage is now increasingly done over the Internet, thus gradually eliminating a segment of previously extensive brokerage services by brokerage firms.

Owners may, understandably, want to build their own relationships with key market contacts to develop their own intelligence vis-à-vis their customers. They may hope to have a better dialogue with them, understand their needs better—in short, to be partners with their customers. We see the development of extensive in-house brokerage organizations in such shipping companies, for example, A. P. Moller-Maersk, Norden, The Torvald Klaveness

Group, Leif Hoegh and Farstad. These organizations tend to deal directly with the customers/shippers, not via brokers.

As we have seen, it is important to be able to differentiate oneself vis-à-vis one's competitors, i.e., to develop one's organization to focus on the customer. This is positive differentiation. In contrast, by working through brokers, it is the broker who will need to differentiate his or her offering to the customer, and so for him or her it is important that the customers—the shipowners—are all more or less of the same type, all substitutable. There is therefore a potential built-in conflict between brokers and owners, in the sense that while the owners will wish to differentiate themselves, the brokers will want to keep the owners' services as standard as possible. The brokers will want to do the differentiation on their own hands. As Morits Skaugen states: "To have a direct access to the market is key, and the brokers can only hamper this."

A major dilemma with brokers has to do with the fact that a broker cannot easily work for only one shipping company. Brokers need to work with several shipping companies. It can therefore be difficult to establish "Chinese walls," i.e. for each customer firm to keep confidential and exclusive data. When the shipbroker gains access to particularly interesting commercial opportunities, he or she will often face a dilemma regarding which particular shipping company on his or her list of clients to offer this deal to. In theory, all new potentially commercial deals should be offered to all of the shipbroker's clients; in practice, this is often not the case. A shipbroker therefore becomes a "deal router." Many of the benefits from the middleman function—creating a more perfect market—are lost. When we work with commodity-type deals, the question of exclusivity is not typically a big issue. And, as indicated above, basic commodity-type deals appear increasingly to be handled directly over the Internet. The problem of exclusivity can, however, be particularly difficult with unique niche deals, where the very nature of the information around the commercial aspects of the deal requires one-to-one handling, not a broad sharing of information. The dilemma is that the traditional broker function thus easily becomes compromised.

The Business Model

The business model of the successful shipping company may itself change in the coming years. We have touched on these changes in the previous chapters, but this is a good opportunity to look at three additional major trends we believe are likely. The first would be for the company to move from more or less complete dependency on market fluctuations for each ship toward more and more proactive management of the entire portfolio composition. This is already the case in many of the examples we looked at in previous chapters; it is, however, perhaps most clearly seen in Norden's strategy. Norden's business model is firmly rooted in the major markets for bulk carrier services and short-term trading, but the company's model is now increasingly long-term relationship oriented. Thus, the portfolio is more stable, while at the same time offering opportunities to take advantage of short-term positive market developments.

Second, shipping companies will abandon many of the old traditions and modes of working, so prevalent in many companies in the sector, and move toward future innovations and more dynamism, more "can do." This means that shipping companies may evolve away from being traditional industrial shipowners to being more maritime logistics partners. They may evolve from being basic ship transportation suppliers to being integrated service providers for customers. All in all, this means a much stronger focus on coming up with new ways to serve the customer, rather than executing the business model in one set way. Understanding how to innovate across the entire spectrum of the supply chain will become key. In bulk shipping, for instance, the initial move toward offering more sophisticated cargo loading equipment has been followed by an emphasis on the entire harbor function, on warehousing and even trucking, i.e., from shipping to logistics.

Third, one would expect that the classic pool manager role of the shipping company might fade, and the shipping company will instead become a tonnage administrator. The classic pools might tend to provide a bias in the networked relationship, perhaps somewhat favoring the pool manager. We can expect that shipowners will resist this, so in future pool arrangements tonnage is much more likely to be administered in a common network.

SHAPING THE SHIPPING COMPANY OF THE FUTURE

Let us now turn—lastly—to another four dilemmas in our discussion. These represent strong, lasting characteristics of many shipping firms and we expect them to continue to shape the shipping company of the future.

Short Term and Long Term

The first dilemma is that we can expect to continue to see shipping companies trying to balance long-term *and* short-term focuses in dealing with the markets. This means that they will depend on the spot market *and* on developing longer-term customer relations and alliances. In the latter case, there might also be a sharing of benefits as well as risks between the shipowners and the shippers.

As noted, in many of the case studies analyzed thus far, we have seen a tendency for a gradual shift away from unilateral short-term market exposure toward a build-up of longer-term relationships, but in a way that would still maintain reasonable flexibility to reap short-term market development benefits. It was perhaps most accentuated in the case of Norden. Thus, the very essence of success in the shipping company of the future will probably be based on long-term *and* short-term focus to take maximum advantage of stability and market swings.

Local and Global

A second dilemma that will continue is to think globally *and* act locally. The reason for this dilemma is that the shipping business is essentially a global business, operating in global markets, with global competition. Thus, the shipping company must take a global point of view when it considers how it operates and acts. At the same time, the shippers are often local; they have their own traditions, their own values and their own organizational styles. It is important for the shipping company to operate locally vis-à-vis shippers, with a strong ability to listen without hubris, i.e., to act as a local organizational entity itself. This dilemma, thinking globally while at the same time acting locally, will continue to characterize the successful shipping company.

Commodity and Niche

A third dilemma that will continue is the emphasis on commodity-type shipping *and* niche-type shipping business activities. As pointed out in Chapter 2, a large part of shipping businesses will be commodity-oriented, with close to perfect, atomistic competition prevailing. At the same time, there will always be opportunities for developing new, niche-oriented businesses. In Chapter 3, we saw many examples. The emphasis in the modern shipping company will be to focus on *both* commodity *and* niche shipping.

It should be pointed out that there will probably always be a very strong tendency toward the rapid commoditization of what initially might be good niche shipping opportunities. It generally takes only a short time for competing shipowners to build tonnage that can enter into the niche shipping areas, which creates more competition, a more fragmented industry structure on the supply side and, as a result, increasing commoditization of what was previously a lucrative niche. Thus, the shipping company must always look for *new* niches as it continues to excel in the more atomistic, commodity-sized business areas. This is again a dilemma—always to be on the lookout for new business opportunities *while* excelling in the existing businesses. The new business development function *and* the ship market trading function must be actively in place and working in an organizational symbiosis.

Intuition and Discipline

The final dilemma is this: Shipping is very much based on strong intuitive decision-making *and* increasingly disciplined decision-making, based on facts, analysis, discipline and data. Again, the dilemma is that intuition and discipline must go together in successful shipping. It is *not either/or*! Experience and heuristics must go hand and hand. Although the modern shipping firm will clearly have to be professional to succeed, it must also maintain the perspective of "the old salt." In many shipping firms this has become a source of tension. Hopefully, the future might bring more respect for both.

CONCLUSION

We can of course, continue to speculate about the future of the shipping industry. For instance, there are clear cases for and against family-held versus publicly held firms in the shipping industry. Needless to say, however, the rather unique nature of shipping has led to a relatively stronger profile of privately held firms in the industry. Still, a perhaps uncomfortable fact remains: This industry has become less and less part of the central focus in the overall world of economic value creation, has less and less of a central function in the large integrated industrial companies, and also has less and less social status in the professional world and society at large. As such, we may perhaps conclude that the shipping industry has become more and more marginalized.

This book is meant to raise arguments against this. It is meant to show that the shipping industry is full of challenges, with ample opportunities for creativity, professionalism and upside economic value creation potential—even at levels many other industries would find hard to challenge. For instance, we have pointed out that the industry offers unique opportunities for the development of sophisticated commodity-based strategies, with unique upside opportunities. Similarly, one can see that the industry also offers great potential for "spotting business opportunities before they are obvious to everyone else" through the development of unique niches. Thus a broad, eclectic variety of competences and viewpoints are called for in order to succeed in this industry in its modern form.

Still, in the end, it is, of course, a matter of whether the industry is able to *attract* its fair share of the cutting-edge human brains that go toward business. My impression is that other industries are picking up more of the key talents. Shipping is not seen as "hot." Can the trend be reversed, to allow shipping to rebuild its status? How?

There is a need for more research on modern shipping, both to raise the level of professionalism in our general understanding and to develop more in-depth curiosity for key issues, above all with regard to a better understanding of the shipping markets. Shipping is perhaps not as unique as has previously been thought when it comes to the markets. The trend toward more emphasis on derivatives, futures and new instruments for tackling the shipping-based commodity business elements is only a start.

The growing research on the value chain largely seems to have "missed" the ocean-shipping dimension—and many interesting business opportunities can probably be investigated further through more of a research focus. For instance, we have seen earlier in this book the enormous importance of the macroeconomic growth of China. This assumes, however, that ports, inward and outward logistics to/from China work efficiently, etc. The entire shipping sector is probably much more central to the macroeconomic growth of China than has often been assumed. This is more broadly a logistics challenge than a shipping company challenge, however. And this is related to the entire reconfiguration of where large manufacturing-based firms might be sourcing from in the future!

Also, more theory is needed to understand how shipping organizations should work, as an interesting "business model." The flat, project-based organization is key here. The research and broader dialogue should probably focus heavily on how to utilize the relatively small size of shipping company organizations to allow their key talents to relatively rapidly get into positions where they can truly create value, truly have an impact, truly take a holistic view.

This would be in contrast to the more silo-oriented, often hierarchical, bureaucratic, large industrial and financial organizations. More research on the innovative organization, as well as a closer link to human resources management in general, would be needed, in order to emphasize the positive work environment that the shipping organization can provide. This can only be further accentuated through the shift toward "brains rather than steel" that we see. This should then impact the way the industry can attract and keep new brains, while evolving the strong industry-based competences that will be needed to succeed.

My hope is that this book will thus represent—in essence—an argument for seeing the shipping company as an intellectually challenging arena for professional talents and cutting-edge managerial work. I realize, however, that it is clearly only a modest argument in this direction. My hope is that business school curricula, for instance, can include shipping firm issues more directly, seeing shipping as a true basis for "global meeting place" learning and professional development, indeed as an example of the practice of broader modern intellectual value creation for international business. We have a long way to go to make the shipping industry more attractive. Hopefully, this book can make a modest contribution toward a positive evolution here.

REFERENCES

Aftenposten (2003), Cruise Ship Statistics, August 20.

Aftenposten (2003), October 29.

Andersen, T. (2003) Farstad Shipping Presentation, Shippingklubben, Oslo.

A. P. Moller-Maersk Group (2003)
http://www.maersk.com/about_values_and_philosophy.asp?nav=1&subnav=11
[Accessed July 5, 2004]

Bakka, D. (1997) *Hoegh: Shipping through Cycles*. Oslo, privately published.

Baughman, J. P. (1972) *The Mallorys of Mystic: Six Generations in American Maritime Enterprise*. Middletown, Wesleyan University Press.

Bhagwati, J. (2004) *In Defense of Globalization*. Oxford, Oxford University Press.

Bischofberger, A. and Ryback, M. (2003) *Basel II: Implications for Banks and Banking Markets*. Zurich, Credit Suisse, Economy and Policy Consulting.

Bodie, Z., Kane, A., and Marcus, A. J. (2004) *Essentials of Investments*. 5th ed. New York, McGraw Hill.

Chakravarthy, B. and Lorange, P. (2004) Leading for Growth: Dealing with Leadership Dilemmas.

Christensen, C. M. (1997) *The Innovator's Dilemma: When New Technologies Cause Great Firms To Fail*. Boston, HBS Press.

Christensen, C. M. and Raynor, M. E. (2003) Why Hard-Nosed Executives Should Care about Management Theory. *Harvard Business Review*, Vol. 81, Issue 9.

Contractor, F. and Lorange, P. (2002) *Cooperative Strategies and Alliances in International Business*. New York, Elsevier Science.

Courtney, H. (2001) *20/20 Foresight: Crafting Strategy in an Uncertain World*. Boston, Harvard Business School Press.

Denison, D., Lief, C., and Ward, J. (2004) Culture in Family-Owned Enterprises: Recognizing & Leveraging Unique Strengths. *Family Business Review,* Vol. 17, No. 1.

DnB Markets. (1997) Offer Document, Oslo, Leif Hoegh & Company.

DiStefano, J. J. and Ekelund, B. (2002) *Management across Cultures : A Model for Bridging the Differences*. Shaftesbury, Donhead Publishing.

DiStefano, J. J. and Maznevski, M. L. (2003) Culture in International Management: Mapping the Impact. *Perspectives for Managers*, Lausanne, IMD.

Eckbo P. L. (1976) *The Future of World Oil*. Cambridge, Ballinger.

Economist, The (2004) Full Steam Ahead, February 19.

Evans, P., Pucik, V., and Barsoux, J. L. (2002) *The Global Challenge: Frameworks for International Human Resource Management*. Boston, McGraw-Hill.

Fairplay Internet Ships Register (2004), www.ships-register.com.

Farstad Shipping ASA (2002) Annual Report, Aalesund.

Financial Times (2004) March 12, p. 12.

Fischer, S. (2004) World Needs to be Open to Globalization. *Financial Times*, May 31.

Fladmark, J. M. (ed.) (2002) *Heritage and Identity, Shaping the Nations of the North*. Shaftesbury, Donhead Publishing.

Fueglistaller, V. and Halter, F. (2003) Perspectives from Basel II and Consequences for Swiss SMEs, *Business Guide to Switzerland*, No. 6.

Goldman Sachs (2003) Annual Report.

Grove, A. S. (1997) Navigating Strategic Inflection Points. *Business Strategy Review*, Vol. 8, Issue 3.

Gulf News (2003) December 15, 2003, p. 45.

Guttormsen, T. J. (2003) Presentation, Oslo, Norwegian Shipping Academy.

Hamel, G. and Välikangas, L. (2003) The Quest for Resilience. *Harvard Business Review*, Vol. 81, Issue 9.

Hale, D. and Hale, L. H. (2003) China Takes Off. *Foreign Affairs*, Vol. 82, Issue 6.

Harbison J. R., Moloney, D., Pekar Jr., P., and Viscio, A. (2003) *The Allianced Enterprise: Breakout Strategy for the New Millennium*.
http://extfile.bah.com/livelink/livelink/80564/?func=doc.Fetch&nodeid=80564
[Accessed July 5, 2004]

Hoegh, L. (1970) *I skipsfartens tjeneste*, Oslo, Gyldendal Norsk Forlag.

Hoegh, B. D. (1997) *Shipping through Cycles – Leigh Hoegh Co. 1927-1997.*

Hornby, O. (1988) *With Constant Care.* Copenhagen, Schultz.

I. M. Skaugen ASA (2002) Annual Report, Oslo.

I. M. Skaugen ASA (2003) Annual Report, Oslo.

Imarex (2003) Investor Presentation, Oslo.

Jakobsen, E. W. (2003a) *Attracting The Winners.* Oslo, Kolofon, Hørvik.

Jakobsen, E. W. (2003b) European Maritime Benchmark, Research Report, Oslo, Norwegian School of Business.

Jeannet, J. P. (1985) *Jan-Erik Dyvi Ship Owners (A) and (B).* Case nos. IMD-5-0292 and IMD-5-0312, Lausanne, IMD.

Klaveness, T. E. (2003) Annual Partnership Speech, Oslo.

Klaveness, T. E. (2003) *The Art of Business,* Private Publication, Oslo.

Kotler, P., Kumar, N., and Scheer, L. (2000) From Market Driven to Market Driving. *European Management Journal*, Vol. 18, Issue 2.

Leif Hoegh & Co. (2002) Annual Report, Oslo.

Levitt, T. (1960) Marketing Myopia. *Harvard Business Review*, Vol. 38, Issue 4.

Levitt, T. (1975) Dinosaurs among the Bears and Bulls. *Harvard Business Review*, Vol. 53, Issue 1.

Lloyd's List (2003) May 5, London.

Lorange, P. (1980) *Corporate Planning: An Executive Viewpoint.* Englewood Cliffs, Prentice-Hall.

Lorange, P. (2001) Strategic Re-thinking in Shipping Companies. *Maritime Policy & Management,* Vol. 28, No 1.

Lorange, P. (2004) The Role and Responsibility of the CEO. In *Mastering Global Corporate Governance* (Steger, U., ed.), Hoboken, John Wiley & Sons.

Lorange, P. and Norman, V. D. (1971a) *Risk Preference Patterns among Scandinavian Tankship Owners.* Bergen, Institute for Shipping Research.

Lorange, P. and Norman, V. D. (1971b) *Risk Preference and Strategic Decision Making in Large Scandinavian Shipping Enterprises*. Bergen, Institute for Shipping Research.

Lorange, P. and Norman, V. D. (1973) *Shipping Management*. Bergen, Institute for Shipping Research.

McKinsey & Company (1985) Excellence in Norwegian Shipping, Oslo.

McKinsey & Company (1989) Challenges in the 1990s: Strategizing in Norwegian Shipping Companies, Oslo.

Marcus, H. (2003) The International Liner Industry: Overview and Challenges, Working Paper, Cambridge, MIT.

Markowitz, H. M. (1991) *Portfolio Selection: Efficient Diversification of Investments*. Revised ed. Oxford, Blackwell Publishers.

Marsoft Inc., Internal Company Presentations.

Miller, M. et al. (2003) The Forbes 400. *Forbes*, Vol. 172, Issue 6.

Mortensen, A. (2003) *European Maritime Benchmark Centre for Value Creation*, Oslo, Norwegian School of Management.

Mossin J. (1968) Merger Agreements: Some Game-Theoretical Considerations. *Journal of Business,* Vol. 41.

Mossin, J. (1973) *Theory of Financial Markets*. Englewood Cliffs, Prentice-Hall.

Norden AS (2002) Annual Report, Copenhagen.

Norden AS (2003) Annual Report, Copenhagen.

Ofer Brothers Group (2004) Shipping webcast, London.

Oldendorff Carriers (2004) www.oldendorff.com, Lübeck.

Pearce II, J. A. and Zahra, S. A. (1991) The Relative Power of CEOs and Boards of Directors: Associations with Corporate Performance. *Strategic Management Journal*, Vol. 12, Issue 2.

Pretzlik, C., Wells, D., and Wighton, D. (2004) The Balancing Act that Is Value at Risk. *Financial Times*, March 25.

Porter, M. (1998) *The Competitive Advantage of Nations*. New York, Free Press.

Reve, T. and Jakobsen, E. (2002) *Et Verdiskapende Norge.* Oslo, Oslo University Press.

Rigby, D. and Zook, C. (2002) *Open Market Innovation.* Boston, Harvard Business School Press.

R. S. Platou Economic Research (2003) Tanker Market Report, Oslo.

Seland, J. (1994). *Norsk Skipsfart År for År.* A Stromme Svendsen (ed.), Bergen, Fagbokforlaget.

Sohmen-Pao, A. (2003) Localization vs. Globalization: A Perspective on the Norwegian Shipping Cluster, Oslo, Speech to the Norwegian Shipping Association.

Stopford, M., (1997) *Maritime Economics.* London, Routledge.

Strebel, P. (1992). *Breakpoints: How Managers Exploit Radical Business Change.* Boston, Harvard Business School Press.

Teekay (2003) Teekay Shipping Corporation Annual Report, Vancouver.

The Torvald Klaveness Group (2003) Annual Report 2002, Oslo

TradeWinds (2004) www.tradewinds.no.

Tufano, P. (1996) Who Manages Risk? An Empirical Examination of Risk Management Practices in the Gold Mining Industry. *Journal of Finance,* Vol. 51, Issue 4.

Ullring, S. (2003) Presentation, Cambridge, MIT.

Verleger, P. K. (1999) The Evolution of Oil as a Commodity. In: *Energy, Markets, and Regulation, Essays in Honor of M.A. Adelman*, Cambridge, MIT Press.

Von Schulz, T. (2004) Die Kulis der Globalisierung. *Der Spiegel*, June 7.

Walton, W. E. (1987) *Innovating to Compete: Lessons for Diffusing and Managing Change in the Workplace.* San Francisco, Jossey-Bass.

Ward, J. and Lief, C. (2002) T*he Torvald Klaveness Group: From Old Traditions to Future Innovations,* Case no. IMD-3-1123, Lausanne, IMD.

Whittaker, G. (2003) Owners Face Stormy Waters. London, *Financial Times*, November 10.

Wilhelmsen, W. (2004) When Our Oil Is Depleted: Why Not Now Focus on Something We Know (title translated), Shippingklubben, Oslo.

Wolf, M. (2004) *Why Globalization Works.* New Haven, Yale University Press.

World Competitiveness Yearbook (2003) Lausanne, IMD.

World Competitiveness Yearbook (2004) Lausanne, IMD.

Zannetos, Z. S. (1966) *The Theory of Oil Tankship Rates*. Cambridge, MIT Press.

Zannetos Z. S. (1999) Oil Tanker Markets: Continuity Amidst Change. In: *Energy, Markets, and Regulation, Essays in Honor of M. A. Adelman*. Cambridge, MIT Press.

Zook, C. (2001) *Profit from the Core : Growth Strategy in an Era of Turbulence*. Boston, Harvard Business School Press.